£7.95
PENNIES

# Rock &Roll
# MEMORABILIA

EG

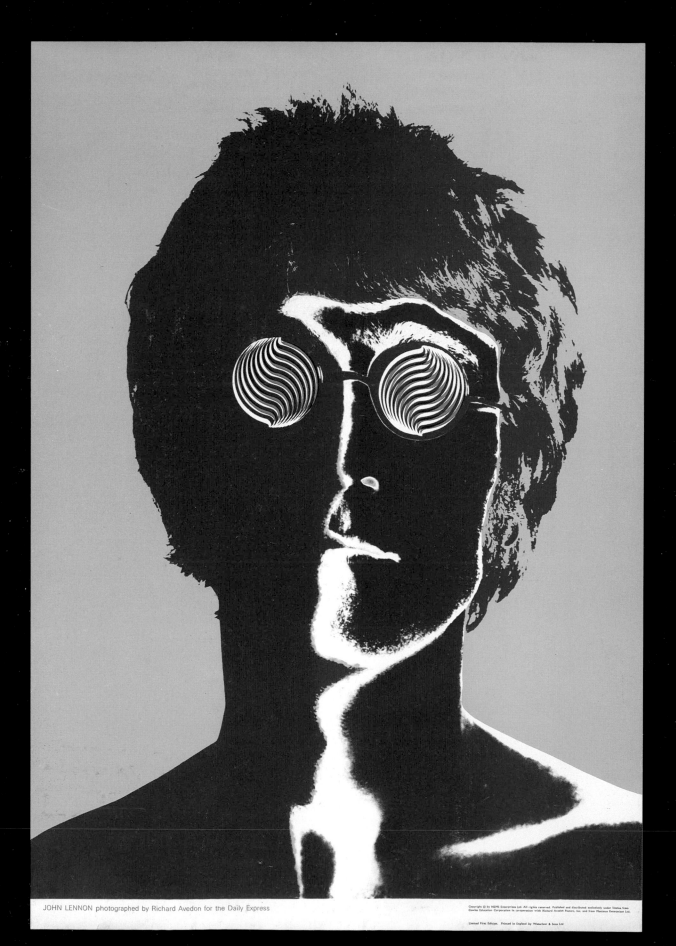

JOHN LENNON photographed by Richard Avedon for the Daily Express

# Rock & Roll
# MEMORABILIA

## A History of Rock Mementos

WITH OVER 600 ILLUSTRATIONS

**by Hilary Kay**

F

A FIRESIDE BOOK
PUBLISHED BY SIMON & SCHUSTER INC.
NEW YORK   LONDON   TORONTO   SYDNEY   TOKYO   SINGAPORE

## DEDICATION
for DD and the K's

### ACKNOWLEDGEMENTS
Mike Evans, Dana Hawkes, Jim Jaworowicz and his assistance with the Isaac Tigrett Collection, Barry Johnson, Judy Jowett, Steve Maycock, Octopus Publishing, Photographic Archivists of Christie's and Phillips, Justin Pressland, Steve Smith, Isaac Tigrett (the first great collector of rock memorabilia and the inspiration for countless imitators), the Victoria & Albert Museum, Tetsuo Hamada, Emily Evans, Jake Evans, Ron Jones and all other contributors who wished to retain their anonymity and all would-be contributors who, through time and space constraints, were unable to be represented.

### Bill Haley Program (Half title page)
The British debut of Bill Haley and the Comets – the first visit by any U.S. rock & roll star – was accompanied by unprecedented hype involving the band being met at Southampton docks by a trainload of fans who had won a place on the "Bill Haley Special" courtesy of a contest in the *Daily Mirror* newspaper. When the train steamed into London's Waterloo station it was met by thousands more fans, prior to the headline-grabbing opening concerts at the Dominion Theatre.

### John Lennon (Title page left)
One of four psychedelic photographs of the Beatles by American photographer Richard Avedon, published as Posters in 1968 and limited edition Portfolios of original photographs in 1990. (Posters out of print.)

### "Elton" Illuminated Spectacles (Title page right)
The oversized frames are constructed of plastic with small electric light bulbs linked by cable to a separate battery powered unit. It is difficult to attribute any one pair of Elton's glasses to any manufacturer as Elton probably does not know himself, but many of them were obtained from "LA Eyewear" in California. These glasses were for stage use only.

F

A Fireside Book
Published by Simon & Schuster Inc.
Simon & Schuster Building
Rockefeller Center
1230 Avenue of the Americas
New York, New York 10020

Copyright © Reed International Books Ltd 1992
Text © Hilary Kay 1992
For copyright reasons this edition may not be sold outside the United States of America.

First published in Great Britain in 1992 by Pyramid Books, an imprint of Octopus Illustrated Publishing,
Michelin House, 81 Fulham Road,
London SW3 6RB
part of Reed International Books Limited

Produced by Mandarin Offset
Printed and bound in Hong Kong

10  9  8  7  6  5  4  3  2  1

Library of Congress Cataloging-in-Publication Data

Kay, Hilary.
Rock & Roll Memorabilia: a history of rock mementos/Hilary Kay
    p.     cm.
"A Fireside Book"
Includes index.
ISBN 0-671-77931-1
1. Rock music - Collectibles.   2. Rock musicians - Collectibles.
I.Title  II. Rock & Roll Memorabilia.

### PHOTOGRAPHIC ACKNOWLEDGMENTS
The Publisher has made every effort to credit the artists, photographers and organizations whose work has been reproduced in this book. We apologize for any unintentional omissions which will be corrected in future editions. (Key: t - top, c - centre, lo - lower, b - bottom, l - left, r - right,)
**Autoclassic:** 8 r, 85, 86 b, 88 t;
**Christie's:** 21 tr, 25 c, 26-27, 28 bl, 29 bl, 34 bl, 34 br, 48 tl, 66 c, 81 b, 92 t, 94, 103 tr, 104 br, 114 t, 114-115, 115 tr, 118 l, 118 l, 118 br, 120 c, 120 r, 126 l, 129 tl, 143 tl, 148 tr, 153 tr, 153 br, 163 tr, 169 tr, 170 b, 171 tl, 172 tl, 173 t, 177 bl, 178 br, 179 br, 182 bl, 182 br, 183 b, 185 t, 191 cl, 196 tc, 196 br, 197 tl, 197 bl, 198 tr, 205 tl, / © Apple Corps Ltd. 62 t, /Atlantic Records 186 bl, /David Bailey 66 b, /K. Burness 57 bl, /David Byrd 59 tr, /CIA Promotions 56 b, / © Tom Connell-Tom Cervenak 52 l, /Davron (Theatrical Managers) Ltd. 51 tl, /Bob Gruen, Pictorial Press 99, /Dezo Hoffman, Rex 72 l, /NEMS Enterprises 48 tr, /John & Tony Smith in association with EG Management 56 tl, 56 tr, /Sun Records 194 tl, /Ron Wood 141 tr;
**Phillips, The Fine Art Auctioneers:** 8 l, 18 tl, 18 tr, 18 bl, 18 br, 19 tr, 22 tl, 25 b, 31 tr, 32 tl, 35 bl, 52 ct, 60 tl, 60 tr, 78 tr, 107 c, 114 b, 115 bl, 167 cl, 167 br, 168 cr, 178 c, 188 c, 193 b, 200 tr, 201 cr, 201 b, 204 tr, /Cyrus Andrews 62 b, / © Apple Corps Ltd. 130 tr, 171 br, /The Decca Record Company Limited, London 183 t, /GAC Super Productions 49 br, /Courtesy of Yoko Ono Lennon and Bag One Arts, Inc. 133 r, /S&L Ent. Entr. B.V. in association with Jerry Weintraub, Concerts West 79 bl, /Walter Shenson Subafilms-Eastman Colour-United Artists 58 t;
**Private Collection:** 73 tl, 81 tl, 83 tl, /Capitol Records, Hot Rod Magazine 88b, 145 tl, 164 tr, 177 br, 193 tl, 197 br, / © Apple Corps Ltd. 130 b, 131 t, /Harvey Goldsmith Entertainments Ltd. 79 br, /Courtesy Yoko Ono Lennon and Bag One Arts, Inc. 127 t, 148 br, 187 tr, /C. Ann Mason 129 br, /Nixa Records 180 tr, /Pyramid Books 204 cl, /A Sun Recording, London Records 190 br;
**Quadrant Picture Library:** 93 b;
**Reed International Books Ltd/(James Bland):** 7, 16 b, 19 b, 157, 176 bl, 176 br, 177 tl, 177 tr, 178 tl, 179 tr, 180 br, 184 bl, 186 b, 189 br, 190 tc, 191 tr, 196 tl, 200 tl, 200 tc, 202 br, 203 tl, / © 1964 The Decca Record Company Limited, London 160 b, /Louis Benjamin and Leslie Grade 51, /IBC Sound Recording Studios, Decca 199 tl, /Courtesy Yoko Ono Lennon and Bag One Arts, Inc. 6, /Don Pennebaker 59 br, /Studio Films 41;
**Photographs courtesy Sotheby's:** 3, 10, 11, 12-13, 14 t, 14 b, 15, 16 t, 17, 19 tl, 19 c, 20, 21 tl, 21 b, 22 tr, 23 tl, 23 r, 23 bl, 24 r, 25 t, 26 t, 26 b, 27 l, 27 r, 28-29, 30-31, 30 br, 31 c, 31 br, 32 tr, 32 bl, 32-33, 33 tl, 33 tr, 34 t, 35 t, 35 br, 36 tl, 36 bl, 36-37, 37 tr, 37 br, 38 tl, 38 bl, 38 tr, 38 br, 39 tl, 39 bl, 39 r, 39 c, 40, 46 r, 50 bl, 60 br, 61 tl, 63 bl, 64 t, 64 br, 65 b, 66 t, 70 t, 70 b, 71 tr, 72 r, 73 br, 73 bl, 74 tl, 74 b, 76 b, 77 tl, 80 b, 81 c, 82 l, 84, 87, 89 tl, 89 tr, 89 b, 90, 92 b, 93 tl, 93 tr, 95, 96 b, 97, 98, 100, 101 tl, 101 tc, 101 tr, 101 bl, 101 br, 102 tr, 102 br, 103 tl, 103 b, 104 tc, 104 tr, 104 bl, 105 tl, 105 tr, 105 bl, 105 br, 106 tl, 106 tr, 106 bl, 107 b, 108 tl, 108 tr, 108 b, 109 tl, 109 tr, 109 bl, 110 tl, 110 tr, 110 bl, 110 br, 111 tl, 111 bl, 111 br, 112 tl, 112 bl, 113 l, 113 r, 115 br, 116 tl, 116 b, 117 tr, 117 c, 117 br, 118 tr, 119 tl, 119 tr, 119 bl, 119 br, 120 l, 121 l, 121 r, 134 bl, 139 tr, 140 tl, 140 br, 141 tl, 142 cl, 142 b, 143 b, 146 tl, 146 tr, 146 bl, 147 tr, 148 l, 149 tl, 149 bl, 149 br, 155 bl, 155 c, 156, 158, 159, 161 l, 161 r, 162 tl, 162 bl, 162 br, 163 tl, 163 bl, 163 bl, 164 tl, 164 tc, 164 br, 165 tl, 165 tr, 165 bl, 165 br, 166 tl, 166 bl, 166 tr, 167 tl, 167 tr, 167 cr, 167 br, 168 t, 168 cl, 169 tl, 169 b, 170 t, 171 tr, 171 cl, 172 tc, 172 tr, 172 bl, 173 cl, 173 b, 174 bl, 174 bc, 174 br, 174 tl, 174 tr, 175 tl, 175 tr, 175 b, 176 tl, 178 tr, 178 bl, 179 tl, 179 bl, 180 tl, 180 bl, 180 bc, 181 tl, 181 tc, 181 tr, 182 tl, 182 tr, 183 c, 184 tl, 185 cl, 185 cr, 185 bl, 185 br, 187 tl, 187 c, 187 b, 188 tl, 188 tc, 188 b, 189 tl, 189 tr, 189 cl, 190 tl, 190 tr, 190 bl, 192 tl, 192 tr, 192 bl, 193 cl, 194 b, 195 t, 195 br, 196 tr, 198 tl, 198 br, 199 tc, 199 cr, 199 bl, 199 br, 200 cl, 200 b, 201 cl, 201 lol, 202 tl, 202 tr, 202 bl, 203 cl, 203 bl, 203 bc, 204 b, 205 tc, 205 tr, 205 c, 205 bl, /Alan Aldridge 150 bl, / © 1966 American International Pictures 50 br, / © Apple Corps Ltd. 63 t, 63 br, 124, 131 bl, 135 t, 168 b, 172 br, /David Bailey 68 t, 71 tl, /Sid Bernstein 74 tr, /Peter Blake, courtesy Waddington Galleries, London 45, /Karl Buchmann 57 tr, /Capitol Records 203 r, /Dave Clark 67 t, /George Cooper Organization Ltd. 50 tr, /Jon Douglas 150 tl, /EMI Records Ltd. 48 bl, /Endale Associates 61 br, /John Entwistle 155 t, /Bryan Ferry 144 b, /Lew & Leslie Grade Ltd. 48 br, / © 1967 Bill Graham #87, Artist: Bonnie Maclean 53 br, /Hemdale 60 bl, /His Masters Voice, The Gramaphone Co. Ltd. 198 c, /Dezo Hoffmann, Rex 46 l, /Dick James Music Ltd. 170 c, /Jobete Music Co Inc, Belwin Mills Publishing Corp. 184 br, /Elton John 146 br, 147 br, / © 1969 Gunther Kieser 55 tr, /Astrid Kirchherr 64 bl, /Greg Lake 144 tr, 144 cr, /Leach Entertainments 43, /Courtesy of Yoko Ono Lennon and Bag One Arts, Inc. 129 tr, 131 br, 132 tl, 132 tr, 133 t, 134 tl, 134 tr, 134 br, 135 bl, 135 br, 136 b, 137 tl, 137 tr, 137 b, 138 bl, 139 tl, 139 cl, 139 bl, 188 tr, /Bob Mackie 147 bl, /Macmillan, New York 181 b, /Gered Mankowitz 69, 71 b, /Marbet 147 tl, /Oliver Messel 152 tr, /Moss Empires Ltd. 49 c, 50 l, /Music City 42, / © National Portrait Gallery, London 152 tl, /Bryan Organ 142 tr, / © 1968 Osiris Visions Ltd. 44 r, 55 bl, /David Oxtoby 127 b, 150 tr, 151 l, 151 r, 154 br, /Paramount Pictures 51 b, /Polydor 166 br, / © Patrick Proctor, courtesy of Redfern Gallery 145 bl, 153 bl, /RCA, Victor 194 tr, 195 bl, /RCA Popular, Teal Records 193 tr, / © Rocket Records 111 tr, /Rockstar Records 142 tl, /Dave Roe 55 br, /Martin Sharp 52 cb, 55 tl, /Simone & Marijke,"The Fool" 53 tr, 173 cr, /Skolnick 54 l, /John Somerville 126 r, 133 bl, 153 tl, / © 1973 Sunday Promotions Inc. 57 tl, /Supersonic Attractions Inc. 51 c, /Stuart Sutcliffe 138 tr, 138 br, /Tape Head 59 bl, /Jimmy Thomson 132 b, /Ret Turner 109 br, 147 cb, / © The Tuxedo Co. 1981 61 bl, /Twentieth Century Fox 49 t, / © copyright USA for Africa 204 c, /Courtesy of the Trustees of the Victoria and Albert Museum, Harry Hammond 65 t, 67 b, 68 b, /Virgin Records Ltd 61 tr, 154 t, /Bill Watson & #1 K/Men 199 tr, /David Wynne 130 tl;
**© 1991 Sotheby's, Inc.:** 13, 24 l, 28 br, 29 t, 29 br, 30 bl, 31 bl, 33 br, 58 b, 82, 90-91, 91 tl, 91 tr, 96 t, 102 tl, 102 bl, 102 bc, 104 tl, 106 bc, 106 br, 107 tl, 107 tr, 112 r, 116 r, 117 l, 125, 128, 138 tl, 140 tl, 146 bl, 154 bl, 169 c, 176 tr, 184 tr, 186 cr, 192 tc, 201 tl, / © Apple Corps Ltd. 136 tr, 139 br, /David Bowie 140 tr, /Capitol Records 129 bl, /Fab Magazine 205 br, / © 1968 Bill Graham #105, Artist: Rick Griffin 44 l, © 1967 Bill Graham #93, Artist: Jim Blashfield 53 tr, /Kappa Sigma Fraternity 53 l,/Courtesy of Yoko Ono Lennon and Bag One Arts, Inc. 136 tl, /Henri Matinez 145 tr, /Peter Max 54 r, /Motown Recording Artists, GAC 201 lor, /Bob Seidemann 68 c, /Twentieth Century Fox 160 t, / © 1969 by The Visual Thing Inc. 59 tl, / © 1992 The Estate & Foundation of Andy Warhol/ARS, N.Y. 152 b, /Wes Wilson 57 br;
**Courtesy of the Trustees of the Victoria and Albert Museum /Photographer: Brandon:** 1, 9, 73 tr, 75 tl, 75 br, 76 tl, 76 tr, 77 tl, 77 bl, 78 tl, 78 bl, 79 t, 81 tr, 82 br, 83 cr, 83 b, 144 tl, 144 cl, 155 r, 164 bl, 189 cr, 189 bl, 191 tl, 191 br, 196 tr, 197 tr, 198 bl, 201 tr, 204 tl, 204 cr, /Mel Bush in association with Peter Grant 78 br, / © 1967 Bill Graham #96, Artist: Bonnie Maclean 47 tl, © 1969 Bill Graham #159, Artist: Randy Tuten 47 tc l, © 1969 Bill Graham #177, Artist: Randy Tuten 47 tc r, © 1967 Bill Graham #82, Artist: Jim Blashfield 47 tr, © 1967 Bill Graham #79, Artist: Bonnie Maclean 75 bl, © 1968 Bill Graham #110, Artist: Stanley Mouse 75 bc, /Levis 75 tr, / © Osmonds Inc. 80 t;
**The Vintage Magazine Co. Ltd. / © by Richard Avedon, 1968:** 2.

# CONTENTS

# Introduction

Rock music has unquestionably affected the lives of those of us born in the U.S. and Europe since World War II, influencing our choice of friends and lovers, our moods and even our careers. It is no surprise, therefore, to find that rock & roll collectibles, a description devised to describe material which relates to popular music and its exponents since the mid 1950s, have become so widely collected today.

The first auction of rock & roll collectibles was held by Sotheby's in London in 1981. At that time I was heading a department at Sotheby's which held a variety of Collectors' sales of objects which were anything but fine art or works of art and included toys, dolls, jukeboxes, cameras and scientific instruments; in a department without real boundaries, I wanted to keep pace with new collecting trends and interests and reflect these in our auctions. I discovered, by speaking to a wide cross-section of people, that my own enthusiasm for rock music memorabilia was shared by a great many others, and the decision was taken to hold a rock & roll collectibles sale. The atmosphere at the first auction was likened to a Beatles concert by those who attended, with fans lining up in the streets for hours in late December before the start of the sale, and with standing room only in the auction room.

The different groups of sellers in the first sale were similar to the groups who sold in all the subsequent auctions. There were outgrown fans who had lost their teenage obsession with Marc Bolan or Roxy Music, who might have accumulated concert program, signed albums, and a poster or two; mothers who had cleared out their children's bedrooms long after they left home to find boxes holding Beatles wigs and stockings, an autograph book filled with the signatures of stars of the 60s, a cigarette pack which Mick Jagger had thrown for a fan to catch. They were all treasured in their time but were now being sold to pay for a special vacation or to mend the hole in the roof. People within the music industry delivered their gold disks, letters and acetate recordings; others brought in original artwork for album covers or posters. Photographers and designers provided examples of their published work and fascinating material which had never been seen publicly before. The performers themselves donated personal items to be sold to raise money for charity, while their friends, ex-band members, or former employees entered letters, contracts, instruments, and small pieces of furniture.

To date, more than $10 million worth of rock & roll memorabilia has been sold through public auction. Undoubtedly a very popular and financially important collecting area, few people outside the circle of serious collectors have an idea of the wealth of material which has been available over the last decade.

Rock'n'roll collectibles cover a wide range, from cars to T-shirts, but all linked by their connection to an individual rock musician or band, to a particular record, concert, film or event. The world record price for any rock & roll collectible remains the $2.3 million paid for John Lennon's psychedelic Rolls Royce Phantom V in 1985. Cars and other motor vehicles attract wide interest, particularly if, as with Lennon's Rolls Royce, they are inextricably linked to a certain performer (ZZ Top's red hot-rod which has appeared on album covers and videos is an example.) The cross-pollination between car enthusiasts and rock & roll devotees can lead to engaging battles when a buyer only interested in the vehicle pits his wits against a dedicated rock memorabilia collector.

Perhaps the most obvious of the collectible rock icons are musical instruments associated with particular performers and certain monumental concerts, films, videos or hit records such as the white Fender Stratocaster which Jimi Hendrix used at the Woodstock festival in August 1969 when he performed his widely acclaimed and revolutionary version of "The Star

**Handwritten Lyrics for "Instant Karma" and Lennon Photo**
The last two verses and chorus of "Instant Karma" handwritten by John Lennon in black felt-tip on card. This is mounted next to a color photograph of Lennon performing the song live on BBC TV's *Top Of The Pops* in February 1970. (From the Isaac Tigrett Collection)

**Signed CSNY Guild Acoustic**

The Guild Acoustic was played by the folk-rock supergroup that formed in Los Angeles in 1968, made up of David Crosby from the Byrds, Steven Stills and Neil Young from Buffalo Springfield, and Graham Nash out of the U.K. Hollies. Young left the outfit to become Crosby, Stills and Nash, and had to be tracked down to Dallas, Texas, to add his signature to this collectors' item. (From the Isaac Tigrett Collection)

Spangled Banner". Such rare and desirable instruments appear in auction very seldom, indeed it is perhaps extraordinary that they come onto the market at all and the results are unpredictable when they do. The Hendrix Woodstock Stratocaster, for example, was estimated before the sale to fetch between £60,000 and £70,000, but actually realized £198,000 when auctioned in 1990, a figure unlikely to be bettered by any other rock & roll collectible in the foreseeable future.

Costumes made famous by concert appearances – or more recently in video performances – as well as trademark streetware and accessories, are some of the more personal pieces of rock memorabilia to be offered for sale and are generally bought by institutions or museums rather than individual collectors, since the space needed to present costume effectively cannot be found in most private homes. But possible difficulties in displaying costume did not deter enthusiasts as they bid fiercely in competition for Madonna's gold lamé Jean Paul Gaultier corset (worn in the 1990 'Blond Ambition' tour) when it was offered to the collecting world in 1991.

Dedicated collectors and, occasionally, museums are attracted by the very scarce manuscript material which occasionally appears on the market such as concert playlists, letters, and original handwritten song lyrics – like Lennon's highly influential 'Imagine' of which two handwritten examples have appeared in auction to date. Original two-dimensional works of art are some of the easiest items to display successfully in a home environment and are sought after by individuals and institutions interested in the design aspect, as well as more specialized collectors of memorabilia. These two-dimensional images include paintings and self-portraits by musicians, celluloids for animated films such as *Yellow Submarine* or *The Wall*, artwork for album covers, posters and photographs.

Photographs captivate another group of enthusiasts who are attracted by different aspects of photography. Some regard photographs as decorative works of art and look for well-known, published images of their idols by the original photographers. Indeed, several professional photographers have become permanently associated with rock musicians such as Astrid Kirchherr who was responsible for recording the earliest images of the five Beatles in 1960 Hamburg. Others include Robert Whittaker, Gered Mankowitz, Robert Freeman, Dezo Hoffmann, Harry Hammond and Jurgen Vollmer. Other devotees look for slightly quirkier likenesses; alternative versions to well-known printed images (a progressive from the Beatles' "Sgt. Pepper" album cover for instance), or shots of performers

### Jackson's "Bad" Boots

A pair of Michael Jackson's shoes which are signed by the artist on the sole and bear the words "Bad picture session." The bondage look for the album was a strange choice of image and, to many the always executive Jackson looked faintly ridiculous. Although the album outsold its predecessor in the U.K. (with nine Top 30 singles taken from it) and was number one in some 24 countries, it failed to outsell "Thriller."

in their formative years, or unpublished snaps taken backstage by fans.

The silver, gold and platinum records presented to top-selling performers lure a great many fans, and the awards do look impressive when hung in some quantity on plain walls. Whilst those disks presented to the performer responsible for the record are scarce and expensive, versions conferred upon other individuals involved are more plentiful and cheaper for the collector on a limited budget.

Merchandise, manufactured goods which relate in some way to a popular performer or band, was produced in quantity in the 1960s and was perhaps the easiest rock memorabilia to collect at the time since it could simply be bought over the counter. Barbie-style dolls of Sonny & Cher, wallpaper, curtains, blankets, rugs and dishes decorated with the four smiling faces of the Beatles, badges and T-shirts printed with the name of a popular group; all were available from general stores at that time without the need to attend a concert or join a fan club, and are still relatively plentiful and inexpensive.

The question most often raised about rock memorabilia is "Who buys?" – there is no easy answer. Private collectors have always had a significant part to play in memorabilia auctions and include those who were influenced directly by the music and musicians the first time around, and younger collectors who may have only just diskovered a particular band or sound. At pre-auction exhibitions, dedicated fans view carefully and buy selectively, while others may buy on impulse for themselves or to give as gifts. Another small group of private buyers are those

### Mick Jagger's Galaxy

The powder blue 1964 Ford Galaxy convertible, which belonged to Rolling Stone Mick Jagger until 1978. It was then acquired by *The Sun* newspaper, who offered it as a prize in a competition; the lucky winners eventually passed it to a car showroom in Harrogate, Yorkshire, UK, from where it found its way into a collector's car auction and finally the Peter Black Collection, now known as the Yorkshire Car Collection.

**Blackbushe "Picnic" T-Shirt**
Blackbushe, a disused airfield some miles outside London in the middle of the Surrey countryside, was the site for the "Picnic" on July 15, 1978, a one-day open-air event which starred Bob Dylan – it was during his "Street Legal" tour – with Eric Clapton and others in support. Promotional items such as T-shirts, with the sky-writing logo, are now highly prized among Dylan (and Clapton) archivists. (Courtesy of V&A Theatre Museum)

who purchase for long-term investment. In the early 1980s Japanese private buyers were very influential, particularly feverish in their enthusiasm to acquire Beatles memorabilia and paying high prices for mass-produced merchandise as well as the scarce manuscript material. There were very few memorabilia dealers in the early sale years, but recently this group has become stronger and their impact on the market has increased. Occasionally rock performers themselves take part in the sales either personally or, more usually, through an agent. Commercial enterprises are unpredictable buyers and their importance in the market can fluctuate widely from one year to the next; sometimes a radio station, restaurant or newspaper will buy in order to use the memorabilia as a publicity vehicle to attract customers, but once they have what they want they may disappear completely from the field of action.

While this book focuses on material which has appeared in public auction since 1981, there are other ways of building a collection, although they may require more research and patience. Memorabilia has been collected by people attending concerts, perhaps catching a hat or part of a guitar thrown to the audience, perhaps standing at the stage door and getting a signature on a program. Conventions are held regularly which focus on particular performers or a certain type of item (the many Beatles conventions for instance, or record fairs) where material can be purchased or swapped. Charity auctions are held from time to time which include objects donated by the performers to raise money for a good cause, but these events are generally not publicized widely.

Whether your interest as a collector is general or specific, this book aims to serve as an introduction to rock & roll collectibles, to demonstrate the richness and breadth of the subject, and to show some of the treasures which have been seen briefly before being purchased and disappearing once more from the public arena.

### Lenny Davidson's Rickenbacker

Lenny Davidson's Rickenbacker electric guitar with a mother-of-pearl inlaid neck dating from the 1960s. The Dave Clark Five were successful on both sides of the Atlantic with even more hit albums in the U.S. in the U.K. Despite not being taken seriously by critics, they had hits and toured until 1970. Davidson left the band in 1971 to concentrate on his antique dealing. Dave Clark produced the West End musical *Time* in London in 1986.

# Musical Instruments

Rock & roll groups were a natural progression from the black R&B dance combos of the early 1950s who, with their honky-tonk pianos, saxophones and guitars, were so popular in roadhouses and at dances. Developments in electric guitar design during the 1950s led to the instruments producing a wider repertoire of sounds and this, linked to the increasing sophistication of sound amplification, meant that performers no longer had to rely on the powerful sound of the piano or brass instruments, nor mere force of numbers to fill a large hall with sound. Lead and bass guitars, drums and/or keyboard were the standard line-up for many

▶

### Bolan's Second Flying V

An appropriately entitled "Flying V" guitar purchased by Marc Bolan in 1971. According to the vendor who sold the guitar in 1991, Bolan purchased it from a shop in Denmark Street in London, primarily because he liked the design. It was second-hand dating originally from 1967/8. Bolan subsequently sold it in 1975 to the South Eastern Music Shop.

successful rock bands from the early 1960s onward. Today, technology has progressed to the extent that performers can take to the stage with little more than a drum machine and computer to produce synthesized sound.

With the renewed interest in the music of the 1960s, performers have sought out instruments and equipment dating from that period in order to produce a more authentic sound. Good vintage instruments, immaterial of their original owner, can fetch thousands of dollars, but the highest prices are paid for those instruments which can be firmly linked to a particularly popular performer. Jimi Hendrix's guitar, for example, realized $198,000 at auction in 1990, while Buddy Holly's sold for $275,000 at auction two months later. The focus of this chapter is on those instruments which have strong links with famous rock musicians.

### Hendrix Woodstock Stratocaster

This Jimi Hendrix Fender Stratocaster guitar must be rare not least because it is still in one piece. The neck is stamped with the manufacture date, "13MAR68 C," and the guitar has clearly been restrung for left-handed playing and the strap-peg has been moved. Not unexpectedly it has various chips and dents including cigarette burns on the headstock. The guitar was used by Hendrix at the Woodstock festival in 1969 and he is seen playing it in the film of the festival. He was one of the most important musicians to perform and received the highest fee for doing so. Although the Experience had split from Hendrix in July, drummer Mitch Mitchell also played with him at the festival and it was he who sold the guitar in 1990 for a world record price of £198,000.

The guitar in its various forms has been with us since the 15th century and the flat-top and arched-top acoustic guitars are still used extensively by some bands. The American company, Martin, has been responsible for producing some of the best acoustic guitars this century, suitably braced in the 1920s and 1930s to take the additional strain of steel strings. One particularly popular style was Martin's "Dreadnought," designed in 1916. Elvis Presley was using a Martin Dreadnought in 1954 and 1955 when recording for Sun Records and he played one in his television debut on January 28, 1956 on the Dorsey Brothers' *Stage Show*.

Surprisingly, Jon Bon Jovi's first guitar was also an acoustic, brought home for him by his mother from a trade fair. In an interview in 1987 Bon Jovi described how as a child he had liked to wrap the instrument in a blanket and throw it down the stairs, "to hear the weird twang of the strings as it crashed." Bon Jovi also described his first guitar lesson, aged 14, from a club band guitarist: "He asked me, 'Why do you want to learn to play?' I said, 'To get chicks, what else?' 'Good thinkin',' said the guitarist," and the first song Bon Jovi learned was appropriately enough 'House Of The Rising Sun', about a whore house in New Orleans.

Fender, Gibson, Rickenbacker, and Gretsch are names synonymous with the electric guitar and although country singer Les Paul had constructed a prototype electric guitar in 1928, it was not until 1950 that Fender produced the first commercially manufactured guitar with a solid wooden body, bolt-on neck and electric pickups. Originally christened the "Broadcaster,"

### Buddy Holly's Leather Covered Gibson

A gem among historic instruments. This acoustic country Gibson dated from 1945, so was a prized possession when it came into Buddy Holly's hands in the mid 1950s. Displaying his talent in leatherwork – it was a hobby of his – Holly covered the guitar in tan, gray, white and black leather which he then handtooled with intricate decorative motifs and the legends "Buddy Holly," "Love Me," "Blue Days, Black Nights," and "Texas."

the name was changed to "Telecaster" in 1951 and the solid body successfully reduced echo resonance from one note to the next while giving a certain depth to each tone. Popular from the start, the Telecaster has remained in production ever since. The same year Fender produced the first bass guitar, the "Precision," which replaced the unwieldy double basses which had been used to provide the bass line melody in the rhythm and blues combos.

Gibson employed Les Paul to design a solid-bodied electric guitar for them, and the "Les Paul" model launched in 1953 has continued to inspire manufacturers of electric guitars ever since. Eric Clapton popularized the Les Paul when he played with John Mayall in 1965 and 1966, and when asked in an interview in 1989 what had excited him about this particular guitar at the time, he replied, "The LP cover for 'Freddie King Sings The Blues' on the King label, and he was playing a Les Paul! I went out after seeing that cover and scoured the guitar shops and found one. That was my guitar from then on, and it *sounded* like Freddie King. It had everything; it was it."

The most popular solid-bodied electric guitar ever made, the Fender "Stratocaster," was first available in 1954. With its sculptured and contoured body, three pickups, vibrato arm and recessed socket for the jack plug, the Stratocaster was advanced for its time, both in terms of design and technology. Used by many of the great names in rock music since, both in live performances and on recorded tracks, the Stratocaster is perhaps the best known of all electric guitars.

George Harrison had an early 1960s pale blue model which he described in conversation in 1987: ". . . in the late 60s I painted

it psychedelic – it was the one I used for the 1967 satellite thing for 'All You Need Is Love' and also on 'I Am The Walrus'." Harrison may have repainted his Strat, but that was nothing compared to the torture Jimi Hendrix inflicted on his. At the Monterey Pop Festival in the summer of 1967, as he was drawing his wild set to a close, Hendrix poured lighter fuel over his still resonating guitar, set it on fire, then left the stage accompanied by the Strat's last drone which continued to play over the speakers during its cremation.

The 1950s saw Gretsch, Rickenbacker and Hofner launch electric guitars, while Gibson and Fender consolidated their positions. The year 1954 witnessed the production of Rickenbacker's first modern electric guitar, the "Combo." The following year Gretsch unveiled their "Jet" series while Fender introduced the "Jazzmaster" in 1957; Gibson launched both the "Les Paul Standard" and their modernistic "Flying V" in 1958.

There have been countless developments in electric guitar design since then and many of the instruments made subsequently have maintained their popularity. The Vox Mk VI (nicknamed the "Teardrop") became Brian Jones' trademark; the British "Bison" made by the Burns-Weill company and Japanese guitars such as those by Ibanez, Tokai and Yamaha were original designs (it was only in the 1970s that the Japanese began to copy the American classics). The Paul Reed Smith guitar introduced in the late 1980s combined the best elements of Fender and Gibson, and the "Superstrats" by Grover Jackson,

13

**Gibson Sold by Noel Redding**

Bass player Noel Redding left the Jimi Hendrix Experience in 1969, a year before the guitarist's death. After a spell with Fat Mattress in the early 70s, he formed the Noel Redding Band. Redding sold this Gibson Eb bass, which he had used throughout the 70s, in 1983.

whose styling did much to refine Fender's Stratocaster design, is now the most popular guitar worldwide.

Since the futuristic Flying V of 1958, some revolutionary styles have been offered on the market. The twin necks, usually with a combination of six and 12 strings were widely seen at one time, but playing could be difficult with one neck positioned perfectly for play while the other was always slightly difficult to reach. At one stage, exotic tropical hardwoods were used to construct instruments of quite outstanding beauty, but environmental concerns led to the general demise of this style. Other, ecologically sound materials are now being used for the construction of guitars, including molded epoxy resins which are strengthened by carbon and glassfiber (the finished material widely known as "graphite"). Steinberger's "Headless" bass, introduced in 1982, used this revolutionary material coupled with a striking design which did without a headstock, a style which was subsequently mimicked by several manufacturers.

Most of the greatest rock guitar exponents have fond feelings towards their guitars, and several have expressed emotional sentiments about the instruments. A lonely Jimi Hendrix wrote to his father from the 101st Airborne Unit in Fort Campbell, Kentucky, in 1962 asking him to send down his Stratocaster (which Jimi played upside down as he was left-handed). When it arrived, Jimi painted "Betty Jean" on the side in memory of an old flame and spent evenings alone in the barracks playing it. Les Paul described the comfort he gained from playing his electric guitar, comparing the experience to talking to a psychiatrist, a bartender, or his wife, adding . . . "You can't say that about a saxophone or a clarinet or a tuba." Keith Richards, recounting his personal feelings for the electric guitar confided . . . "You can hug it, you know."

A guitar was often the first instrument owned by aspiring rock musicians. B.B. King is reported to have said: "The one reason why the electric guitar revolutionized the music industry is that it is so accessible . . . you can pick up a guitar and immediately play a couple of notes," and there are many touching stories of how the great acquired their first guitars. John Lennon's mother, Julia, bought him a second-hand model. Paul

McCartney's first guitar was a present from his father who helped Paul find chords by playing along with him on the piano. Stuart Sutcliffe was encouraged by John Lennon to buy his first guitar, a Hofner "President" bass, when he sold his first painting in January 1960, and he became the Beatles' original bass player.

One of the greatest contemporary rock guitarists, Eric Clapton, began playing his own electric guitar when he was 17, the purchase made possible with financial help from his grandparents. He described the instrument in a recent interview, "It was a double cutaway Kay electric," (possibly a 1962 Jazz II K775), "and very expensive at the time. And a bitch to play. Had a big thick neck, and very high action which you couldn't lower without touching the fret bars. It was heavy and unbalanced,

**Clapton's Strat**

Eric Clapton's Fender Stratocaster electric guitar, donated by the artist to raise funds for a cancer unit. Having successfully conquered drug and drink problems, Clapton's popularity has increased in recent years with his annual Royal Albert Hall performances in London. He is very much a part of the rock establishment, generously donating assorted goodies and his time to many worthy causes. As with his contemporaries, such as George Harrison, Bob Dylan and Jeff Lynne, he now produces solid rock albums with healthy sales.

and sort of a copy of the ES335 that Gibson was making – without the refinements." It cost Clapton's grandparents about £100, "which was a fortune then. It just goes to show how much faith they had in my ability." Clapton used the Kay guitar in the early 1960s when he played in a group called Rhode Island Red and the Roosters.

Bo Diddley's sister, Lucille, bought him his first Gibson, and Jerry Garcia reminisced in 1989, "When I was first loving rock & roll and I was fumbling around with my first electric guitar, my old Danelectron." Keith Richards, who was given his first guitar (costing £7) by his mother, recalled childhood sojourns to his grandfather's house in a 1988 interview, "When I'd go to visit him, he had a piano and on top of it used to be this guitar. It was like an icon up there, so beautiful. I always wanted to touch it. I can't see the guitar losing its image appeal."

Successful performers have favourite guitars which are treasured and used for "special occasions." Paul McCartney explained, "I got myself the little Hofner violin bass because it was symmetrical for left-handed playing, meaning if you turned it upside down it still looked all right." Paul still has a Hofner bass, given to him by the manufacturer at the Royal Variety Show in 1963 and which he used for the Beatles' last public performance as a group, a live concert on the roof of 3 Savile Row, London, in January 1969.

When someone observed recently to George Harrison that he'd come a long way since he quit school at 16 in 1959, he quipped: "Well, yes and no, because the Gretsch guitar I got several months after splitting from Liverpool Tech is the very same one I'm holding on the cover of 'Cloud Nine'!"

For some, it was not the guitar which inspired them, but the piano. A much more expensive instrument, it needed a greater financial investment than a second-hand guitar. The story goes that Jerry Lee Lewis's parents noticed his talent for music while he was a child, so they mortgaged their house to buy him a piano; after it arrived, Jerry Lee apparently taught himself to play it in two weeks! Bryan Ferry, after shifting pianos as part of his first post-university job (a truck driver and furniture mover), described how he ". . . got myself an old piano and tried to teach myself a few chords, and started writing songs."

Billy Joel, who admitted to being ". . . a terrible guitarist who has bizarre substitutes for decent bar chords," started to show an aptitude for the piano as a toddler and, at the age of

### Elton's Upright

Elton John's upright piano dating from the early 1970s and marked "British Piano Action Ltd. 6297." Many find Elton's writing partnership with Taupin strange, as Bernie writes the lyrics first and then Elton finds a tune. The album of cover versions of their songs and the subsequent book are titled "Two Rooms," so called due to the nature of their method of working. In their early writing days when they both lived with Elton's mother, Bernie would write the lyrics in the bedroom and Elton would be in the living room on the piano. Elton remembers this period very fondly, especially the buzz they would get when Elton had found the perfect tune for a set of Taupin words.

**Jon Lord's Minimoog Synth**
This early Moog synthesizer was used extensively with Deep Purple and Whitesnake. Lord played with Deep Purple from 1967 until 1976 in which time they recorded ten albums, including two U.K. number ones. They became a significant live act with concerts as loud as anything the Who could muster. After more line-up changes than albums Lord left in 1976. He joined David Coverdale's Whitesnake in 1978 producing six albums with them before leaving to join the re-formed Deep Purple.

four, his mother lost patience with his untrained torture of their living room Lester upright and sent him to lessons with a teacher. In an interview in 1982, Joel described his style of playing: "Most of the people who play piano in rock & roll aren't pianists, they're piano bangers of some quality, and I fit into the latter category." He also went on to list his (then) current collection of keyboard instruments, 13 in all, including a Baldwin 9 foot grand piano in his living room, a Hammond B-3 organ, a Wurlitzer D-40 electric piano, a Mellotron and an accordion!

Elton John is perhaps the greatest contemporary rock pianist and, with his vibrant live performances, has helped to make piano accompaniment popular once again. Describing his own and Elton John's playing styles, Steve Winwood confided to an interviewer, "I'm not that good a piano player. Elton John is much more accomplished on the piano; it's a percussion instrument, and he knows how to get the most out of it in terms of figures, chording, and live performing. But I don't think he's as good an electric piano, organ, or synthesizer player as I am."

Comparatively few keyboard instruments appearing on the market have belonged to well-known rock musicians, but two notable exceptions were Lennon's and McCartney's instruments which were sold in 1981. In a chance conversation between myself and the head of Sotheby's Musical Instrument department earlier that year, the latter had described a photograph of a ". . . rather beat up-looking upright piano" which had been received, and while it was too far gone to be of any value as a musical instrument, he wondered if it would be of interest to me since the piano had definitely come from Paul McCartney's family home in Allerton. The vendor agreed to wait until December for a sale and the first lot for the first ever auction of rock collectibles was consigned. The sale, held December 21, 1981, consisted of 196 lots relating to rock & roll, and the piano, illustrated in the catalogue, was estimated to realize between £1,500 and £2,500. On the day, however, it fetched £9,900 – the highest price in the auction.

Percussion instruments increasingly appear at sale as current rock drummers realize that the drums which they had considered selling anonymously as second-hand instruments can be sold for a premium to fans and enthusiasts. Some of the more interesting to be included have been those of Ginger Baker, Mitch

**Dylan Autographed Harmonica**
Certainly, along with Elvis, the most influential American performer in rock music, Bob Dylan has undergone regular changes of style which have often perplexed both fans and critics, but retain a basic relationship to American folk music, blues and rock & roll. His affinity to the first two forms no doubt influenced his use of the harmonica – including this autographed Hohner Marine Band – from his debut gigs in New York's Greenwich Village. (From the Isaac Tigrett Collection)

Mitchell, Keith Moon, Carl Palmer, Paul Cook, Don Powell and John Coghlan. Charlie Watts revealed, "I was just a teenager when I first got interested in drums. My first kit was made up of bits and pieces. Dad bought it for me and I suppose it cost about £12. I don't think I ever wanted to play any other instrument instead of the drums."

Paul McCartney, not widely known as a drummer, did own a drum kit early on (he is illustrated playing them in his brother's book *Thank U Very Much*). His early enthusiasm with drums held him in good stead when he was let down by Wings' drummer just before they were all due to leave to record 'Band On The Run' in Lagos. In a subsequent interview McCartney described how Keith Moon had once asked ". . . 'who was that drummer on 'Band On The Run'?" That was the biggest accolade I could get . . . my favourite drummers are Ringo, Bonham, and Keith. Mooney had more flash, and Bonham was a lot more flash, but Ringo is right down the centre, never overplays. We could never persuade Ringo to do a solo."

The sight of Ringo seated behind his drums inspired many would–be rock drumnmers; one was Frank Beard who saw

### McCartney's First Drum Kit

Paul McCartney's first drum kit consisting of a snare, base, tom-tom, side base tom-tom, a Zyn cymbal, two High Hat Krut special cymbals and a clash cymbal. Although McCartney is best known for his bass playing he is a genuine multi-instrumentalist. He played all of the instruments on his first solo album and claims to have done most of them on "Band On The Run" although it is credited to Wings. This drum set dates from his early teenage years.

Ringo on the *Ed Sullivan Show* in 1964. He went out and bought himself a set of blue pearl Lyra drums, the closest he could find to those that Ringo was playing.

Large and unwieldy, drums and pianos are difficult to display in average-sized homes, and their auction prices reflect the restricted number of potential buyers who may be able to both afford and exhibit objects of this size. With guitars the story is very different. Easy to present either on stands or hanging on walls, guitars have an enormous following among those who buy rock & roll collectibles and a good quality instrument with a strong provenance always stimulates frenzied bidding.

# Guitars

### Chuck Berry's Gibson

A classic in guitar styling, the jet black Gibson Firebird V as illustrated on this tour program had a remarkable history of users. During the 1972 Rock & Roll Show at London's Wembley, it was used onstage by Chuck Berry (he never traveled with his own musicians, so maybe this time he arrived in England without an instrument as well!), then backstage it was played in the dressing room by Bo Diddley. It was also used in studio sessions by Gene Vincent on the London recordings for the ''Battle Of The Bands'' LP, before eventually falling into the redoubtable hands of David ''Screaming Lord'' Sutch.

### Marc Bolan's Flying V

Having no necessity for a hollow ''soundbox'' body, the solid electric guitar allowed for previously impossible flights of fancy on the part of designers, no more so than in the celebrated Gibson Flying V, with its aerodynamic lines reminiscent of 1950s American motor cars. This model belonged to Marc Bolan from 1968 until the time of his death in 1977.

### Autographed Dylan Gibson

An Epiphone-Gibson guitar signed by Bob Dylan. Dylan used the guitar at the CBS Records Convention in 1988. Dylan worked his way through the Rock & Roll hall of fame during the late 1980s, teaming with many of the greats including the Grateful Dead, Eric Clapton, Mark Knopfler, Dave Stewart, and Ron Wood. He also worked with such diverse performers as Full Force and former Pistol Steve Jones. His best-known collaboration was as Lucky Wilbury, working with Nelson, Otis, Lefty, and Charlie T, Jr., as The Traveling Wilburys.

### Marc Bolan's Custom Valeno

Marc Bolan's custom-built, polished, aluminum electric guitar which he ordered from the American firm, Valeno Institute, in Florida. It has the inscription ''Marc Bolan J V'' and it is believed that Bolan ordered two further models of a similar design and gave them to Eric Clapton and Jeff Lynne. The guitar has a stylized ''flying head'' design mounted with a red cut stone. T Rex never mirrored their U.K. successes in the U.S. with the exception of the single ''Get It On (Bang-A-Gong)'' and so Bolan's trips to the U.S. were few and far between.

### Billy Bragg Silverstone

Billy Bragg's first electric guitar. This Silverstone guitar is signed by the artist and was donated by him to raise money for a cancer appeal in 1989. Bragg started in a group called Riff-Raff in 1977, but his sheer determination during his solo tour (if that is not too grand a title) during 1982 gave him a strong base from which to build his support. He signed to Go! Disk records in 1983, a genuinely independent label which tends to favor the less glamorous performers of whom Bragg was a perfect example.

### Trent D'Arby Stratocaster

Terence Trent D'Arby is better known as a singer than guitarist, though he played lead on some tracks on his 1987 debut album ''Introducing The Hardline According To . . .'' and features it in his stage act. This smashed Fender Stratocaster dates from around 1985, and was used by D'Arby – who had moved to Europe from his native America when serving with the US Army in Germany – after he established himself in London in the late 1980s. (From the Isaac Tigrett Collection)

Lightning guitar

"The Axe"

"Tommy" 'guitar

Transparent-bodied guitar

Red Flame guitar

## John Entwistle's Customized Guitars

Five of John Entwistle's customized bass guitars all dating from the middle 1970s. Entwistle had an Elton John-style re-assessment of his collection in 1988 and auctioned off a sizable amount of his Who memorabilia. The lightning guitar was customized by Peter Cook and was the one on which Entwistle based his self-portrait on the cover of the 1975 "Who By Numbers" album. The red flame guitar was also by Cook and was used by the bassist on the U.K. TV show *Top Of The Pops*. Ray Bunker airbrushed the cover of the album "Tommy" onto the next Fender, and it is dated 1976. My favorite is the one known as "The Axe," again by Cook, with the head in the form of a pole-axe. Finally, Charvel-Ellsworth designed this transparent-bodied bass which presumably gives a very clear sound. Despite these spirited designs, Entwistle maintained the lowest profile of the group, although he was the first to make a solo album, the enticingly titled "Smash Your Head Against The Wall" in 1971 and followed it in 1972 with "Wistle Rhymes."

## Harrison Lewis Guitar and Amp

This Lewis six-string guitar and Fender Champ amplifier, which were sold for several thousand pounds in the early 80s, had belonged to George Harrison before being passed on by the Beatle in 1974.

## George Harrison's First Guitar

In 1956 George Harrison's mother Louise, giving in to much pressure from her son, gave him £3 to buy this, his first guitar – a steel-strung Spanish-style Egmond, manufactured in Holland – from a school friend. George managed to break the neck while trying to adjust the action some time later, and the instrument was subsequently repaired with screws by his brother Peter. The guitar, still with machine heads missing and screws in the damaged neck joint, appeared in a London rock & roll sale in the mid 80s.

## Bill Haley's Guitar Strap

In many ways, Bill Haley was something of a sad figure; one of rock & roll's true founders, and certainly its very first international star, he and his brand of rock sounded out of date almost as soon as it had disappeared from the charts the first time around. But what he did have going for him was stamina – he plugged away with the same repertoire over the years, not always enjoying the best of health, until a couple of months before his death in 1981. The engraved guitar strap seen here, that appeared in a London auction in 1990, was used by Haley on his tours in the late 1970s, before he passed it on to his lead guitar player, Jerry Tilley.

### Jimi Hendrix's Fender Mustang

This Fender Mustang, made around 1964, and reputed to have belonged to Jimi Hendrix, was part of the ''L'' Series which were among the last Fenders made before the company was taken over by CBS, and regarded as some of the best guitars ever made by the company. This guitar was a collectors item in its own right, regardless of its provenance.

### Custom-Built Hendrix Gibson

''Custom-built for left-handed play, finished in tobacco sunburst, the frets inset with mother-of-pearl and lined in ivorine, in rexine case lined with synthetic fur,'' this Gibson ES335 Stereo guitar, according to the 1985 sale catalogue description (but sadly without any documentary evidence to support the affidavit of the vendor), was ''purported'' to have been owned by Jimi Hendrix.

### Eric Haydock's Precision Bass

Before they made it nationally, Manchester's Hollies were almost as big on the northwestern England circuit as the Beatles, and often used to share the bill with the latter at the Cavern. Eric Haydock was bass player with the group during their years as single-orientated beat stars, from 1962 to 1966, and a letter of authenticity from Haydock accompanied this Fender Precision bass (made in 1955) when it was sold in 1989.

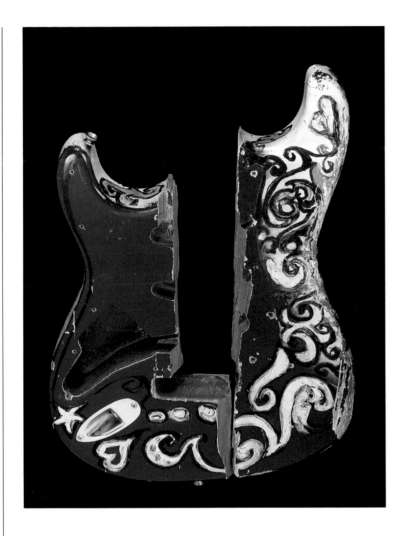

### Remnants of Hendrix Strat

The remains of a Jimi Hendrix Fender Stratocaster guitar, smashed by the musician during one of his concerts. The back has been crudely overpainted by hand and has a poem written by Hendrix. The piece is also dated "JUNE 4 1967 . . AVILLE . . LONDON" which should read "Saville", the venue for some of the earliest Hendrix concerts in England. The performance has been well documented by Hendrix historians and so the guitar is a highly prized addition to any collection – which goes some way to explaining the multi-thousand pound price achieved by this item in 1991.

### Hendrix Champ Amp

Jimi Hendrix used this "Champ Amp" before giving it to Mitch Mitchell shortly before his death. It is amusing that by this stage Hendrix was giving amps away, yet when he first toured in France in 1966, the band's manager, former Animal Chas Chandler, had to sell some of his guitars to buy the band two Marshall amps which they had nagged him for. The amp was sold by Mitchell in 1988 together with a letter to authenticate it.

### Holly's Fender Strat

A classic Fender Stratocaster dating from 1958, unique because it was one of Buddy Holly's small collection of guitars. He played it both on stage and in the studio in the latter part of his career, and it was actually in the station wagon on its way to the next gig with the rest of his band's equipment when Holly met with his fatal airplane accident.

### Dobro Belonging to Steve Howe

A rare National Dobro Reso-Phonic guitar produced in the early 1950s. Steve Howe of Yes sold a part of his collection of guitars; this was one of the finest, representing a good example of a pre-electric resonator guitar. Yes have an immensely complex history of group albums, followed by solo projects, no group activity for a couple of years, legal disputes on who can and cannot use the name, and finally reforming about every five years. As with so many of the rock groups who formed in the late 1960s and early 1970s, they consist of genuine musicians, often with formal music training, and are hence not limited to creativity only within a group 'environment.

### Brian Jones' Vox Guitar

This instrument was sold with a removable knee pad enabling it to be played horizontally. Jones became increasingly alienated from the other Rolling Stones, mainly due to the creative partnership which developed between Jagger and Richards with their songwriting. Initially, before that success, Jones, together with Mick, had been the public and private focal point of the group. His guitar riffs were vital to the sound the band was developing and had an influence on the way the others would write in the future. He continued to write himself but his confidence *vis-à-vis* the group was so eroded he never showed them to others.

### John Lee Hooker's Signed Gibson

One of the all-time legends of modern country blues, John Lee Hooker was a key influence on a generation of white British and American guitarists who changed rock & roll in the 1960s. Numbers like "Crawling King Snake" and "Dimples" were seminal classics in their own right, and his 1989 album "The Healer" saw him in the best-selling lists once again. His Gibson ES-345 semi-acoustic was sold in 1990, signed and inscribed in white "John L. Hooker J.L.H.," and accompanied by a photograph of John Lee holding the same instrument.

### Aria Belonging to Robin Le Mesurier

A six-string Aria guitar which was sold with a personal note from the owner, Robin Le Mesurier, which read "This is my guitar which was used on the '80-'81 Rod Stewart World Tour and was smashed (with great glee) on *Saturday Night Live* in New York in October 1981 – and consequently wonderfully repaired."

### Robbie Krieger's Gibson

Robby Krieger's Gibson SG Standard Guitar which is signed by the Doors player. Krieger used the instrument on a variety of the group's live appearances and albums. The Doors have retained all the cult status they first achieved with their eponymous debut album in 1967. The band was only moderately successful in chart terms in the U.K. but their reputation and influence extends well beyond statistics. In the U.S. they had two number one singles and often flirted dangerously close to the law with their concert performances – Morrison finding it increasingly hard to keep his clothes on. When Morrison moved to Paris in 1971 the Doors were effectively closed. Krieger continued to work, forming the Butt Band in late 1972 and releasing a solo album, ''No Habla'' in 1989 as well as writing numerous scores.

### Brian Jones' Guild Semi-Acoustic

A certain amount of mystery surrounds the history of this Guild semi-acoustic guitar, which originally belonged to Brian Jones of the Rolling Stones. In the early 1960s, a guitarist – who used to sit in with the Stones from time to time – had his equipment stolen from the Rolling Stones' van. A decade later, Ian Stewart, the "sixth Stone" who used to play piano with the group and acted as personal road manager, gave the Jones instrument to the guitarist as a gesture to replace his stolen "axe" of ten years earlier.

### Phil Manzanera's Yamaha

This guitar was used by Phil Manzanera of Roxy Music on their 1975/6 "Siren" tour and has been signed by the player. He donated the guitar to raise money for charity in 1989. The tour helped to produce the biggest single at that point, which was their only significant U.S. hit, "Love Is The Drug". After the tour the group was put on hold for a number of years, and Manzanera formed 801, whose album cover pictures him using the guitar.

### Lennon's "Imagine" Amp

John Lennon's Fender De-Luxe amplifier which he used in the recording of the album "Imagine". Many consider this 1971 album the only truly significant work of Lennon's solo career. It was a genuinely very successful album, not just selling on the strength of the Lennon name. Quite the reverse in fact; it was a brave listener who purchased a Lennon album at that time, as you could never be sure what you would get. "Imagine" earned its success and finally spent just under two years on the U.K. chart.

### Rare Burns "Marvin" Prototype

A rare Burns "Marvin S" prototype guitar with the serial number 2592 and dating from 1967. This is one of only three prototypes made, possibly as a replacement for the original Burns Marvin model. The guitar pictured here was used by Hank Marvin during the Shadows' Australian summer tour of 1967, but due to a change in company policy after the takeover by Baldwin, the model was never developed. Of the three models made, a white version was destroyed by the factory but the fate of the third is unknown. This period was not a productive one for the group as their singles started to fail regularly. They would not hit the U.K. Top Ten again until 1979.

### Page's Prize Yamaha
Donating the guitar as a prize in a local radio contest in 1982, Jimmy Page inscribed the Yamaha acoustic which he had used on the Led Zeppelin 1975 world tour "This guitar was stolen from Jimmy Page, Led Zeppelin (Officially of course)."

### Oldfield "Abbey Road" Guitar
This guitar, which originally belonged to multi-instrumentalist Mike Oldfield, was actually sold at a charity auction dubbed "The Sale of the Century" at EMI's famous Abbey Road studios in London in the early 1980s.

### John Lennon's Compensator Acoustic

John Lennon's Hofner Compensator steel-string acoustic guitar which was sold in 1984 with a letter of authenticity from George Harrison stating ''the Hofner is one of the first guitars of John's, going back to the early days in Liverpool (1960-ish).'' It is difficult to find a photograph of John using the guitar as he tended to keep to his electric on stage.

### Los Lobos Strat

Tex-Mex band Los Lobos, relative newcomers in the annals of rock music had their big break via the Richie Valens biopic La Bamba, and so a Stratocaster bearing their signatures immediately becomes collectible, as its appearance in a recent New York auction proved.

### Roy Orbison's Gibson

A regular Gibson electric, with mother-of-pearl inlaid neck and black wooden body, acquires collector status although it isn't signed or marked in any way, because it was sold with a letter authenticating the fact that it belonged to rockabilly pioneer, million-selling pop stylist and latter-day Traveling Wilbury, Roy Orbison, who died in 1989.

### Bon Jovi's Kalamazoo

Even relatively recent and contemporary rock names immediately confer collectability on personal effects and instruments once they appear in the salesroom – as with this Kalamazoo Oriole acoustic guitar signed in black felt-tip pen by Bon Jovi, leader and superstar of the late 1980s Jon Bon Jovi.

### Iggy's Marauder

Once one of the wild men of rock, Iggy Pop has calmed down in recent years, with a return to the commercial success that had eluded him for some time. Whether Mr. Pop got rid of his Gibson Marauder in the flush of recent fame or driven by not-so-long-ago bad times is not clear. Whatever, it appeared signed (with a picture of Iggy actually signing it), at a London sale in 1991.

### Eric Stewart's 10cc Stratocaster

A Fender Stratocaster guitar bearing the serial number 72013 and dating from 1962. The guitar has a refinished maple neck and is refretted with Gibson frets. The item was sold by Stewart in 1990 at Sotheby's, and he confirmed that it was used on all of 10cc's albums. Stewart has an impressive resume, playing with the Mindbenders, Hotlegs, Wax, and Paul McCartney, along with his 10cc successes. The demise of the band was quite extraordinary for, having had their third number one with "Dreadlock Holiday" in 1978, only one of their next 11 singles made the charts, and that only to number fifty.

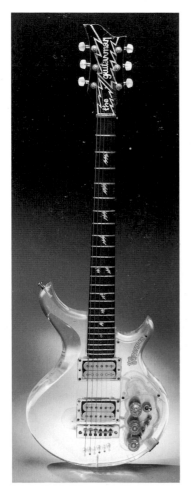

### Custom-Built Lou Reed See-Through

A genuine piece of pop art from one-time Andy Warhol acolyte, Lou Reed, this custom-designed Guitarman guitar featured a "see-through" plastic body which displayed the internal electrical wiring of the instrument. The ex-Velvet Underground guitarist and singer used the instrument during his "Street Hassle" tour of 1978.

### Keith Richards' 1965 Acoustic

Keith Richards' Framus acoustic guitar which was sold in 1983 at Sotheby's complete with a battered carrying case, lettered "Rolling Stones". Also included was a photograph of Keith Richards using the guitar in a room with Brian Jones standing next to him. The guitar dates from 1965 and may have been used on some of the band's ballads such as "Ruby Tuesday".

### Sting Signed Strat

Particularly in his days since playing bass with Police, singer Sting has frequently moved over to guitar. Socially aware, he's been associated in recent years with his exhaustive work toward saving the Amazon rain forests. This cream Fender Stratocaster, signed by Sting, was donated by him to a charity auction in the U.S.

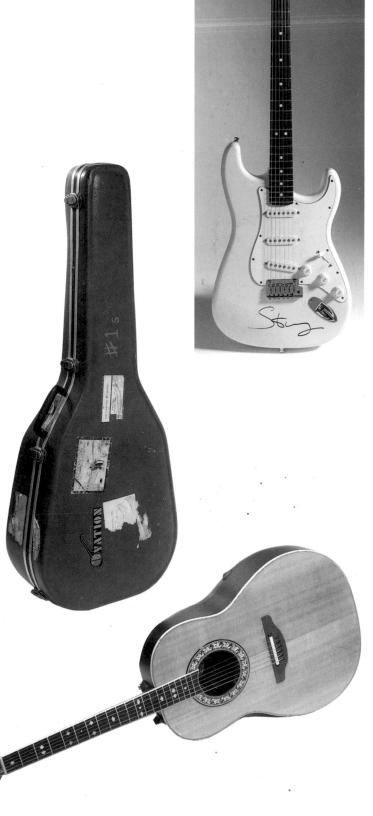

### Early Springsteen Bass

A primitive-looking instrument, this Japanese-made bass guitar dates from the mid 1960s when it was used by Bruce Springsteen's first-ever band the Castiles. With its single pickup, dual control knobs and regular design, it was clearly an inexpensive instrument which Springsteen, though not the actual bass player in the band, probably bought for them, and which he certainly owned in later years before passing it on to a friend.

### Cat Stevens' Ovation Acoustic

Cat Stevens' Ovation Legend acoustic/electric guitar dating from 1974 with the model reference number 1617-4. The case has several stickers on it, promoting his albums. Stevens was becoming increasingly involved in religion at this stage, as the title of his seventh album confirmed – ''Buddah And The Chocolate Box.'' His final three albums were too moody and complex for the broad audience he originally attracted and in 1981 he auctioned all the trappings from his past pop life to concentrate on studying Islam.

### Andy Summers' Autographed Guitar

Even if a memorabilia auction is not specifically for charity, individual items sometimes crop up where it is stated they are being sold for some worthy cause or institution. This Hamer custom-built Phantom guitar, signed by Andy Summers of the Police was sold on behalf of The Young Variety Club of Great Britain.

### Pete Townshend Guitar Splinters

A frustrated musician's guitar? No, it just suffered the same fate as many guitars belonging to Pete Townshend. The guitar was used to record the demo versions of most of the songs on the "Who's Next" album of 1971. It was later smashed by Townshend who donated it to raise money for charity in 1989. It was signed with the comment "I'm not very proud of all this."

### Stu Sutcliffe Early Beatle Bass

Stuart Sutcliffe's Hofner President bass guitar. This German guitar is instantly recognizable to any historical Beatles buff as Sutcliffe was often photographed with the instrument (usually half-hidden because he could hardly play it). Sutcliffe joined the Quarry Men in January 1960. John Lennon had persuaded him to use the £65 he received from British millionaire John Moores, for a painting, to buy the guitar. The guitar came from Frank Hessey's Music Shop in Liverpool. In August, now calling themselves the Beatles and with Pete Best on drums, they traveled to Hamburg. Sutcliffe remained behind in Germany to concentrate on his Art studies and to be with his fiancée, Astrid Kirchherr.

### Bruce Welch Shadows Strat

Before the advent of the 60s beat and blues boom, the Shadows epitomized the instrumental guitar sound in British pop, and the Fender Stratocaster, complete with tremelo arm, summed up the image of the Shadows. Many a would-be Hank Marvin mimed in front of the full-length mirror with a tennis racket in place of the much desired Strat. Here then, a real collectors item, the Strat Anniversary owned by Bruce Welch which was sold with a letter of authenticity signed by Bruce himself.

### Rare Ex-Townshend Gibson Doubleneck Acoustic

The first example of a Gibson electric 12-string, (in fact one neck accommodated 12 strings, the other the usual six) this double-necked semi-acoustic dates from 1957. Less than 40 examples were made between then and 1962, so when Pete Townshend bought this model it was already a collectors item of sorts.

### Wreckage From Typical Who Performance

Rock & roll collectability knows no bounds, as instanced by these remnants of instruments smashed by the Who. They include (left to right) bass drum pedal, drum sticks and drum keys belonging to Keith Moon, John Entwistle's Hofner "violin" bass with the neck separated from the body, and Pete Townshend's Rickenbacker guitar. The instruments were wrecked during the "auto destructive art" period of the group's stage act; this particular musical mayhem took place during a broadcast of the BBC TV *Top Of The Pops* program.

### Paul Weller's Rickenbacker

Paul Weller's Rickenbacker electric guitar. The body has been applied with "Biff," "Bang" and "Pow" stickers and the instrument was used as his back-up stage guitar and featured

heavily on the "Setting Sons" album.

The emergence of Weller as a talented songwriter was one of the byproducts of the punk/New Wave era in the U.K. The Jam's early albums suggested little more than another set of moderately good musicians who had managed to get a record contract. However the "All Mod Cons" album hinted at a writer capable of uncannily good tunes, allied to harsh and only occasionally subtle lyrics. The success that followed genuinely surprised the group, achieving four U.K. number ones in just three years. The "Setting Sons" album is seen as the breakthrough as this provided their first Top Five single, "The Eton Rifles."

### Wyman's Framus

Bill Wyman's Framus Star-Bass guitar used by the bass player during 1964/5 in studio and live work. Won as the first prize in a raffle by the vendor, it was sold together with the winning ticket and a letter confirming the use of the guitar. Wyman never forgot the first song that excited him with its use of the electric guitar – the Les Paul and Mary Ford song "How High The Moon" in 1951. The guitar here was donated by Wyman to be raffled on behalf of ARMS, the Multiple Sclerosis charity, in 1983.

### Signed ZZ Top Explorer

A Gibson Explorer guitar dating from 1986 and signed by ZZ Top. Along with the beards and that car, the ZZ's must be as renowned for their guitars as they were rarely seen without them in their promotional videos. Although formed in 1969 the band's first international success did not emerge until 1983 with the "Eliminator" album. Prior to this they had toured relentlessly, especially in their native Texas, and had achieved five Top 30 US albums.

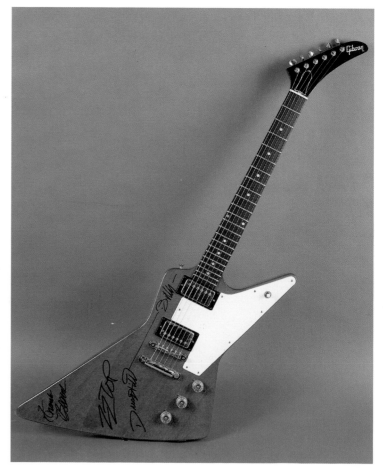

### ZZ's Custom Coyote

A most amazing looking guitar, this custom-shaped Coyote, which was made in Japan, was built for the wild Texas rock trio, ZZ Top. It was signed by the band – Billy Gibbons, Dusty Hill and Frank Beard – when they donated it in 1985 to a special sale in London, in aid of the Samaritans organization.

# Drums

### John Coghlan's Slingerland Kit

John Coghlan's Slingerland drum kit which he purchased in 1962. Previously it had belonged to the jazz drummer Louie Bellson, and the kit still bears his initials and name plaque. Coghlan joined a fledgling band called the Spectres in 1962, who later signed to Piccadilly Records and, like the label, disappeared without trace. They returned in 1968 on Pye as Status Quo but did not develop the 12-bar groove until 1972 when they signed to Vertigo. The band never achieved a major break in the U.S. since adopting their rocker look. Coghlan left the band in 1982 to pursue other solo and group projects.

### Drums Used by Sex Pistol Paul Cook

Despite the fact that they rejected the rock "star" syndrome, the black Gretsch drum kit used by Paul Cook throughout the Sex Pistols' career eventually made it to the salesrooms, authenticated by Cook himself.

### D'Arby's Ambassador Snare Drum

Terence Trent D'Arby's Pearl Ambassador snare drum with a message that finishes "Never lose your determination" followed by his signature and the words "Now Beat it." The singer donated the drum from his personal kit to raise money for The Arvon Foundation. After his first album sold over 1 million copies in the U.K. and having had a U.S. number one single, great things were expected of D'Arby.

### Lovelady's snare drum vertification

Part of the Brian Epstein "Scouse stable" of groups, the Fourmost had several chart entries with numbers written for them by Lennon and McCartney; the Ludwig snare drum given to their drummer Dave Lovelady at Abbey Road Studios by its original owner, Ringo Starr, in 1964, was sold by Lovelady twenty years later accompanied by this letter of verification.

I, David Lovelady, wish to certify that the "Ludwig" snare drum which was purchased from me by Mr. Patrick McCann was formerly the property of Richard Starkey or "Ringo" as a member of "The Beatles".

The drum was given to me by Ringo, whilst I was a member of the group known as "The Fourmost".

It was given to me at "Abbey Road Studios" whilst the Beatles were recording there. This was witnessed by William Hatton, also a member of "the Fourmost" at the time.

We were recording in another studio at Abbey Road under the supervision of Mr. Ron Richards, since George Martin, who usually recorded us, was occupied with the Beatles.

Ringo stated that he had played the drum in the morning session and stated that I could have it if I wished. I will be willing to provide any further information if asked to do so.

David Lovelady (EX FOURMOST).

### Various Keith Moon Percussion Items

A collection of Keith Moon's drums used between 1969 and 1975. The Chinese gongs at the back cannot fail to bring a smile to the faces of "Moon the Loon" fans as you picture him with these at his side. It is said that Moon joined what was to become the Who when, drunk as usual, he started to play the band's drums on stage during an interval. He was a significant asset to the band, combining energy and outrageousness with a genuine talent for playing drums. He is considered by some to have been the best drummer that rock & roll has ever seen.

## Carl Palmer's ELP Kit

Carl Palmer's custom-built drum kit from 1971 which was used on tour with Emerson, Lake and Palmer. A typical early 1970s rock combination, ELP were predominantly an album and touring band who achieved substantial sales on both sides of the Atlantic. They formed just too late to appear at Woodstock but made it to the Isle of Wight in 1970, and they continued to tour extensively before their split in 1978. It is best to check the music press weekly to discover if they have reunited or split once again.

## Kit Used by Don Powell of Slade

Slade drummer Don Powell's drum kit dating from 1971 and used by the artist on every Slade single, album and tour from that date until it was sold by Powell at Sotheby's in 1988. It was sold with all its fitted flight cases. Slade is a uniquely British band with sound and lyrics that are not vicious enough to be classified as heavy metal, but with more guts than the middle-ground, soft rock market that dominates the U.S. charts. They are still performing today and occasionally dent the charts with either a ballad or an interesting "thumper."

## Ringo's Sticks

A pair of Ringo Starr's drumsticks with a letter from Ringo, dated March 24, 1987, confirming in general terms the authenticity of the "beat bashers." Naturally the sticks conform to the type that Ringo used in the period.

# Pianos, Organs and Synthesizers

### Lennon Mellotron

John Lennon's Mellotron electric organ dating from the 1960s. The instrument was used by Lennon on the "White Album" of 1968 and still features in its memory the introduction to the track "Bungalow Bill." The "White Album," so called because the cover was plain white with just the group's name embossed and a serial number printed on the front (a stark contrast to "Sgt. Pepper"), was a double long play and is regarded as one of the group's weakest efforts. Producer George Martin attempted to persuade the band to reduce it to a single set but was over-ruled.

### The McCartney Family Piano

Paul McCartney's Chappell and Co. Ltd. upright piano, numbered 38567 and dating back to 1902. The young McCartney learnt his craft on this very piano until it was sold by his father in 1955. It re-emerged in 1981, together with a letter of authenticity, to be sold at auction for £9,000, proving it to have been a good investment by the original purchaser.

### John Lennon's Steinway Piano

This upright piano, made by Steinway and Sons of Hamburg, Germany, was manufactured in 1970. It belonged to John Lennon, and it was the instrument upon which he composed or partly composed much of his post-Beatles material. Eleven years later, a year after the singer's death in 1980, it realized £7,500 in auction.

### Cat Stevens' ARP Synthesizer

After a string of hits through the 70s, in 1979 singer Cat Stevens converted to Islam and changed his name to Yusef Islam; this ARP "Omni" Synthesizer is clearly earlier than that, so even though it was high-tech in its time, recent developments have rendered it a museum-piece with its now-primitive ability to synthesize the sound of various instruments. It appeared in sale complete with its instruction booklet.

# Miscellaneous Instruments

## Sade Album Saxophone

A saxophone used by Stuart Matthewman on the Sade album "Promise" and the subsequent tour. Another item donated to raise money for charity, it was auctioned with a photograph of Matthewman holding the instrument with Sade by his side, adding to its collectibility. The quality of the brass and wind instruments has always been vital to Sade's success, and Matthewman has been a part of the group since their early days.

## Beatles' "Penny Lane" Trumpet

The piccolo (octave) trumpet in Bb used on the Beatles' single "Penny Lane". The trumpet is made by Couesnon of Paris and is 18 inches in length. The instrument was used to record the solo trumpet part at the Abbey Road Studio 2, on January 17, 1967. It was also used in the same studio on June 25 on the recording of "All You Need Is Love", which was transmitted live in a massive TV world link-up. The "Penny Lane" single is highly significant to those obsessed by the Beatles' chart statistics. It was the group's only single not to reach number one (it peaked at two) in their sequence of 17 U.K. chart toppers, a fact made even more bizarre by its double billing with "Strawberry Fields Forever."

## Wonder's Hohner Chromatic

Stevie Wonder's Hohner Super 64 harmonica which was donated by the singer to raise money for a cancer center. Wonder, next to Dylan, is probably the best-known harmonica player in the rock business. He was specially asked by the Eurythmics to play it on their U.K. number one single "There Must Be An Angel" although, as so often happens nowadays, he recorded his solo in another country and the tape was sent over for the mix.

## Sax Used on Pink Floyd Classic

A Henri Selmer tenor saxophone dating from 1969 which was used by the session musician, John Parry, on the Pink Floyd album "Dark Side Of The Moon." The album is one of those that seem to be in every record collection, and Parry played on the title track and the single "Money" which reached number thirteen in 1973.

**Early R&B Movie Poster**
A cheap 65-minute compilation of footage shot at the Apollo Theatre, Harlem, jumping on the rock & roll bandwagon as *Rock'N'Roll Revue*, this cinema release from 1956 featured some of the biggest names in jazz and R&B, including Nat "King" Cole, Duke Ellington, Joe Turner, and Ruth Brown. (From the Isaac Tigrett Collection)

# Printed Memorabilia

Posters, concert programs, photographs and other printed memorabilia, whether a simple snapshot or an intricate design from the psychedelic era, were essentially produced for a short life, to publicize a specific event or group at a particular stage in their career. With Elvis Presley, the first, young white exponent of rock & roll music, it was important to show his color and smouldering good looks to an audience who at that time would have been unlikely to buy "black music" by African–American recording artists. Plain billboards announced concerts in movie theaters, sports arenas and theaters; ephemeral and scarce today, these posters would have been

▶

**Apple Portrait of Lennon**
A psychedelic portrait of Lennon from the Beatles' Apple Boutique collection of colored lithographic posters. These were commissioned by the group to be sold in their store which was located at 94 Baker Street. The store opened on December 7, 1967 but closed on July 31, 1968 with the remaining stock being given away.

generally torn down or pasted over a few weeks after they first appeared.

Printed memorabilia reflects the popular design styles of the period. The 1950s saw considerable development in graphic design, influenced by stylistic movements such as Surrealism, Abstractionism, and Bauhaus. New typefaces were designed which gave printed material a clean and innovative style and, with the use of photolithography which allowed full-color photographs to be printed with ease, photographs of objects were often shown floating in white space. A good example of this stark design can be seen on the cover illustration of the program for Helen Shapiro's February 1963 concert tour (with the Beatles as support), which consisted of a floating cutout color portrait of Shapiro laid over a cutout (British) Columbia label LP record.

Corporate identity, the use of a consistent design image throughout one company or institution was a novel innovation in the 1950s, but a design strategy which was to be used extensively in the next decade by rock bands who wanted to promote their own style or publicize a certain aspect of their repertoire. Graphics were increasingly affected by the results of market research into the buying patterns of the public which indicated that bright colors and gimmicks gained the greatest commercial impact over a limited timespan.

In the early 1960s artists such as Eduardo Paolozzi, Andy Warhol and Roy Lichtenstein were influenced by the popular or "pop" graphics of comics, packaging and advertisements and used them in collages or carefully created two-dimensional painted icons inspired by canned supermarket produce – Warhol's Campbell's soup can from 1962 is an example of the "pop" art created at the time. Gradually the word "pop" was applied to other areas, pop music and pop clothes for example, both of instant appeal to the young and generally regarded as ephemeral at the time.

Mass communication in the 1960s fueled a proliferation of strong images for posters, television commercials, magazines and the color magazine supplements which accompanied weekend newspapers. These were concerned with the promotion of consumer goods, but also helped to stimulate public awareness of new design styles. Arresting designs were printed on an array of novel items including shopping bags and lapel badges; before long promoters and record companies themselves realized that the record sleeve could be an important vehicle both for the graphic designer and, more importantly, for the band to use in self-promotion.

Stark black and white images were the vogue in the early-to-middle Sixties, popularized by trendy and influential magazines, a style which was widely used by artistic editors. The now memorable image on the front of the Beatles' second album, "With The Beatles," took the austere form of dramatically side-lit and grainily shadowed faces of the group members which appeared to float against the black background (released on November 30, 1963, it was the first album of any type to sell 1 million copies in the U.K.).

The later 1960s saw a merging of styles; a retreat into retrospective graphic design and fashion inspired by Art Nouveau and Art Deco and their exponents, including Alphonse Mucha and Aubrey Beardsley. Alongside the use of Art Nouveau's flowing lines developed psychedelia; swirling shapes and brightly mixed colors influenced by drug culture and the hallucinogenic experiences stimulated by drugs such as LSD.

The plain printed billboards of the 1950s and early 1960s which had been used to publicize concerts or events and which were thrown away immediately afterwards, began to develop into inexpensive works of art which were used to enhance living spaces. Posters became less typographic and more pictorial, and much greater use was made of the photolithographic process which had so revolutionized graphic design in other printed material of the time. Alongside the development of more

**"James Brown Revue" Advertisement**
Even straightforward concert posters, like this James Brown Revue advertisement for Oakland Auditorium in the mid 60s, now change hands for hundreds of dollars. Catalogue descriptions like "printed in purple on black and white" are important to serious collectors to whom color variants can have a bearing on collectibility.

Despite numerous threats, Brown has never stopped touring, and although he has had few highly placed chart hits, his sales remain strong.

**Early Beatles Concert Poster**

An advertising poster for Emile Ford, and the Beatles, April 6, 1962, with the "Beetles" misprint. The poster was the property of Pete Best, who was ejected from the group in August 1962. The poster dates from an important period in the group's development, having just signed with Epstein in February that year who began to polish their image. Shortly afterwards they were destined to meet with George Martin.

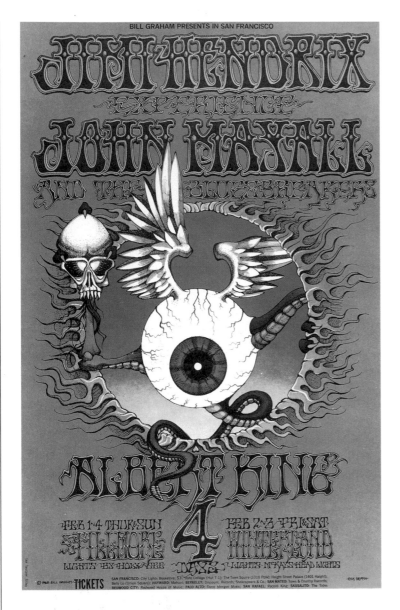

### Hendrix/Mayall San Francisco Poster

This double poster for the Jimi Hendrix Experience and John Mayall's Bluesbreakers – plus blues guitarist Albert King – advertised four West Coast concerts at two famous venues, the Fillmore and Winterland, both in San Francisco. It was sold in New York in 1990 along with various other similar posters for concerts that included the Doors, the Grateful Dead, Jefferson Airplane and the now almost-forgotten Moby Grape.

psychedelic style which is so inexorably linked with the hippy movement that flourished there. The Fillmore posters of the late 1960s combined blocks of color with innovative typographical styles (which often required concentration to decipher), intricate drawn detail and photolithography to create a style of poster art in which the overall design elements were more important than just putting across a simple message which could be read from a distance.

In England the fusing of psychedelia and retro motifs was developing along similar lines. A particularly influential design partnership established by Michael English and Nigel Waymouth in 1967 was christened "Hapshash and the Coloured Coat" in true hippy style. English was known in design circles for creating wildly popular fashion accessories such as the Union Jack sunglasses which had invaded Carnaby Street during the mid 1960s. Nigel Waymouth, the owner of "Granny Takes A Trip," a popular shop in the fashion Mecca of London's King's Road, commissioned English to decorate the boutique. The frontage was duly covered with the enormous face of an American Indian and became a landmark in the street. A boutique much favored by those involved in the music business, the publicity and decorative posters which Hapshash and the Coloured Coat produced for the store may have stimulated work in this industry. However the first introductions were made, Hapshash went on to produce impressive and innovative psychedelic posters for influential bands over subsequent years.

The mid-to-late 1960s saw the revival of the emphasis on sophisticated and decorative posters, the living conditions and lifestyles of most householders changed. Cluttered homes which had remained largely unchanged since World War II were revolutionized by a new fashion. Stark interior design influenced by Scandinavian style created clinical expanses of plain white walls; posters began to be used as cheap and novel home decorations.

Rock posters were originally bought, begged, or "borrowed" from the venues where groups were appearing. But in the 1960s mail order companies began placing advertisements in magazines offering a wide cross-section of different posters for sale. The advertisements appeared in the growing number of magazines dedicated to "pop" music, teenage fashion, culture and interests and the magazines themselves would often feature large centerfold portraits of performers which could be taken out and used as posters.

Wes Wilson, the American artist who designed startling posters for rock concerts held at the Fillmore Auditorium in California, is generally credited with having developed the

### "Granny Takes A Trip" Poster

Hapshash and the Coloured Coat was the collective name of artists Nigel Waymouth and Michael English, who produced some of the most accomplished British "psychedelic" artworks of the late 60s, including a number of influential rock concert posters and album cover designs. This "Granny Takes A Trip" poster – also the name of Waymouth's fashionable King's Road boutique at the time – is typical of the poster-as-art, when they were designed as decorative objects rather than just a commercial advertising medium.

illustration rather than photography in the 1966–1970 period which was apparent in many different types of printed material. Martin Sharp, an Australian artist, was the center of this style in the music industry and was responsible for creating many striking images; the album cover for Cream's "Disraeli Gears" (released on November 18, 1967) is a good example of his graphic style. Sharp's works include the Donovan *Sunshine Superman*, the Bob Dylan *Blowing in the Wind* and the poster for the "Legalize Cannabis" demonstration held at Speaker's Corner in London which adorned the walls of many university bedrooms in the late 60s and early 70s. All these designs placed the emphasis on highly detailed illustration mixed with limited photolithography. However, perhaps Sharp's best known poster, *Hendrix Explosion*, is very different in timbre to his other work; a startling image of an abandoned Jimi Hendrix playing his guitar with shafts of psychedelic color exploding from the instrument in every direction.

Rock posters in the early 1970s continued the tradition of illustration mixed with photolithography, but increasingly designers used stark, monochrome photolithography overlaid with brightly colored typography. But it was not until the end of that decade that the Sex Pistols and punk bands brought a new graphic style to the billboards. The artist, Jamie Reid, was responsible for the creation of some of the most memorable posters and album covers of the late 70s. He was the first British designer to exploit stickers to advertise rock music; his "No Future" Sex Pistols stickers were used all over London by fans; fluorescent pink, green and yellow streamers were also printed with the Sex Pistols' logo and anarchic messages such as "Believe In The Ruins," "Never Trust A Hippie," and "They Swindled Their Way To The Top." Using his threatening ransom note-style typography and startling images, including a portrait of Queen Elizabeth II with a safety pin through her lips, Reid redefined rock poster design. One memorable poster for a Sex Pistols performance at the 100 Club incorporated photographs of letters (banning the group from venues nationwide) into the overall poster design.

The common thread which links most of the wide diversity of graphic styles during the 1980s is retrospection; the culture of the 60s was the focus of a popular revival which affected music and the design of much fashion, printed and mass-produced material including those associated directly with music and musicians.

Posters have to be in near perfect condition if they are to be of interest to collectors and they are bought for many different reasons. Some enthusiasts are attracted by only the visual quality of a poster; others may purchase to illustrate the stylistic development of this very immediate and ephemeral art form. A number may collect posters from one period which may have been particularly influential in their lives, or those which relate to just one venue (such as the Fillmore Auditorium posters). But it is generally a preoccupation with one performer which attracts collectors who may buy a poster as part of a general collection concerned with a single band.

Rock music is fortunate in that every twist and turn in its sinuous history has been recorded by photographs, television

programs, movies and video. From the birth of rock & roll in 1950s America, when record companies were anxious to show that their performers were white and not black, to present-day rappers who want to prove to their potential audiences that they are black and not white, photographers have helped to project the image and style of the performers. While portraits of rock performers by well-known photographers are widely collected and expensive today, some of the photographs taken by fans and members of the group's entourage can provide some of the more interesting insights into their lives. Often sold with negative and copyright, these unposed, amateur shots are generally of more importance to enthusiasts of rock & roll collectibles than collectors of photographs who require particular photographic or design qualities which this type of shot may lack. In England some of the most influential photographers who specialized in portraits of musicians were Dezo Hoffmann, Harry Hammond,

### Live Aid Illustration by Peter Blake
Growing out of the success of his Band Aid record project, Bob Geldof's vision of a worldwide rock audience for African relief came true on July 13, 1985. This poster, designed and created by painter Peter Blake, was signed by all the Wembley participants except for Adam Ant and some of the backing musicians and appeared in a sale four years later.

**The Stones by Dezo Hoffmann**
Although mainly associated with his work with the Beatles, Dezo Hoffmann photographed hundreds of stars from the world of movies, pop music and jazz. This original print of a portrait of Mick Jagger dates from the early days of the Rolling Stones' success, circa 1964, and was auctioned, mounted and signed by Hoffmann (who died in 1986), in 1984.

Gered Mankowitz, Linda McCartney, Robert Freeman and Robert Whittaker, with Cecil Beaton, David Bailey and Annie Leibowitz, being well-known portrait photographers who took rock portraits from time to time.

The photographer who, during his lifetime, had the largest archive of rock portraits, was Dezo Hoffmann whose offices were bursting with transparencies and negatives of the famous as well as the one-hit wonders. The scale of the archive was extraordinary, but it should be noted that most groups trying to make it in the business would be sent somewhere by their managers or record companies to get their "monkey shots" or publicity photographs taken. Hoffmann was fortunate during the 1960s to be one of the few photographers who specialized in this type of portraiture.

Harry Hammond was working as a photographer between 1948 and 1963 and recorded the images of many performers, both from England and the U.S., at the peak of their profession. Hammond captured the excitement of performers and audience in close contact with the development of the first television programs in the U.K. designed to attract younger audiences, *6.5 Special* launched in 1957 and *Oh Boy!* (1958). A photographer whose early experiences included photographing for society magazines including *The Tatler, Bystander* and *Illustrated London News*, Hammond used a similar sympathetic style in his portraits of musicians. Much of Hammond's work is known through exhibitions, particularly those in London's Photographers Gallery in the 1980s, and through his numerous books; several of his images have been bought by The National Portrait Gallery and the Victoria and Albert Theatre Museum. His best-known portraits include those of Buddy Holly and the Crickets performing in England during their brief tour in 1958, a young Cliff Richard captured in 1958 looking at a concert poster which showed him topping the bill for the first time, and Eddie Cochran in action at the *NME* Poll Winners' Concert at Empire Pool, Wembley in February 1960 less than two months before his fatal car crash.

**Redding and Hendrix Color Set**
One of 21 unpublished color photographs of Jimi Hendrix and his bass player Noel Redding, all taken at London's Royal Albert Hall during a 1969 appearance by the Jimi Hendrix Experience. The Cibachrome prints, along with corresponding Ektachrome transparencies, were sold complete with copyright.

  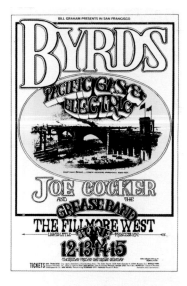 

| Valid Saturday Only $3.00 | Valid Friday Only $3.50 | Valid Friday Only $3.50 | Valid Friday Only—$3.00 |

A young Hamburg girl, Astrid Kirchherr, was responsible for some of the most imaginative early rock photographs. Posing unsmiling Beatles against army trucks and freight cars in a rail classification yard in 1960, Kirchherr created a feeling of smoldering danger which made the group appear older and more experienced. Her studio portraits were generally harshly lit and stark, but posed with great verve and originality, capturing a sense of mystery and romance. Kirchherr's work appears very seldom outside the auction market, although her images are widely known.

A fashion photographer, Robert Freeman, was the man responsible for creating some of the Beatles' most lasting images including the covers of their second album "Meet The Beatles" (1963), their fourth "Beatles For Sale" (1964) and their sixth, "Rubber Soul" (1965), plus those of their two film albums *A Hard Days Night* and *Help!*. Accompanying the group on tour to America and to the Bahamas for the filming of the movie *Help!*, Freeman has taken many memorable monochrome and color portraits which are widely sought by collectors of photographs as well as rock memorabilia. Freeman toured internationally during the 1980s with exhibitions of his photographs, and much of his work both previously published and unpublished, appears in his recent book.

Gered Mankowitz was a young successful theatrical portrait photographer when he took his first photograph for an LP cover. Through Marianne Faithfull Mankowitz was asked to photograph the Rolling Stones and became the group's official photographer from 1965 until 1967, taking shots which were used on the album covers of "Out Of Our Heads" (1965) and "Between The Buttons" (1967) as well as numerous other familiar images which were used for programs and other promotion purposes. Mankowitz was generally commissioned by artist's managements rather than record companies who did not appear to have art departments in the early 60s and he was given every encouragement to experiment. Many memorable images can be

## Byrds Tickets

Four tickets that were presented as a set to a London museum specializing in the theater and live entertainment, from late 1960s events featuring the Byrds. All four concerts were at the San Francisco Fillmore Auditorium; the first (top left) dates from 1967, the second (top right) a Byrds bill with seminal West Coast band Electric Flag and blues guitarist B.B. King from the same year, a concert doubling at the Winterland Ballroom. Mike Bloomfield tops the bill on a Byrds gig with Pacific Gas and Electric in 1969 (bottom left), while the Byrds headline again in 1969 over Joe Cocker and PG & E. Given the now cult status of the Byrds, and the long ago demise of some of the other bands – together with the historic importance of the Fillmore itself – such a set of tickets would command considerable interest on the collectors market. (Courtesy of V&A Theatre Museum)

credited to Mankowitz, Hendrix exhaling smoke dressed in his military frogged jacket, Shakin' Stevens as a matinee idol, cricket player Elton John on the cover of his "Greatest Hits Volume II" album, and the Tourists' white room. Gered Mankowitz continues to experiment with his photographs and has, in recent years, produced some arresting "photo-paintings" in which the monochrome print is colored and progressed by being subject to "emulsion manipulation" during development.

The printed image (whether still or moving) and graphic design have been recognized as the most important weapons in the battle for record sales. Over the decades a great deal of material has been produced to launch artists and groups and subsequently to promote them, and enthusiasts today can still be fortunate enough to find concert programs, theater front-of-house stills, and fan club photographs at yard sales and conventions. Excluding the very best photographs and posters, printed material remains a relatively inexpensive and satisfying collecting area.

# Posters

## THE KING OF ROCK N' ROLL

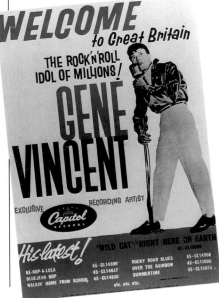

### Bill Haley Poster

No pretender to the throne, for a brief few months in 1955-56 Bill Haley really was the "King of Rock & Roll" as this poster claims, before the younger, earthier and undeniably sexier Elvis Presley stole his crown forever.

### Gene Vincent British Debut Material

An original Capitol Records poster to promote Gene Vincent's 1959 first tour of Britain. Despite a lack of chart hits for several years, he made a successful debut with Marty Wilde at the Tooting Granada in London. He went on to appear regularly on the British TV rock show *Boy Meets Girl*.

### Rolling Stones 1963 Poster

When the Rolling Stones first played in the north of England, in 1963, they were often billed as "London's answer to the Beatles." But Brian Epstein's NEMS Enterprises would have none of this – for obvious reasons, as this poster advertising a concert he promoted at the Tower Ballroom, New Brighton suggests. Titled "Southern Sounds '63," the event was subsequently canceled.

### Buddy Holly British Tour Poster

An original poster from Buddy Holly's final concert on his only British tour in 1958. The tour consisted of 25 twice-nightly performances throughout March. Together with various TV appearances the tour helped promote four Holly songs into the Top 20 in just one week.

### Love Me Tender
### Front-of-House Bill

An original poster for the Elvis Presley film *Love Me Tender*. Elvis's movie debut met with indifference from the critics but not from the fans. Twentieth Century-Fox was to issue an unprecedented 550 prints for distribution in the U.S.A.

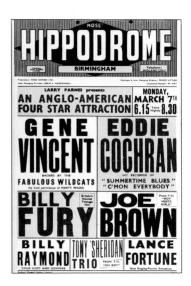

### Vincent/Cochran Package Poster

A poster from the ill-fated Gene Vincent/Eddie Cochran U.K. tour of 1960, its collectability is obvious; it was the tour during which Cochran was killed on April 17, on the way from a gig in Bristol. The bill also featured Marty Wilde's group the Wildcats backing Vincent, "Britain's Newest Teenage Idol" Billy Fury, and Tony Sheridan, who the following year was to record with the Beatles in Hamburg.

### Vintage R&B Bill

This poster for a typical rhythm and blues package show from 1961 advertises a line-up in Baltimore, Ohio, featuring names like Fats Domino, Bo Diddley and the Drifters who were to be regarded as legends a decade later. Note the inclusion of Chubby Checker just before he was being hailed as "King of the Twist" – here, his claim to fame is his second million-seller "Pony Time." Although he had smashed in 1960 with "The Twist," it was only after the success of "Lets Twist Again," later in 1961, that he became permanently associated with the dance craze.

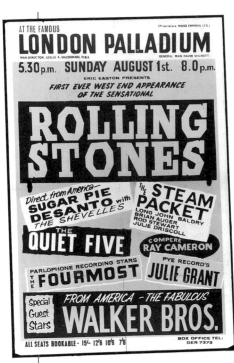

## The Stones at the Palladium

An original poster for the Stones headlining the London Palladium, in August 1965. This was the only time they ever played at this venue and on this occasion they rented it themselves and booked all the support acts. The Walker Brothers were eventually replaced by the Moody Blues.

## Poster for Brenda Lee One-Nighter

Brenda Lee was on a 17-date U.K. tour having performed in the Royal Command Performance. Despite efforts with several British record producers, she could not recapture her success of the early 1960s.

## Four Vintage Movie-House Bills

The quick-and-cheap pop exploitation film was a Hollywood response to each new chart trend right from the days of *Rock Around The Clock*. A set of four posters that typified the genre appeared at auction in 1989, framed and glazed, including Chubby Checker in *Don't Knock The Twist, Play It Cool* with Billy Fury, and a thrown-together collection of film cameos, produced by Phil Spector, called *The Big T.N.T. Show*, featuring "all time greats" that included Tina Turner, Ray Charles, and the Byrds in "the biggest bash in the history of show business!"

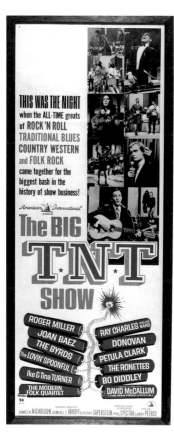

## Rare Who Club Poster

A rare original poster for the Who at the Marquee, November 1964. Having just changed their name from the High Numbers, the band did not have a record contract, having failed with "I'm The Face" on Fontana. By January 1965 they had secured a deal with Brunswick, having been rejected by EMI.

### Chuck Berry/Animals Tour Bill

An original concert advertising bill dated May 21, 1964, just before ''The House Of The Rising Sun'' hit number one for the Animals. Chuck Berry had spent two years in jail, but his popularity on both sides of the Atlantic was underpinned by the Beatles' covers of his songs.

### 1963 "Soul Extravaganza" Poster

Package tour posters make fascinating historic documents, if only because of the secondary billing given to support acts who later became world superstars. The ''Soul Extravaganza'' of 1963 featured among 11 acts Gladys Knight and the Pips, who were to eclipse the short-lived success of bill-toppers Gene Chandler and Jerry Butler in years to come.

### Mama Cass Poster

A poster for Cass Elliot at the London Palladium, dating from July 15, 1974. Billed with a package of names which have not withstood the test of time, it was a sad end to the career of the ex-Mama And Papa's star; Mama Cass died in England just two weeks after this concert. (From the Isaac Tigrett Collection)

### Elvis *Roustabout* Movie Bill

An original poster to promote the 1964 Elvis Presley film *Roustabout*. Elvis's sixteenth film continued the trend of poor reviews and box office success. The plot followed the by then familiar romantic drama theme.

### "Freak Out" Poster

A real period piece, this 1966 poster advertising a "double – giant – freak – out – ball" was in fact for two gigs on consecutive nights at London's Roundhouse featuring Geno Washington, the Cream, the Who, Pink Floyd, and others. Note the reference to "late bars, central heating, psychedelic lighting" and "new improved entrance." The Roundhouse was a regular venue for the more esoteric "happenings" and "raves" that characterized the flower power era, which came into its own in 1967.

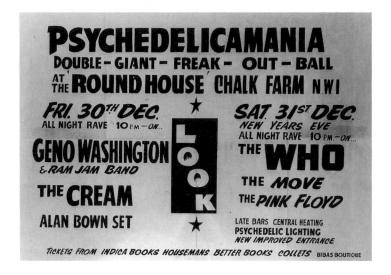

### "Lucy In The Sky" Illustration

A poster from 1967 by artist Tom Cervenak printed by Impulse of San Francisco, illustrating the Beatles song "Lucy In The Sky With Diamonds." The newspaper taxi, a boat on a river, a plasticine porter and kaleidoscope eyes are all represented. It is a tribute to the Beatles that their album tracks are as familiar as many bands' singles.

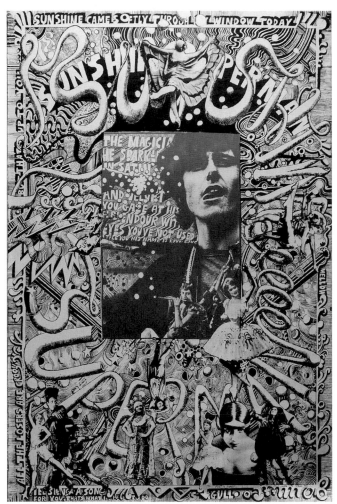

### Donovan Poster by Martin Sharp

Martin Sharp produced some of the most visibly complex posters and album covers of psychedelia, in an area where legibility had been sacrificed to design in most cases.

This photolitho evocation of Donovan's 1967 anthem "Sunshine Superman" was a case in point, and the quality of much of the graphic style of the era was only emphasized further when it appeared under glass in a salesroom.

### Psychedelic Fillmore Advertisement

Bill Graham's Fillmore Auditorium in San Francisco – it only became the Fillmore West after he opened a New York branch as the Fillmore East – was a catalyst for the whole West Coast scene, and as a consequence produced some of the classic artefacts of "psychedelic" graphics. This one advertises a gig by Quicksilver Messenger Service and others.

**The Doors at the Fillmore**

A typically stylized poster of the San Francisco hippy era of 1967. Advertising the Doors concerts at the Fillmore Auditorium and at the Winterland in San Francisco – both venues managed by Bill Graham. By this stage the band had achieved their first U.S. number one and were the most significant live act of the time.

**Doors Poster**

Since the 1991 Oliver Stone movie about the band and lead singer Jim Morrison, any ephemera associated with the Doors has become even more collectible, such as this and one other early poster advertising the band in 1967, sold in New York in mid 1991.

**Poster by "The Fool"**

An Apple Publishing Co. Ltd. Dream poster designed by Simone and Marijke of "The Fool," signed and dated 1967. "The Fool" design team contributed heavily to the Apple Boutique and specialized in innovative images and forms.

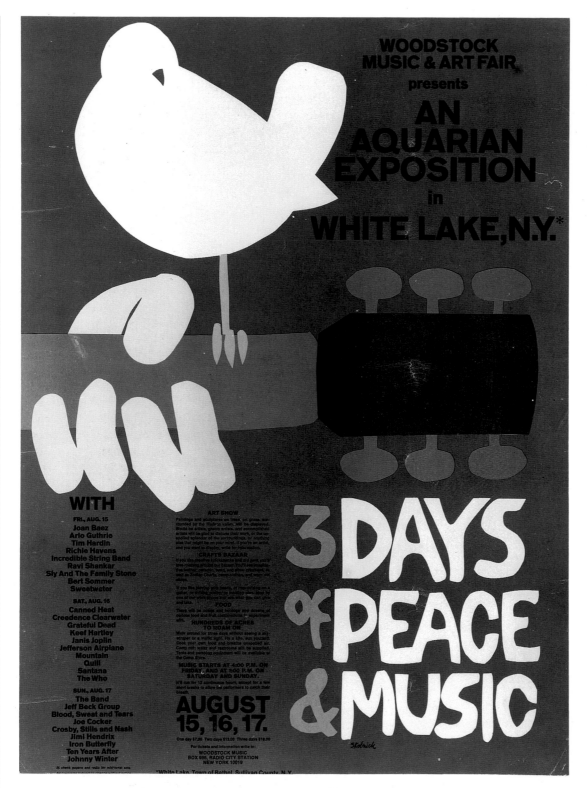

### Dylan Portrait by Peter Max

Peter Max was a highly successful graphic designer in the heyday of "psychedelic art," his work appearing in books, on record covers and most notably on posters. His style, like that of most of his contemporaries working in the same field, very quickly became dated, such as in this case with a poster portrait of Bob Dylan. In hindsight the rather quaint feel of the poster does mean that the material is even more collectible.

### Poster Announcing Woodstock

Posters, by their very nature (as advertisements in advance of events rather than commemorations afterwards), are essentially temporary and disposable. Highly collectible, therefore, in later years – especially when the event was to become a slice of rock & roll history, as with the three-day festival "of peace and music" in upstate New York that became known forever as Woodstock. By the time it hit the salesroom the poster was being described in works of art terms – "printed in black, blue, green and yellows on red, mounted, framed and glazed, overall size 89.5 by 76.5 cm (35 by 30 in)."

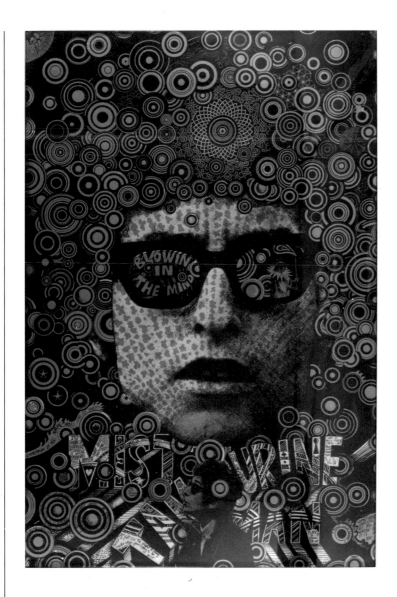

### Psychedelic Dylan Poster

Mind-expanding drugs and their effects were clearly near the surface in most "psychedelic" imagery , no more so than in this Martin Sharp poster that uses Bob Dylan lyrics and song titles along with the *de rigeur* swirling "op art" shapes and colors to evoke the sensation of an hallucinatory "trip."

No hippy home should be without one.

### Isle of Wight 1970

The nearest Britain got to its own Woodstock was at the Isle of Wight Festivals of 1969 and 1970. The three days in 1969 — just two weeks after Woodstock — were climaxed by Bob Dylan and the Band in front of a crowd of 250,000. The festival the following year was marked historically by the appearance of Jimi Hendrix less than a month before his untimely death. The Saturday headlining of the Doors also marked one of the last appearances of another of rock's doomed legends.

### German Hendrix Concert Bill

Not as often reproduced as some of the more familiar American and British items, this German poster for a Jimi Hendrix concert in Stuttgart has a rarity attached to its collector value. The work of designer Gunther Kieser in 1969, it shows a move away from the decorative excess of psychedelic graphics to a more formal — and readable — style toward the end of the decade.

### UFO "Coming Events" Advertising Bill

The "UFO Coming" poster, a typical piece of 1967 psychedelia, was designed by Hapshash and the Coloured Coat. "UFO" refers to the once-a-week "underground" club of that name in London's Tottenham Court Road; the rest of the time it functioned as an Irish social center. The upcoming events advertised, in addition to The Crazy World of Arthur Brown and Soft Machine, include a "Liverpool Love Festival" which was a mixed-media "happening" that helped launch the Liverpool poetry scene in the capital.

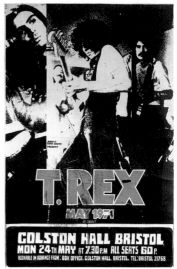

**T. Rex Concert Bill**

An original poster for a T Rex concert in May 1971. "Hot Love" had become the group's first number one in March and the "Electric Warrior" album, released in October, would stay at number one for six weeks. Within a year, T. Rex would play to audiences in excess of 100,000.

**Tour Poster for T. Rex 1971**

An original concert promotion poster for T. Rex on October 24, 1971. The tour had a significant effect on the fate of "Electric Warrior" which first hit number one in December 1971. At this time Bolan changed from Fly Records to his own T. Rex Wax Co. label, backed by EMI.

**Move/ELO "Peace And Love" Concert Poster**

An original concert poster dated September 4, 1971 to promote "a day of peace and love." The poster is significant as it promotes both The Move and, as the group was to become, The Electric Light Orchestra. Roy Wood originally intended to run ELO concurrently with The Move, but eventually lost interest in both projects, leaving Jeff Lynne to lead the group.

### Stones in Honolulu Poster

Grandiose (in fact often over-the-top) graphics characterized rock visuals in the early 70s. With a band like the Rolling Stones, it seemed in stark contrast to the essentially earthy nature of the music. Bill Graham promoted the Honolulu concerts during their 1973 world tour.

### Rolling Stones Cardiff 1973 Concert Bill

A poster for the Rolling Stones canceled concert at the Cardiff and Pembroke Castle in 1973 which was part of their U.K. tour that began on September 11. The poster uses a Gothic style and incorporates the famous Stones tongue motif by Andy Warhol which they adopted for their own label launched in 1971.

### 'Stones 1967 Poster

An original Rolling Stones poster dating from 1967. The group were tired of touring and proposed that the 16-date tour of Europe be their last for a considerable period. The tour included a concert in Warsaw which, partly due to Jagger's high jinx with some Stones 45s, ended in the use of tear gas by the army.

### Advertisement for Beatles' Final Concert

Though the poster for the event appears to have been designed in something of a hurry, little did the promoters know that this concert at San Francisco's Candlestick Park on August 19, 1966 was to be the Beatles' last ever, therefore conferring historic status on the event and a commensurate premium on the sale price of the poster in later years.

### Help! Movie Poster

Nothing quite captures the feel of a film's original release like the theater poster of the time. There is a great collectability for movie posters as such, and much other film memorabilia, and it crops up among rock & roll artifacts from time to time. This poster for the Beatles' second feature *Help!* evokes perfectly the inevitable excitement of any new release, on record or celluloid, by the Fab Four in the mid 60s.

### Early Springsteen Promo Material

After the Castiles, Bruce Springsteen's second band in 1969 was called Child. Any ephemera concerning the group is highly sought after, as the singer changed the name to Steel Mill after a couple of months when he discovered there was another outfit using the same name. Sold with this Child poster, in New York in 1991, was a slightly later but equally rare one from 1974, advertising "New Jersey's own" in a gig at the local Seton Hall University.

## PHI ZAPPA KRAPPA

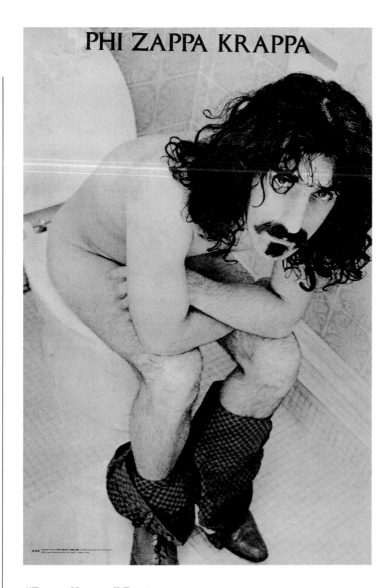

### Stones Ad by David Byrd

Among the many visual influences that were incorporated into the graphics of the late 60s, the Victorian pre-Raphaelites and turn-of-the-century art nouveau were both evident in the work of British artist David Byrd, as in this poster for two Rolling Stones concerts in December 1969.

### Dylan Movie Poster

A poster for the Don Pennebaker movie made on the road with Dylan during his 1965 British tour, *Don't Look Back*; since hailed as one of the best rock documentaries; the film – made in black and white – was released in 1967. (From the Isaac Tigrett Collection)

### "Zappa Krappa" Poster

During the heyday of the poster-as-decoration, certain images – like the ''Would you buy a used car from this man?'' picture of Richard Nixon – became ''best sellers'' of their kind. One famous, or notorious, example was the ''Zappa Krappa'' poster of shock-rock *avant garde* musician Frank Zappa sitting on the toilet . . . satirizing, as he did in his records, the rather serious tone certain rock & rollers had adopted in the late 1960s.

### Floyd "Fantasy" Illustration

An example of ''sword and sorcery'' imagery featuring in rock illustration. Eventually associated with Heavy Metal music, this 1970 poster shows its use in the so-called ''progressive'' field – as it continued to be with 70s bands like Yes – advertising a Salt Lake City appearance by Pink Floyd.

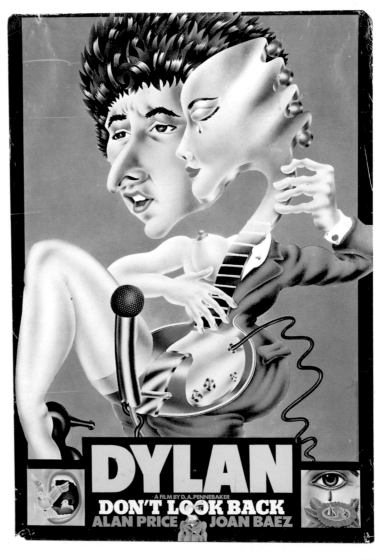

### Early Bolan Promo Poster

Originally the property of Andy Ellison (top right), who shared vocals with Marc Bolan (top left) in John's Children, this poster for their minor hit "Desdemona" was sold at a 1987 charity auction in aid of a drug rehabilitation trust. The salesroom concerned waived charges on the sales, most of which comprised material donated by the stars themselves.

### Bolan "Keep Britain Tidy" Advertisement

An early example of environmental concern on the part of a pop star: Marc Bolan, who had moved from "underground" name to glam-rock teenybop idol in the early 70s, endorses the "Keep Britain Tidy" campaign on this rare poster that was sold in a London auction in 1990.

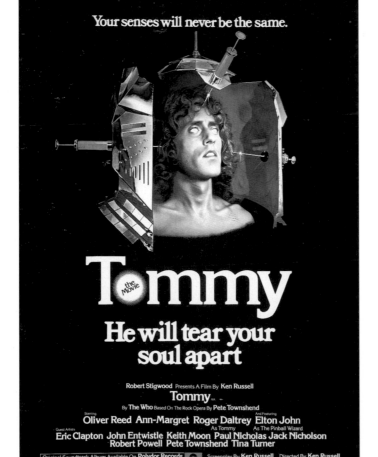

### Tommy Billboard Material

Ken Russell's 1975 film version of the Who's *Tommy* now looks decidedly dated, but that probably enhances the value to collectors of associated ephemera. Of three posters up for sale in 1989, two – a standard 101 by 152 cm (39 by 59 in) – were literally dwarfed by the third which was a ten-section billboard poster.

### Signed Elton-in-Russia Poster

An original concert poster for Elton John's tour of Russia in 1979 and signed by John, which was sold in 1988. Having announced his retirement from live work in 1977, he toured the U.K. in March 1979 and followed this with the eight Russian dates in May. Towards the end of his first concert, Elton decided to play "Back In The U.S.S.R." despite not knowing the words or chords, so merely repeating the chorus. The authorities advised him to drop the song for the subsequent events on the tour but it was too tempting to resist.

### Cliff Richard Leningrad Poster

A rare Russian concert poster for Cliff Richard's September 1976 dates. Believed to be the second of only two posters to have been used to advertise the event. Richard played at the Hall of the October Revolution in Leningrad (St. Petersburg), becoming the first western rock star to do so.

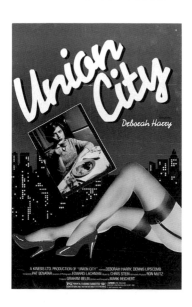

### Debbie Harry Film Poster

An original poster for the film *Union City* starring Blondie singer Deborah Harry. Her first feature film, with soundtrack by her long-time boyfriend Chris Stein, the film failed to capture the imagination of the public and Harry's film career has been limited to date.

### 'Pistols "Pretty Vacant" Poster

Its visual image was central to the impact of punk, coming as it did from the art schools and fashion trend-setters rather than the music mainstream – in fact it was the latter it sought to challenge. No surprise, therefore, that the main creator of the Sex Pistols' graphic image was a designer, Jamie Reid, who established the "paste-up" look of their posters – this one is for the 1977 single "Pretty Vacant" – album covers, and other promotional material.

### Punk Promotional Material

Punk memorabilia, by its very design throwaway, is now ironically, highly collectible. A collection of Sex Pistols ephemera sold at Sotheby's in 1987 included this poster for their debut U.K. tour. Note the Clash at the bottom of the bill, also the plug for the Damned's first single "New Rose" (actually, the first record by a punk group to be released).

# Photographs

### "All You Need Is Love" Pics

Previously unpublished pictures of the most widely collected groups like the Beatles become rarer as the years go by, so when a set of color positives from the celebrated 1967 "All You Need Is Love" session on the global TV link-up *Our World* appeared for sale, it naturally generated much interest, reflected in a sale figure of around £1,000.

### Cyrus Andrews Archive

Cyrus Andrews, born in 1902, was a newspaper and radio journalist who became fascinated with the British popular music scene, and during the early to mid 60s became something of a photographic entrepreneur, hiring photographers to take casual shots of stars, particularly at the studios of the famous *Ready Steady Go!* TV program between 1964 and 1966. His amazing collection, comprising over 15,000 negatives, prints and contact sheets, was eventually sold in 1987. Among the hundreds of stars featured in the archive were (left to right, top) the Beatles, Mick Jagger, David Bowie, (bottom) Cliff Richard, the Supremes and the Beach Boys.

### Limited Edition "With The Beatles"

Perhaps the most familiar of all the Beatles iconography, Robert Freeman's celebrated 1963 photograph in grainy black-and-white epitomized the group's image in the mid 60s. Collectors, of course, want a limited edition print: this one was signed by the photographer on the back of the mount and the bottom right-hand corner of the matt, image size 46 by 38.5 cm (20 by 15 in).

### Alternative "Sgt. Pepper" Photographs

Alternative takes of familiar images such as record covers are highly collectible; this picture of the Beatles during the shooting for the middle spread of "Sgt. Pepper," presumably by the sleeve photographer Michael Cooper, was in a collection of 13 color prints auctioned in 1984.

### Early Beatles Interview Photo

Among an unrepeatable collection of scrapbook material that was sold in 1986 was this photograph of the Beatles being interviewed by a local hospital radio presenter in 1962, and a playlist from the same period, the latter illustrating the broad-based nature of their repertoire – from R&B covers like "Some Other Guy" and "Slow Down," oldies such as "Ain't She Sweet" to current chart hits including the Crickets' "Don't Ever Change" and Joe Brown's "Picture Of You" – plus just one original, "Love Me Do."

### The Beatles in Hamburg
A surprisingly large number of pictures have emerged over the years of the Beatles in their early days in Hamburg. Here they are in a casual snapshot leaning against the bar of the Indra club, the original five (left to right) Paul, John, George, Stuart and Pete. This original print was sent by Paul to his then girlfriend in Liverpool, a lady named Dot, to whom he inscribed on the reverse.

### Sutcliffe in Studio
The Bohemian art student personified, from the open-toed sandals to the attic garret studio, Stuart Sutcliffe – as in this picture taken in Hamburg by girlfriend Astrid Kirchherr – was the first of the early Beatles to adopt the ''flat'' haircut, inspired by Kirchherr, that later became their trade mark.

### The Beatles on *RSG*
Cathy McGowan, co-presenter of the trend-setting British TV show *Ready Steady Go!*, represented the archetypal image of mid 1960s ''swinging London''; this photograph of her with the Beatles was sold with the copyright and two negatives.

## The Beatles Backstage

A backstage photograph taken during one of the Beatles' first U.K. pop package tours, early in 1963, when they still shared the top billing with other acts – in this case, American chart stars Chris Montez (center left) and Tommy Roe. The 16 by 20 in print was signed by Harry Hammond, a celebrated photographer of British show-biz personalities in the 1950s and early 1960s.
''Love for ever, Yours Paul.''

## Lennon and McCartney 1961

When it appeared at a London sale in 1982, this 1961 picture of Paul McCartney and John Lennon was attributed to their first-ever out-of-Merseyside date in Aldershot, but actually was taken on the August 19, 1961 at one of their regular Liverpool venues, the Aintree Institute, a good four months before the disastrous trek south to Aldershot where they attracted only 18 paying customers.

### Marc Bolan with John's Children

Barely recognizable early manifestations of the later famous are guaranteed to stimulate bidding among collectors, as with this picture of T. Rex star Marc Bolan (left) when he led an early psychedelic group called John's Children; he joined the group on the suggestion of his manager Simon Napier-Bell in 1967, after turning down an offer to join the Yardbirds, and apparently wrote their one minor hit "Desdemona" in 25 seconds flat!

### Geldof by Bailey

A David Bailey portrait photograph of Bob Geldof, taken backstage at the Wembley Stadium Live Aid concert on July 13, 1985. It was signed by Bailey and numbered No. 2 of a limited edition of just three. Christie's of London, who auctioned the picture two years later, announced in the sale catalogue "It is hoped that the photograph will be signed by Bob Geldof prior to the auction."

### Marianne Faithfull *circa* 1964

A previously unpublished photograph of Marianne Faithfull, taken around the time of her debut disk "As Tears Go By" in 1964. Although unsigned, or even credited to a particular photographer, it merited inclusion in a memorabilia sale due to its rarity as an image and came with a similarly anonymous picture, apparently taken in Glasgow, of singer Max Bygraves plugging his record "You Need Hands." This would have dated the latter to 1958.

14 Gold Records — Oops! Sorry about that, it is now 18

### Dave Clark Five with Awards

A great contemporary photograph of the Dave Clark Five in 1965. The group's first big hits were in 1964 with the single ''Glad All Over'' (which reached U.K. number one in January 1964) followed by ''Bits And Pieces'' (number one in February 1964). Dave Clark, singer, composer and drummer of the group is photographed with Lenny Davidson, Rick Huxley, Denis Payton and Mike Smith surrounded by their 14 gold awards. Dave produced all of their records and managed the group at the same time which was unheard of in its day. The Dave Clark Five went on to sell over 50 million records throughout the world.

### Haley's Debut Date

Opening the first-ever British tour by an American rock & roll act, the London concerts of Bill Haley and the Comets at the Dominion, Tottenham Court Road, London, in February 1957 were truly historic. This picture, from the archive of showbiz photographer Harry Hammond, captures the Comets' frenetic show perfectly, complete with onstage acrobatics from bass player Al Rex and saxophonist Rudy Pompilli; it was one of several Hammond originals sold at the first London rock & roll memorabilia auction in 1981.

### Live Aid Bailey

Taken by David Bailey, in the 60s the most fashionable fashion photographer, on the occasion of the Live Aid concert, this 20 by 16 in print featuring (clockwise from left), Elton John, songwriting partner Bernie Taupin, Kiki Dee and George Michael was signed on the front by the photographer and on the reverse by Elton John and George Michael.

### Cliff Richard 1959 by Hammond

A cool-looking Cliff, with black shirt and white tie (shame about the socks!) which was his trademark at the time, contemplating top-of-the-bill fame early in his career. Note the reference to the *Oh Boy!* TV show which helped launch many of the British rockers in the late 50s. A vintage piece of pictorial history by Harry Hammond from 1959.

### Mankowitz Hendrix Portrait

Gered Mankowitz's photographs of the rock stars of the latter half of the 60s were among the most enduring images of the time. This 42.5 by 35 cm (16 by 13 in) portrait of Jimi Hendrix entitled ''Hendrix Smoking 1967'' was sold as a print from the original negative, signed and annotated by the photographer from his own archive.

### Joplin Nude Portrait

Though easily reproduced, and often over-familiar through constant use in books and magazines, original prints of photographs signed by the photographer can attract a significant market among collectors. This 1967 nude study of Janis Joplin was signed by photographer Bob Seideman and printed in a limited edition of 500, protecting its rarity value in years to come.

Mason's Yard - 1967

## Cliff and the Shadows

Otherwise run-of-the-mill photographs have a certain premium if sold with negatives and copyright, for instance by this mid 60s shot of the ever-youthful Cliff, and the Shadows: (left to right) John Rostill, Hank B. Marvin, Brian Bennett, Cliff Richard and Bruce Welch.

## Presley Family Photo Album

Just one page from a remarkable photo album discovered in a photographic studio in Memphis, Tennessee when the proprietor, Eli H. Jaffe, died in 1969. Elvis Presley's family had moved to Memphis from Tupelo, Mississippi in 1948, and the album was a 13-page record of the young Elvis and his family from the late 40s to mid 50s, tracing the singer growing up from a kid in baggy pants to rarely smiling but snappily dressed teenager. The 100-plus pictures included candid shots of the earliest stage appearances of the "Hillbilly Cat", as he was billed locally.

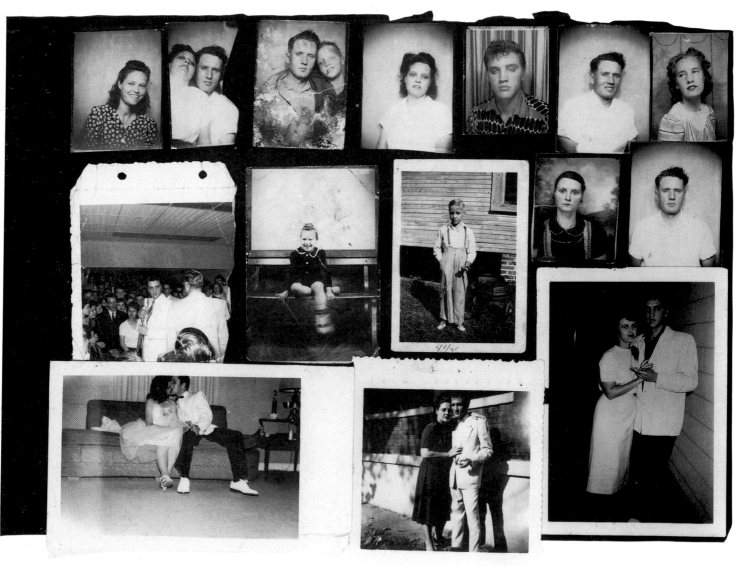

### Style Council Live Aid Portrait

The Style Council, formed by Paul Weller (top left) and Mick Talbot (top right) are no more, so a photo taken by David Bailey during Live Aid is even more collectible. This and many other related items actually first appeared in auction during a special Band Aid charity sale held at Sotheby's in November 1985.

### Mick Jagger, 1966

Part of the many "package" lots that find their way into the auction rooms, this 1966 picture of Mick Jagger was among 20 photographs of the Rolling Stones dating from that period that went up for sale in 1982, along with 112 negatives.

### "Between The Buttons" Alternative Shot

Entitled "Between The Buttons 1967" this photograph was from the archive of photographer Gered Mankowitz, taken during the same session that produced the similarly soft-focus cover picture for the "Between The Buttons" album. What was sold at auction was in fact a black-and-white print from an original color negative. Because of the Stones' nocturnal lifestyle, especially when they were recording which they always chose to do at night, Mankowitz realized the only time he could get them together for this shoot – on London's Primrose Hill – was at dawn, immediately after a nocturnal session in the studios.

Between the buttons 1967

### Very Early Who by Hoffmann

Mods to a man, the Who started out as the High Numbers (a Mod term for style) — and the High Numbers they were in this Dezo Hoffmann picture taken in 1964 — before their manager, film director Kit Lambert decided they should change their name because he thought High Numbers on posters could look like an advert for a Bingo session!

### Photograph of the Who

Even the Who, hard-edge protagonists of mod teenage rebellion from the start, found themselves in the favorite photographers' role of happy-go-lucky beat stars during picture sessions — although in this shot Pete Townshend (left) seems to find it all a bit tiring. From a collection of pictures and negatives of the group taken in 1966, that went on sale at the second rock memorabilia auction in 1982.

# Programs, Tickets, etc

### 'Rollers Concert Program

Frightening to think that the "tartan terrors," the teeny-hordes who followed the Bay City Rollers around early 1970s Britain are now thirty-something mothers with kids of their own. Nostalgia indeed then nestles between the covers of this 1974 program for the lads in plaid. (Courtesy of V&A Theatre Museum)

### Tour Tickets, The Alarm

Formed in their native North Wales in 1981, the Alarm were very much a band of that decade, briefly denting the U.K. charts and achieving cult status in the U.S. with a unique brand of post-punk rock with Welsh overtones. Hence this "Celtic Folklore" ticket, complete with national emblem, already a collectors item.

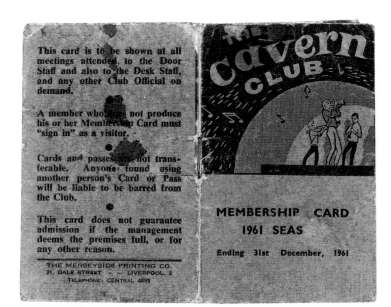

### Cavern Club Membership Card

The Cavern Club logo on this 1961 membership card was indicative of the fact that although the Beatles and other rock & roll groups were playing there, it was still primarily a venue for traditional jazz — a position that was to be completely reversed by the end of the year, when the jazz combos were overtaken by the burgeoning army of beat groups.

### Beatles Concert Programs

Concert programs feature strongly in collectors' fairs and auctions. Kept for years as souvenirs by dedicated fans, they are often in particularly good condition for their age.

Programs for concerts by the Beatles, who finished touring in 1966, are of course at a premium.

### Quarry Men Business Card

Bob Wooler, the DJ at Liverpool's Cavern Club and the man responsible for much of the Beatles' initial promotion on Merseyside, sold this Quarry Men business card at an auction in 1984. The Quarry Men was John Lennon's group before the Beatles (or even the Silver Beatles), so the card – offering "country, western, rock & roll and skiffle" – certainly dates no later than early 1960.

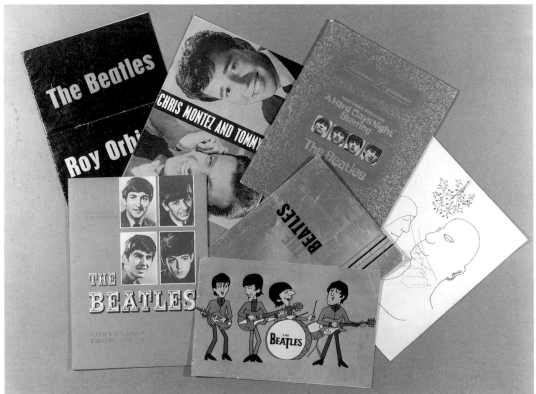

### Beatles Shea Handbill

Certainly the Fab Four's most famous concert during their hectic American tours, anything pertaining to the legendary Shea Stadium appearance on August 15, 1965 – like this handbill and ticket – is of increasing interest to collectors. The concert, filmed for British television, was in front of 56,000 screaming fans, a world record at the time. One collector claims to have one of the only two posters for the gig left in the world – but who knows what is hidden away in the suburban attics of New York?

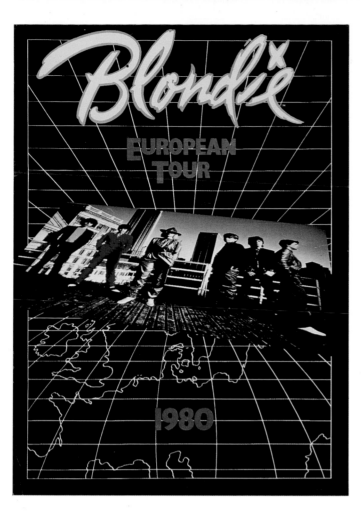

### Blondie "Eat To The Beat" Program

Tour programs often make it plain that the whole exercise is a blatant plug for an artist's current record release, as with Blondie's European trip of 1980. Although the decorative (and talented) Deborah Harry was featured heavily throughout, the cover settled for a straight variation on the "Eat To The Beat" album artwork. (Courtesy of V&A Theatre Museum)

### Bowie Tour Souvenir Book

Just how ambitious programs were becoming on the megastar circuit is illustrated by the souvenir book that accompanied David Bowie's "Serious Moonlight" European tour of 1983. Glossy, with 56 pages in full color, it featured text in three languages – English, French and German – emphasizing the international nature of such enterprises. (Courtesy of V&A Theatre Museum)

### Clapton/Harrison Japanese Program

Currently changing hands at well over the retail price, the souvenir book of George Harrison's concerts with the Eric Clapton Band at the end of 1991 is already a collectors item – especially in the West, as the tour only took place in Japanese cities. (Courtesy of V&A Theatre Museum)

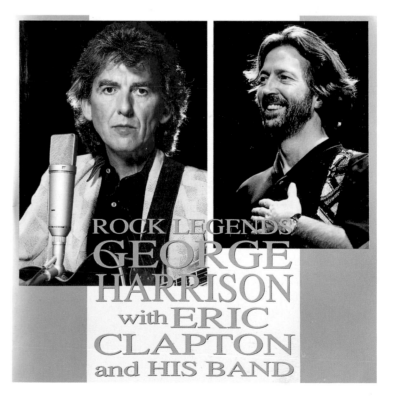

### Tickets For Two Cream Concerts

Like most aspects of rock & roll printed matter from the late 1960s on, even the humble concert ticket often incorporated sophisticated graphics and design, thereby rendering it highly collectible in its own right. These two tickets for Cream concerts dating from 1967 and 1968, are both for San Francisco events promoted by the pioneering West Coast entrepreneur Bill Graham, at the Fillmore Auditorium and Winterland Ballroom. (Courtesy of V&A Theatre Museum)

75

### Culture Club Program, 1984

Fashions change so quickly in pop – this year's trend quickly becomes last year's old hat. Culture Club, with the flamboyant Boy George singing lead, were the most popular manifestation of the early 1980s "New Romantics" – George's effeminate image even being accepted by normally conservative American audiences ("Karma Chameleon" topped the charts on both sides of the Atlantic). Hence for the "Multi-Cultural World Tour" of 1984, the program for the U.S. dates was subtitled "A Kiss Across the Ocean." (Courtesy of V&A Theatre Museum)

### Elton John Backstage Passes

Backstage passes and guest tickets are highly collectible, if only because of their originally exclusive nature. This group of 28 guest and VIP tickets from various Elton John tours formed part of the collection the singer offered at auction in 1988, and included items from "Xmas at the Odeon," "Back In The USSR," "Jump Up" and other tours.

### Dylan's "Street Legal" Tour Souvenir

By the late 1970s the simple running schedule-plus-potted biography program was giving way to the glossy, full-color "souvenir book" which – often without reference to specific venues or even territories – served for a whole tour, taking in several continents in as many months. This 1978 Bob Dylan book was published to accompany his "Street Legal" tour, though the omission of references to this album suggests it was prepared some months before. (Courtesy of V&A Theatre Museum)

### Various Elton John Tour Memorabilia

From Elton John's collection, and highly personalized with his name and photo on many of the items, was a group of 52 backstage passes for tours and events including ''A Single Man,' (1980), ''Jump Up'' (1982), ''Summer of '84,'' ''Rock Of The Westies'' (1975), ''Back In The USSR,'' ''Breaking Hearts,'' Live Aid, the Tube, and the 1986 British Record Industry Awards.

### Glitter Farewell Tour Program

All the razzmatazz of Gary Glitter's glam-pomp image had one redeeming feature – it was done, at least on his part, with tongue planted firmly in cheek. Whether he genuinely thought his concert trek of 1976 was to be his ''Farewell Tour,'' as advertised at the time, is hard to tell – but in retrospect it gives the program even more novelty value. (Courtesy of V&A Theatre Museum)

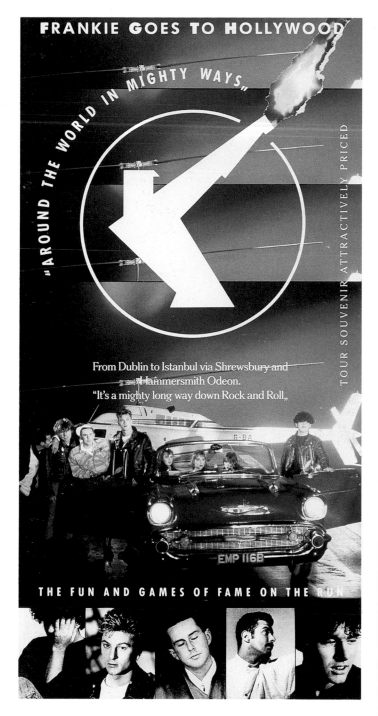

### Frankie Goes To Hollywood Programme 1985

For a couple of years, Frankie Goes to Hollywood's anthemic hits ''Relax,'' ''Two Tribes'' and ''The Power Of Love'' became the pop sloganeering of the 1980s – often in a very graphic sense, with the titles appearing on everything from album ads to fashionable Katherine Hamnett-style T-shirts. The program for their 1985 tour, ''Around the World in Mighty Ways,'' reflected this use of language as a visual device, a blast from the very recent past that is already history. (Courtesy of V&A Theatre Museum)

### Gerry's "Christmas Crackers" Program

A 1965 Christmas show at the Granada Cinema, Shrewsbury, England, "Christmas Crackers" was an attempt to get away from the seasonal pantomime formula, but still present crowd-pulling pop stars – in this case Gerry and the Pacemakers – in a mixed bag of variety acts. Gerry and the lads found themselves performing alongside ventriloquists, TV compère Norman Vaughan and "pub piano" virtuoso, Mrs. Mills! (Courtesy of V&A Theatre Museum)

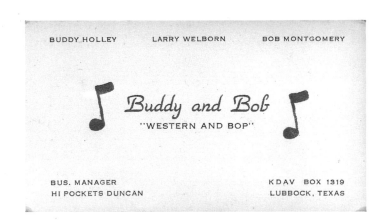

### Buddy Holly Business Card

Of great importance to collectors, this business card for "Buddy and Bob" refers to the country and western trio which Buddy Holly formed with his friend Bob Montgomery while still in high school, in their home town of Lubbock, Texas. Note that it pre-dates Buddy dropping "e" from his surname. The card, which also names their "business manager" as one "Hi Pockets Duncan," was sold in a London auction for four figures in 1990.

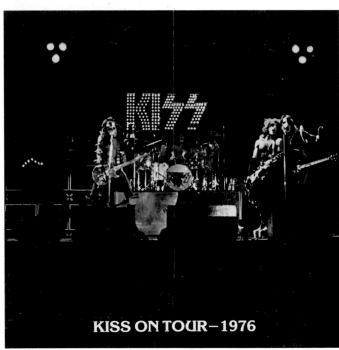

KISS ON TOUR – 1976

### Kiss '76 Program

"Glam" taken to its extreme, Kiss represented stadium rock at its most extravagant, and by the end of the 1970s the group was beginning to look decidedly dated with their stylized make-up and stage pyrotechnics. Programs, like this one from their U.S. tour of 1976, are now eagerly sought at collectors fairs in Europe and the U.S. (Courtesy of V&A Theatre Museum)

### Led Zeppelin Earls Court Souvenir

As bands like Led Zeppelin became bigger, and their stage shows more extravagant, so did their concert programs. This booklet for their Earls Court, London, concerts in 1975 came at a time when the band were at their peak of popularity, and is now keenly sought by both fans and collectors. (Courtesy of V&A Theatre Museum)

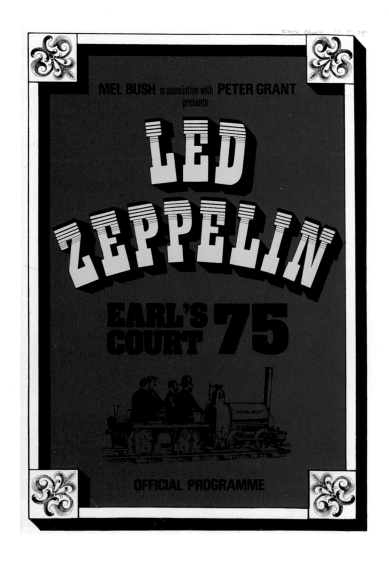

## Bob Marley "Scrapbook"

Bob Marley, and his band the Wailers, almost single-handedly popularized Jamaican reggae at an international level, and with it the now familiar red-gold-and-green livery of Rastafarianism – seen in this case on the 1976 ''Scrapbook'' which served as a tour souvenir booklet.
(Courtesy of V&A Theatre Museum)

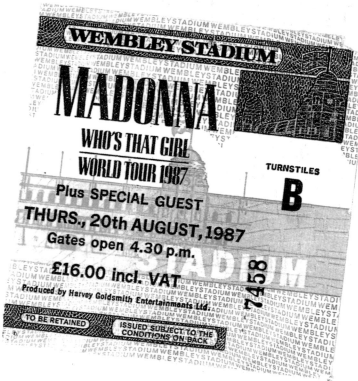

## Zeppelin Chicago Concert Tickets

Even something as essentially throwaway as a concert ticket has its value among collectors, often almost immediately; this set of eight from the same Chicago Stadium appearance of Led Zeppelin in 1980 were sold less than nine years later for about five times their original price, and there was no show to go to!

## Madonna Wembley Ticket

London fans would have to pay a lot more than $30 to see a Madonna concert today, such has been the escalation of both her superstar status and ticket prices generally since the ''Who's That Girl'' world tour of 1987.

**Osmonds British Tour Program**

It's hard to imagine now why the Osmonds were as popular as they were in the mid 1970s, among the teenybopper fraternity at least. It was all big business, of course, a family business, with the Utah brothers (and sister) managed by their father, and in complete control of records, their TV show, and million-dollar merchandising. (Courtesy of V&A Theatre Museum)

**Elvis Shop Window Display**

Like the Beatles in the early 60s, Elvis Presley's big break nationally in America came partly via the *Ed Sullivan Show* which reluctantly featured "The Pelvis" after he'd decimated Sullivan's audience by appearing on the rival *Steve Allen Show*. This 1956 shop window display for *TV Guide* – advertises articles that ask if Elvis is "Sullivan's secret weapon?" It emerged nearly 30 years later at auction in London.

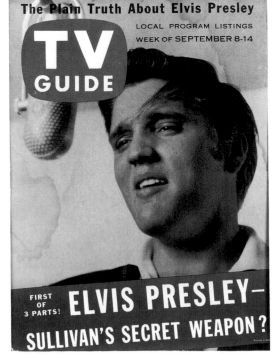

**Johnnie Ray Program, 1959**

Known variously as the ''Cry Guy,'' the ''Nabob of Sob'' and the ''Prince of Wails,'' Johnnie Ray's outbursts of emotion were part of a sensational stage act that pre-dated Elvis' gyrations by a couple of years in the early 1950s. This program, from a British tour in 1959, illustrates how the pop music scene was still regarded as part of the world of the variety stage, with a bill that included ''up and coming'' comedians, Mike and Bernie Winters, and Des O'Connor, who became top British stars. (Courtesy of V&A Theatre Museum)

**1986 Tour Program for Queen**

Since the death of singer Freddy Mercury late in 1991, anything associated with Queen has acquired even greater collector value, like this 1986 tour program from their ''Kind Of Magic'' European trek.

**Ron Wood's Tour Ephemera**

Tour memorabilia and the like take on a special quality when they have come from one of the artists themselves. These photographs and backstage passes were formerly the property of Ron Wood, and part of a sizable collection of material sold at auction in 1987.

**Various 1960s Pop Programs**

More than most other form of collectible, programs are often offered for sale in batches — part or all of a collection, usually accumulated over a seller's teenage years. This is just a selection from a batch of 26 that was sold in London in 1988, including concerts by Cliff Richard, Roy Orbison, the Small Faces and Adam Faith.

## Collage of New York Concert Items

Obviously put together by a keen fan with artistic ambitions, this collage of tickets, passes, news items and program clippings went on sale for over $1,000 in New York in 1991. The ephemera included items relating to performances by the Rolling Stones, Blind Faith, Led Zeppelin, and the Doors, all from the late 1960s and early 1970s, and was dominated by material from Bill Graham's Fillmore East venue in New York City.

## 'Stones Press Clippings Book

This press book, containing clippings relating to the Rolling Stones' U.S. tour of 1975, was presented to Ron Wood prior to that tour. It has a print of the tour logo attached to the front cover, which is embossed with the name Ron Wood.

## The Smiths' Tour Program

A bleak image of Britain in the 1980s, the promotion for the Smiths' "Meat Is Murder" tour of 1985 hardly promised a fun night out. Nevertheless, the band developed a cult following in Britain and the U.S., and the tour program has become a genuine collectors item. (Courtesy of V&A Theatre Museum)

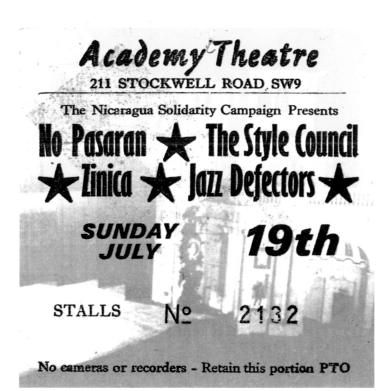

**Ticket for Style Council Benefit Concert**

Paul Weller was always ready to embrace radical causes with both the Jam and later with the Style Council; this ticket for the London venue Brixton Academy was for the Nicaraguan Solidarity Campaign.

**Wings Program, Japan 1980**

Rejuvenating the thumbs-up, happy-go-lucky image that had characterized the Beatles' first years of fame – summed up in the cover photograph for the program – Paul McCartney's 1980 Japanese tour with Wings was unfortunately marred by a drugs bust that kept him out of the country for the rest of the decade. (Courtesy of V&A Theatre Museum)

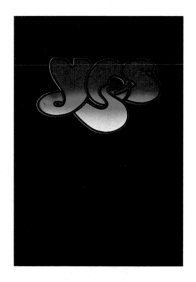

**Program for Yes Tour, 1974.**

The epitome of early 1970s "progressive" rock, the Yes logo created by Roger Dean appeared on all their albums, publicity material and of course concert programs. The "serious" nature of this strand of rock music ("rock & roll" seemed hardly appropriate any more) was emphasized in this program for their 1974 tour of the U.S., with the two halves of each concert given over entirely to their previous ("Close To The Edge") and current ("Tales From Topographic Oceans") albums respectively. Now regarded as part of rock's dinosaur past, artifacts of this kind look almost quaint and are therefore highly collectible. (Courtesy of V&A Theatre Museum)

**Plant's Pink Imperial**

The Pink 1959 Chrysler Imperial Crown convertible, once owned by Led Zeppelin vocalist Robert Plant, is shown here on display at a 1991 exhibition of "Cars of the Stars" held at the National Exhibition Centre in Birmingham, England. Now part of the Yorkshire Car Collection, it carries the motto "50s Rock'n'Roll For Ever" above the number plate.

# Cars of the Stars

Cars have, almost since their invention, been linked with high society, beautiful women, glamour and the good life; they are symbols which demonstrate wealth, superiority and virility. In particular, the *nouveau riche* from the world of entertainment, even dating back to the era of the silent movie, often used the car to display their new status; Mary Pickford chose a Rolls Royce, Clark Gable a Duesenberg SJ short-chassis roadster and Jean Harlow a Packard dual-cowl, dual-windshield sport phaeton. The most stylish and opulent cars came to be regarded as the ultimate symbols of success both by the movie stars and the moviemakers.

**The Elvis Silver Cloud**

Elvis Presley's 1966 Rolls Royce Silver Cloud III. This model carries the standard steel body and has no modifications. The engine is an eight-cylinder 6.2 liter with overhead valves allied to a four-speed automatic transmission. The Silver Cloud is one of the most famous of all Rolls, being introduced in the late 1950s. Presley acquired the car from the actor Michael Landon in 1970 and kept it until 1976. The registration was "No 1 ELVIS." Private plates in the U.S.A. do not carry the prestige or price that they do in the U.K.

The movie industry was also quick to assess the possibilities the motor car afforded in terms of story lines and excitement. Automobiles quickly found their way into films, facilitating romances and elopements, helping to catch criminals, getting stuck on level crossings or being used as props in numerous comedy situations. These early films illustrated cars in a very positive light, showing them as the means of bringing about success and creating happiness, excitement and fulfillment. Julian Smith, professor of Film Studies at the University of Florida, puts forward the theory that: "Automobility has been consciously marketed and both consciously and subconsciously embraced by the American public as a form of emotional transport, the state or condition of being transported by ecstasy, of being enraptured. As Hollywood and Detroit came of age, they both learned how to supply dream vehicles that would carry us away from danger or boredom, transport us to better times and bigger adventures."

Indeed, some of the most popular movies in more recent years have featured cars and motorbikes, including *The Wild One, Genevieve, Vanishing Point*, the early James Bond films, *The Great Escape* (with its memorable sequence of Steve McQueen and motorcycle), *Bonnie and Clyde, Bullitt, The Cannonball Run, The Love Bug, The Italian Job, Easy Rider* and *American Graffiti*.

Anybody growing up in a Western democracy since the 1950s has undoubtedly been influenced by the potent image of the motor car, whether on the movie screen, on poster billboards, in children's story books, in comics and magazines, or through images on television. This latter medium, whether showing reports of the great road and circuit races, advertisements for cars, or entertainment programs such as *Batman, The Saint, Knight Rider, The Dukes of Hazzard, Starsky & Hutch* or *Miami Vice*, has accomplished more than any other medium in cementing once and for all the connection in impressionable minds between the automobile and action, adventure and achievement.

There is also, unquestionably, a link in the subconscious between cars and sex. Through the car, young single people for the first time had a place of their own, somewhere to spend time with their partners away from the constraints of the family home or chaperoned entertainment venues. This led to the inevitable unchaperoned experiences! An American survey of women taken in the 1950s suggested that 38 per cent of women born between 1900 and 1910 had discovered sex in the back seat of a car. More recent surveys would undoubtedly raise this percentage, the figures helped on their way by interesting technical handbooks such as *Harmonie Sexualle dans une Automobile* (the definitive car sex manual featuring 63 photographs and trilingual text).

Advertising agencies have for decades used various images of sex and dominant virility to sell their products. Dr. James Hemming, a British psychologist, sees the direct link between sexual symbolism and the relationship with a car, explaining: "A man gets into his car, he switches on the power, he then has almost a passionate relationship and a passionate satisfaction out of controlling the power of the car. He admires its line, he admires its performance and this immediately cross-references to sex."

Another psychologist, Dr. Joyce Brothers, believes that the motor car is one of the most dominant contemporary icons and the choices of model is often very meaningful. "For some," Dr. Brothers claims, "it's a sexual extension. Their car says to

**The "Penny Lane" Mini**
A real 60s oddity, this customised Mini is covered in 8,500 old pennies. It was one of two made at the end of the decade in celebration of the Beatles song "Penny Lane," one ending up in the Guiness Hall of Fame in San Francisco and the other in the Yorkshire Car Collection in Keighly, Yorkshire, UK. The coins, supplied by a deal in Bradford, Yorkshire, to the now-unknown customiser in Wales, doubled the weight of the vehicle and added just £33 to its immediate value (there being 240 old pennies to the pre-70s pound sterling) – though the Yorkshire museum paid £6,000 for the car in 1988.

others, 'I'm a very successful being. I've got lots of power and lots of drive'."

It is in this environment, then, that today's successful rock musicians grew up. It is only to be expected that many involved with the rock music business have built up collections of automobiles and motorcycles, have commissioned custom cars or have owned during their careers some of the most desirable and expensive motor cars. It was Freddie Gorman of the Originals who described the car buying habits of Motown recording stars and executives at its peak ". . . everybody was buying Cadillacs. It was the thing to do to be prestigious. There'd be all these Cadillacs all lined up in front of Hitsville. Every time a producer or a writer got a number one, he'd run out and buy a Cadillac that was better than the one bought by the last producer or writer."

Many successful car collections have been built up by contemporary rock stars, perhaps the best known being Nick Mason's which includes several of the most desirable automobiles ever produced. Ranging from magnificent examples of veterans from the turn of the century to the Ferrari 250 GTO (of which only 39 were built between 1962 and 1964 and which is widely regarded as the ultimate road vehicle) the collection is one of the finest in the world and includes some of the rarest motor cars still in private hands.

A record of motor vehicle transactions relating to the Beatles and their colleagues and contemporaries between November 17, 1964 and January 11, 1967 listed a staggering 596 vehicles, which included an Aston Martin DB5 for George Harrison, a Ferrari 330GT coupé and a Porsche 912 coupé for John Lennon, a Mini Cooper for Paul McCartney, a Bentley S3 for Brian Epstein, both a mini and an Aston Martin DB6 for Mick Jagger. With such a high number of car purchases by well-known pop people over such a short period of time, undoubtedly many of the original 596 vehicles must still survive today just waiting to be rediscovered.

The best cars, immaterial of past ownership, hold their own intrinsic value and are frequently sold anonymously or part-exchanged through specialist companies and dealers. Subsequent purchasers have often been completely unaware of the interesting provenance attached to their vehicle, generally finding out by chance, through the sight of the original log book or vehicle registration document, that the car in question had first been owned by an influential (or at least celebrated) rock musician. One such vehicle was Ringo Starr's 1970 Mercedes which had for many years, since its anonymous purchase, been used as a wedding car.

Several interesting custom cars belonging to well-known names have appeared on the open market in the last ten years including those that were basically modified for practical purposes and those which were re-worked for fun. John Entwistle's Rolls Royce Silver Shadow estate car dating from 1975 was a useful conversion whereby more space was created for an individual who needed to regularly transport instruments and bulky equipment. In a similar way Ringo Starr had his Mini Cooper adapted and the rear seats removed to allow his drums to fit inside.

Jeff Beck imported a head-turning customized Model T

**The *Let It Be* Merc**

George Harrison's Mercedes 300 SEL. Yet another Beatle with a Mercedes. The German manufacture has always been very popular with rock stars, combining quality and luxury without the ostentation of a Rolls Royce. This car dates from 1969 and features a 6.3 liter engine with fuel injection and a host of luxurious internal features. The car also appeared in the Beatles' last film *Let It Be*, which premiered in New York on May 13, 1970.

Ford from America in 1969. Styled as a hot rod drag racer and finished in scarlet and chrome, the machine was described in *Custom Car* magazine in 1981 as ". . . one of the fastest street rods in the country." Later sold to John Bonham, the car featured in the 1976 Led Zeppelin film *The Song Remains The Same*. John Lennon used his "psychedelic" Phantom V Rolls Royce Touring Limousine extensively in the late 60s and the car at that time was one of the most dominant icons of pop culture. Finished in yellow and overpainted with decorative panels worked by an artist more familiar with the decoration of fun fair rides than the world's most prestigious make of automobile, this memorable motor sold for $2,300,000 in 1985 and basks in the glorious reputation of being the most expensive rock & roll collectible to have ever been sold at auction.

Billy Gibbons, who readily admits to have been obsessed with car culture since he was a boy, has had love affairs with two particular automobiles, one of which was a 1966 Chevrolet Impala which had been converted to a "low rider", a custom car much loved by the working class Chicanos in the U.S.. Based on any large second-hand American car and fitted with small wheels, airbrushed paintwork, plush bordello-buttoned and velvetted interiors, the most extraordinary feature of the low rider is its suspension. With hydraulics fitted, the car's suspension can be raised or lowered at will; at the lowest setting the specially fitted titanium skid pads make contact with the road surface and send out sheets of sparks which light up the tough streets in the areas where the low rider gangs are based. The focus of Billy Gibbons, other four-wheeled infatuation is much better known, the crimson custom 1933 Ford three-window coupé which has featured so extensively in ZZ Top's video pro-

### Bonham's Custom Ford

John Bonham's "Blown Model T" custom car. Based on the 1923 Ford Model "T" this is a classic "pic'n'mix" car incorporating a 500bhp Chevy unit, 1932 Ford dropped beam, 1942 Ford front drums, 1962 Chevy rear axle, Corvair steering boxes, and a Holeshot torque convertor. The Model "T" has always been a very popular base for a hotrod conversion principally because they made over 15 million of them. Known as "The Boston Strangler," it was originally bought by Jeff Beck in 1969, before being sold to the Led Zeppelin drummer. It was featured in their 1976 film *The Song Remains The Same*.

### Little Deuce Coupe

The Beach Boys were the most popular hot rod-and-surfing groups. Their 1965 album on Capitol, "Little Deuce Coupe," featured Clarence "Chili" Catallo's highly-desirable '32 Ford Model A coupe on the album cover, picture courtesy of Hot Rod magazine. The Pearl and translucent Oriental Blue Ford was customized by George Barris after seeing some use as a drag racer (best time 112 mph in 12.90 seconds). The Beach Boys provided twelve automotive-inspired tracks.

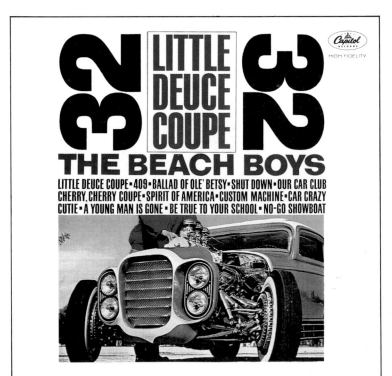

motions and album cover artwork. In an interview Gibbons told all: "I wanted a facsimile of a car I'd seen on television. Four and a half years later the cost was up to $100,000 with no end in sight, and it was too late to turn back . . . we thought of naming the car and the next album after a drag-racing term . . . we wanted to use the car in a photo shoot for the album cover . . . but we had to settle for a drawing of it on the jacket. By the time we took possession of the coupé, it had become our "Top Eliminator" our "Top Icon" and our top priority."

With all the subconscious connections between cars and glamour, sex and success, cars are understandably strong images in rock music, both the songs themselves and their packaging. ZZ Top's "Eliminator" album, John Lee Hooker's "Mr Lucky" album cover which shows him seated on a Buick bearing that registration, the Trabant which featured so extensively in U2's promotion of their recent "Achtung Baby" and Bruce Springsteen's white gas guzzler on the cover of "Tunnel Of Love." Since the immortal works of Chuck Berry in the 1950's, a great many songs have been written about cars and driving, since the automobile has been the focus of so much teenage obsession. The instrument through which authority can be taunted, risks can be taken, experiences and adventures can be achieved will certainly remain an important source of inspiration for many rock performers, and the last word should remain with one of them:

*"Eldorado fins, whitewalls and skirts*
*Rides just like a little of heaven here on earth*
*Well buddy when I die throw my body in the back*
*And drive me to the junkyard in my Cadillac"*
**(Bruce Springsteen)**

### The "Abbey Road" Beetle

The real "fifth Beatle," as it appeared on the cover of the Beatles' tenth studio LP, "Abbey Road," in 1969. The Volkswagen ("people's car") was commissioned by Hitler and first appeared in 1936; it is still produced today, in Mexico. The license plate of the Beatles' Beetle fueled a rumor that Paul McCartney had died and been replaced by a lookalike, as the plate read "28 IF," referring to his age "if" he had lived. The story started in a university rag called the *Northern Star* in Illinois, and I rather suspect it has more to do with a fevered imagination than fact.

### George Harrison's Mercedes

Harrison acquired the vehicle, a 250 CE two-door coupé from his father in the late 1970s and then passed it on to Paul Harrison, his cousin, in 1979. Some of the garage bills that were present when the car was sold in 1990 indicate that the car was run on George's company, Harrisongs Ltd. In the year he sold the car, Harrison launched his Handmade Films company.

### Elton John's Hand-Built Panther

Elton John's 1977 Panther De Ville coupé. Panther Cars, based in Byfleet, Surrey, in England, made only 100 of these hand-built cars over a ten year period and the styling they adopted was influenced by the Bugatti Royale. The car sat on a rectangular section steel-ladder chassis and had all aluminum coachwork, although the doors are made of pressed steel and taken from hardly the most classic of English cars, the Austin Maxi. The engine is the superb Jaguar V12 5.3 Literwhich is still one of the smoothest units available today despite being past the age when most people wish to celebrate birthdays. The vehicle was specifically built for Elton and features his name on the engine plate. It also appeared in the 1983 video for "I'm Still Standing."

### A Beatle Moped Bike

A Raleigh Super 50 moped, once owned by John Lennon. Lennon purchased the bike from Brian Epstein in January 1967, possibly to escape the clutches of London's ''Rita'' meter maids. As the vehicle cannot exceed 30 mph it is really only useful for town travel and Lennon may have used it to get to and from the Apple offices and boutique which opened toward the end of the year. The bike was sold at the first rock & roll memorabilia sale in 1981.

### Lennon's Celebrated Rolls

John Lennon's psychedelic Rolls Royce Phantom V touring limousine with coachwork by Milliner/Park-Ward. A product of the 1960s without a doubt, the car was purchased by Lennon in 1966 with a more traditional coat of paint. In 1967 Lennon and a friend repainted the car. It is reminiscent of the decoration on fairground rides with polychrome scroll work and floral motifs on a gold and yellow background. The interior included an eight-track cartridge system and a record player. The car was used by other groups in the late 1960s before it was shipped to the United States in 1970. It was donated to the Cooper-Hewitt Museum in 1977 and was sold by them for $2.3 million in 1985 to raise money.

## Two Lennon Cars

Two cars which belonged to John Lennon and illustrate the changes in his life. The Rolls Royce dates from the middle to late 1960s and is made by the same coachworkers who produced the body of the psychedelic Rolls. The 1972 Chrysler station wagon is of the style made famous in innumerable TV series of the 1970s. Lennon and Yoko made an extended trip across the U.S.A. in this car in 1975 – presumably before the birth of Sean in October. The two cars seem to illustrate how Lennon's priorities and needs changed from, if not an excessive, certainly a typically rock star lifestyle, to the very ordinary househusband days of his latter six years.

### Lennon's Mercedes Pullman

John Lennon's Mercedes 600 Pullman four-door limousine. This is a significant vehicle. The car has a 6.3 liter V8 engine coupled to a four-speed automatic transmission. The suspension is air-independent, and self-leveling and the car sits on the extended 12¾ foot chassis. It incorporates features which are only now just reaching the best standard production cars (such as the current Mercedes S class introduced in 1991) and included an air pressure system to assist the closing of the doors, trunk and fuel tank. The car was delivered to Lennon on February 19, 1970 and had been custom-made to his requirements – to include a Phillips Mignon record player, a Pioneer eight-track cartridge system (although no one under 20 will know what that is!) and tinted passenger windows. Lennon sold the car to Harrison who then sold it to Mary Wilson of the Supremes in 1978, which increases the significance of a car, already outstanding by itself. In 1991 the car was rebuilt at the Mercedes factory for the present owner at a cost of over £200,000.

### Elvis's Mercedes

Elvis Presley's 1969 Mercedes 600 Sedan. As if proof were needed of the popularity of the German car manufacturer among the rock set, here is "the King's." This model is standard except for the fitting of two jump seats in the back. Presley purchased the car in 1970 from the producer Ross Bagdasarian as a Christmas present for himself. In 1974 he gave the car to Jimmy Velvet of the Elvis Presley Museum, Inc. where it remained until 1990.

### A Presley Phantom

Elvis Presley's Rolls Royce Phantom V touring limousine. A very special Rolls with coachwork by James Young of Bromley, Kent, England. The Phantom, introduced in 1959, was a popular model for special coachwork. The chassis was delivered to Young in January 1963 and completed by March. Elvis specified many extras including a microphone, an armrest containing a writing pad, mirror, clothes brush, and a fitted cabinet with an ice thermos, two decanters and ten crystal glasses (presumably used for parties!). The car was originally midnight blue but has since been repainted in silver gray which suggests that the car had been restored at some stage prior to its sale in 1986.

### Harrison's Aston Martin

George Harrison's Aston Martin DB5. The DB5 is probably the most famous of all Astons due to its use in the James Bond film *Goldfinger*, which reputedly prompted Harrison into the purchase. It was delivered on January 1, 1965. Aston Martin was owned at this stage by a former tractor manufacturer, David Brown (DB), who, when asked by a friend if he could have a car at cost, replied "Certainly, that will be £1,000 on top of the list price please!"

### 'Tailgate' Mini

The Mini Cooper S commissioned by Ringo Starr — and bought for him by Brian Epstein in 1966 — was designed specifically to accommodate the Beatle's drum kit, and has been in a private collection for many years. It was the work of coachbuilders Radford, whose patrons included show business stars and royalty. The similar "tailgate" model shown here was actually built for the deputy chairman of the company, Radford, Freestone and Webb.

**Elton's Fantastic Glasses**

A pair of Elton John's flamboyant glasses with blue and yellow tinted lenses mounted in a simulated mother-of-pearl frame with circular wire extensions embellished with rhinestones. They date from Elton's most exuberant stylistic period in the mid 70s and there are pictures of him in a Captain Fantastic suit wearing them. Although many of the descriptions of Elton's glasses, sound like cake decorations, they all contain prescription lenses and were certainly used.

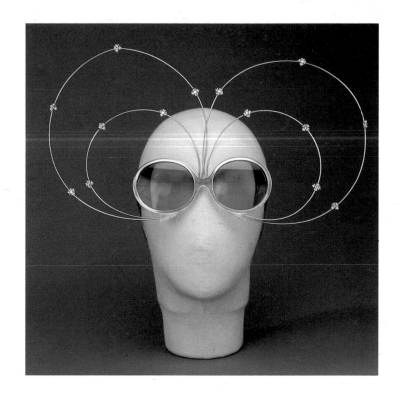

# Gladrags

Elvis Presley will always be associated with his mythical "Blue Suede Shoes", and in a real sense performers are remembered as much for their trademark images as their music: Buddy Holly's heavy-framed glasses, the Beatles and the round-necked collarless suits, Elton John's theatrical performance outfits, the Sex Pistols' bondage trousers, Madonna's underwear outerwear. All are costumes used to create and reinforce different images designed to attract a following, sell records and fill concert arenas.

Since the evolution of 20th century teenage music, some performers chose to adopt images

▶

**Stage Suit Worn by Little Richard**

A Little Richard stage suit which he wore on *The Rolling Stones Special* TV Show. The maker's details read "Fiddlers Costumes & Design, Belew, Los Angeles, CA" identifying it as designed by the influential Bill Belew. Little Richard (real name Richard Penniman) has been widely acknowledged as one of the earliest and most influential rock & roll performers. His style was heavily influenced by the gospel preachers he saw as a teenager, and he designed many of his costumes himself. His later outfits were predominantly by Tommy Rush and Melvyn James, and it is easy to forget that he was glitter and glam in the 50s, long before Elton or Bowie.

### Bill Haley's Tour Tuxedo

Part of British rock & roll mythology, this black-and-white plaid tuxedo jacket was ordered by Bill Haley from D.A. Millings Ltd., the London theatrical tailor who later made stage clothes for the Beatles among others. The occasion was the British debut appearance of Haley and the Comets at the Dominion Theatre, London, in February 1957, and the property tag inside the jacket (reading "Bill Haley – London Dominion") confirmed this.

Dressing in the style of the more fashion-conscious African-Americans, with loose jackets, drainpipe slacks and bright shirts, Elvis – as with his music – defied all contemporary white, middle-class dress codes; his style was categorized as being only fit for "backwoods trash." Bob Luman, a country singer when Elvis was 19, described Elvis's appearance at a concert at Kilgore, Texas, . . . "This cat came out in red pants and a green coat and pink shirt and socks, and he had this sneer on his face and he stood behind the mike for five minutes, I'll bet, before he made a move."

By copying the clothes of these early rockers, whose images were seen on nationwide television and in print, teenagers could show that they rejected convention and identified with all that rock & roll stood for. New wealth allowed the young stars to buy anything they wanted, however outrageous: one of the lasting images of Elvis Presley was on the album sleeve of "Elvis's Golden Records" in 1957 picturing him wearing a suit of gold lamé by Nudie, best known as tailors of western-style costume. Elvis's feelings toward clothes and accessories in the early days are encapsulated in an extract from a contemporary interview . . . "He (Elvis) showed me a gold horseshoe ring studded with 11 big diamonds he was wearing. "Look at all the things I got," he said, "I got 40 suits and 27 pairs of shoes" and I asked him how he knew it was exactly 27 pairs and he said, 'When you ain't got nothing, like me, you keep count when you get things.'" (Extract from the *Daily Mirror*, London, April 30, 1956)

Elvis's contemporaries, Jerry Lee Lewis, Eddie Cochran and Gene Vincent became known for their explosive stage performances while Little Richard was even more outrageous in bizarre glitter suits, heavy make-up "and his hair towering in a bouffant sometimes a foot high." Jerry Lee Lewis, was dubbed "The Wildest of Them All!" by the press. Particularly associated

which conformed to the more conservative dress codes of their day while others chose the path of rebellion. From the time of the dance band and jazz ensembles, musicians in a group dressed alike. The early black exponents of jazz and rhythm and blues wanted to attract affluent white, middle-class audiences and dressed in suits and tuxedos perhaps to appear conventional and thereby more acceptable. In an interview in 1989, Eric Clapton revealed that his interest in stylish dressing had been stimulated by studying album cover photographs picturing impeccably dressed black jazz musicians, . . . "The way these guys presented themselves attracted me to the jazz world much more than the music. They were sharp." The wild men of rock & roll's early years changed all that.

Rough, uncultured and unashamedly blue-collar, Elvis Presley and the other "bad boys" of rock & roll (Little Richard, Gene Vincent, Chuck Berry and Jerry Lee Lewis) caught the mood of the teenager, emerging unsettled and rebellious from the conservative middle-aged middle classes in the mid 50s. They quickly became the rebel heroes of American youth disenchanted with the values and moral codes of their parents and seeking different lifestyles.

### Entwistle Necklace

John Entwistle's silver spider necklace dating from the 1980s. The body of the spider is made of black stone with garnet eyes and well-detailed legs and was designed by Michael Fishberg. The spider is unerringly realistic and for a time became Entwistle's "trademark" symbol.

with garish clothes trimmed with striking fake fur, he wore a leopard skin-trimmed black tuxedo on the *Dick Clark Show* and can be seen in a newspaper photograph in 1958 wearing a jacket similarly trimmed with an arm around his 13-year-old bride – wild indeed!

The American rock & roll toughs inspired several British rebels. Wee Willie Harris with his extrovert costume and dyed pink hair was, in 1958, the first British rock star to really exploit his idiosyncratic visual image. Later came Johnny Kidd with his pirate eyepatch and the sullen-looking Billy Fury. Fury appeared to be little more than a pocket tough, however, as an interview in 1960 proved, . . . "Be a rebel," he suggested, "mind you, when I say 'rebel' I'm not talking about slovenly dressed beatniks who think that long beards, exhibitionism, walking barefoot and just plain defiance and vulgarity, is all that's needed to be 'different'."

The rough image of the rockers, the tough, greasy, blue-collar exponents of early rock & roll, was counterbalanced by rock & roll's "good guys." Buddy Holly, Pat Boone, The Everly Brothers, Neil Sedaka, Paul Anka and Ricky Nelson projected a squeaky clean image which suited the cosy conventionality of the late 50s and early 60s. But their music had been emasculated, it was sanitized and tamed and the performers once again looked reassuringly safe, groomed to appeal to the more conservative record buyers and their parents, who were (in Britain) responsible for the hits of the likes of the Beverley Sisters, Connie Francis and Russ Conway. The state of the charts brought this plea from the pages of *Disk* in 1959, . . . "my Mum knows more about the Top 10 than I do . . . doesn't the record industry realize there is a large potential buyers' market among the teenagers?"

The record industry attracted a growing teenage audience again with the Beatles. The rough Liverpool band who had been raving it up in dark cellars in their home town and Hamburg wearing black leather and grease, had their act cleaned up and were repackaged by Brian Epstein, EMI and a German friend who designed their first round-necked suits, and they emerged with a distinctive image which was to be mimicked by thousands of fans all over the world. Their long hair attracted the young while their stylish suits did not alienate an older age group.

The early 60s saw the emergence of a fashion and lifestyle known as Mod. The Mods, the first yuppies, were able to escape their blue-collar backgrounds through steady jobs which pro-

### A Hard Day's Night Dress

This cotton "shift" dress in typical 1960s polka dot was decorated with a guitar and Beatle heads, specifically designed to be worn by usherettes in various cinemas up and down the U.K. when *A Hard Days Night* was shown in mid 1964. The one illustrated was actually worn by one of the usherettes at the London charity premier of the film and was signed for her by the group while she was wearing it.

vided them with spare cash to spend on consumables, entertainment and clothes. They rejected the Rockers, relics from the "bad boy" rebel exponents of rock & roll in the later 50s; both the Rocker style and music were considered coarse and savage by the Mods. With their short, neat hairstyles and dressed in a combination of pointed-toe winkle-picker shoes, Fred Perry sports shirts, French or Italian suits with neat fitting jackets and narrow pants they were a strong influence on fashion and music. They were devotees of American R&B and encouraged the growth of groups including the Small Faces, the Kinks, the Who, and the Yardbirds. In his Yardbird days, Eric Clapton had a reputation as a sharp dresser; the band's 1964 debut album pictured him in a sharkskin suit, Clapton later confessed . . . "I was mad about clothes . . . I guess I could have been a fashion designer . . ."

London became the hub of fashion and musical trends in the mid 60s with the rise and rise of the miniskirt, Twiggy launched as the "Face of 1966", geometric haircuts, Carnaby Street and the King's Road (the Mecca for the fashion-conscious). The charts both in Britain and the U.S. featured the clean cut sounds of the Beatles, the Beachboys, the Kinks, Herman's Hermits, the Hollies, Manfred Mann, Cliff Richard and the Shadows. Indeed, few of the raunchier R&B or rock & roll bands were represented in the charts at this time, the notable exceptions being Eric Burdon and the Animals and the Rolling Stones who took every opportunity to flaunt their seemingly outrageous nonconformist attitude.

Psychedelia hit the streets in 1967. Growing use of hallucinogenic drugs and the influence of Eastern philosophy led to a more random approach to fashion with ethnic costume and jewelry from the Middle East, India and South America providing the inspiration to the anti-fashion policy of the Hippy movement from 1967 until 1970. The Beau Brummell and Back Britain looks of the mid 1960s were replaced by long-haired groups wearing clothes which appeared to have been thrown together at random and formed a challenge to the consumer culture of the time. The clothes and philosophy of the hippies and "flower children" gradually influenced retail fashion and particular musical styles united youth culture in its rejection of "The Establishment." This was a dress code which could be easily copied; once again dressing in the same way as the psychedelic bands demonstrated a stand against the established moral codes of the time. The demands of these new buyers encouraged the rise of new, mainly West Coast, performers including the Grateful Dead, Janis Joplin, Jefferson Airplane, and Jimi Hendrix; Hendrix, in his dress-up box gypsy costumes, was described as a "technicolor acid dandy."

### John Entwistle Stage Suit

John Entwistle's suede and leather flame motif stage costume which he also wore on the U.K. TV's show *Top Of The Pops* in the early 1970s. The Who drew much of their support from their live performances and were renowned for the noise levels they achieved. Their Woodstock set at the 1969 festival is considered one of their most impressive, and at the Isle of Wight festival in the same year, the sound system was so powerful the audience was cautioned not to venture too close to the stage.

### Sid Vicious's String Vest

The black string cotton T-shirt so often worn by Sid Vicious. The punk era is a highly significant area of collecting which reflects its importance in music history. The Sex Pistols are seen as the parents of punk with Vicious as its most infamous victim. Although the group was really only together for two and a half years they managed to "swindle" (as Malcolm McClaren put it) £115,000 from EMI and A&M who became so disgusted by the group's antics they felt unable to complete the contracts. Virgin Records finally signed the band who notched up seven U.K. Top Ten hits before giving up on "flogging a dead horse."

Even the Beatles metamorphosed from boys-next-door who any parent would have been happy for their daughter to bring home into psychedelic strangers in satin militaria when, on June 2, 1967 their "Sgt. Pepper" album was released. The rebels' rebel, Mick Jagger, went one better and flaunted himself in a white dress at the Rolling Stones' free concert in Hyde Park on July 5, 1969, no doubt causing consternation among many fans!

Perhaps to disassociate themselves from the contrived scruffiness of the hippie groups and the student audiences they attracted, "Glitter Rock" – or "Glam Rock" – emerged as the new style phenomenon in the 1970s. Little Richard, of course, had dressed in outrageous glitter in the 50s, long before it was generally acceptable and had been seen in the film *Don't Knock the Rock* wearing a loose silver lurex suit. It was not until the early 1970s that it became acceptable for performers to transform every performance into a glittering theatrical presentation. The best exponents of the new style were the Osmonds, David Cassidy, the Sweet, Gary Glitter, Marc Bolan, and Alvin Stardust who turned on the glitz to seduce the new group of buyers, the prepubescent "weenyboppers". Older audiences supported Elton John (the Liberace of 1970s rock), Rod Stewart, and David Bowie, who gave spectacular performances dressed in silver lurex jumpsuits, striding out on stacked platform heels; images which enabled the performer to be seen by the audiences in huge arenas or open air concerts without the help of closed-circuit television screens.

Perhaps in rebellion at the peace and love culture of the hippy revolution, and later as a response to the less macho images of the glitter rockers, heavy metal bands rose in popularity during the 70s, led by Led Zeppelin, Black Sabbath, Alice Cooper, Kiss, and Blue Oyster Cult. Performers once again personified tough, rough, uncontrolled music and dressed with increasing freedom and attracted a wide following among students and fans of some of the more experimental groups of the late 60s.

As a contrast to this raw male-oriented sound and style there was the new Disco culture. This burgeoning 70s scene culminated in the John Travolta film *Saturday Night Fever*, from which an album was created which was the 1978 Album of the Year, a Grammy winner and the number one-selling soundtrack album of all time (25 million copies sold). The disco phenomenon, which had previously been largely the province of the metropolitan gay communities, suddenly became a scene which many aspired to; a "Never Never Land" where no costume or form of

behavior was deemed too outrageous. The only musical criterion was that music had to be dancable; chosen performers included the Bee Gees, Donna Summer, the Village People, James Brown, Grace Jones, Rod Stewart, and Labelle, who exploited their freedom to perform dressed as if for a night at the disco.

With such displays of opulence and excess, rock music and young record buyers were ripe for a revolution – in style at least – and, when it came, it was violent. Punk Rock burst onto the music scene in 1975 with the Sex Pistols who represented all that the established order most feared – anarchy. Punk music and fashion were designed from the start to outrage, and attracted those who were looking for belligerent ways to rebel against authority and the superstars of contemporary rock. The Sex Pistols have been described as "blue-collar delinquents" and touched a nerve in 1976 at a time of high youth unemployment, the rise of the neo-Nazi National Front, and a stagnating rock scene in Britain. Punk style was all about stance, aggression and danger; punk style reflected sado-masochism with its references to bondage, razor blades and pins, Nazi decorations and regalia, and clothes were dirty, generally ripped or graffitied. Safety pins pierced cheeks and lips, do-it-yourself tattoos sliced into arms, uncut hair haloed in unkempt spikes; in its purest application, punk style successfully rebelled against style itself in true

**Paula's Mini**
A minidress worn by Paula Abdul at the "Emmy" award ceremony. The dress, made by the Haute Naughty Clothing Co. in a size 34B, is signed inside the corset and inscribed "Live! Love! Dance!" She started her career as a "Laker girl" for the L.A. Lakers basketball team and progressed into choreography with particular success in the Janet Jackson "Control" videos. Her third single reached number one in the U.S. in 1988 ("Straight Up") followed by a double platinum album "Forever Your Girl".

ing more and more outrageous in their dress styles. But as the 80s progressed, "Less Is More" became the style of the more sophisticated performers and the superstar rock bands, such as Pink Floyd, Dire Straits, Bruce Springsteen, and U2, dressed in jeans and T-shirts, heightened street wear or designer labels instead of exaggerated stage costumes. Springsteen wore Levis, Clapton wore Gianni Versace, others chose Jean Paul Gaultier or Armani, but the emphasis on many concert platforms was on understatement.

In contrast to the superstar groups, a style of music developed during the 70s and 80s which could be made without large financial investment in expensive instruments and equipment. Reggae, hip-hop and rap gave voice to disenchanted minorities and then to street gangs, in a similar way to the punk movement in the 70s. As with punk music, a style revolution swept through the performance stages – tough street fashion with an emphasis on sportswear, spandex, and clothes which would allow strenuous activity, coupled with hightop sports shoes and gold chains and charms of increasingly alarming proportions. The first rap album to top the U.S. charts was the Beastie Boys' "Licensed To Ill" (March 1987) and this band's style trademark was able to be copied at no expense by fans. As a result, thousands of owners of VW cars found their emblems removed to be worn on a chain round the neck of a Beastie Boy fan as a medallion! MC Hammer has his own particular style, baggy pants, which appeared as street and party wear in large numbers. Recently (March 1991) MC Hammer's style won him – no doubt surprising many – the "Best Dressed Male Artist" award from *Rolling Stone* magazine.

Some superstars of course persisted as peacock-style 'prima donna' performers and used Hollywood costumiers to create elaborate sequined, feathered and leathered outfits. Prince, Madonna and Michael Jackson, for example, continued to commission extravagant costumes for their shows which more closely resembled theatrical performances than mere concerts. We still live in the reign of these superstars, their gruelling world tours and their promotional videos for singles which cost many millions of dollars to make.

Films, as well as her concerts, have helped to make Madonna the focus of a culture of young "Wannabees"; the world saw many teenage gum-chewing, black-rooted dyed blondes mimicking Madonna as she appeared in *Desperately Seeking Susan*. Perhaps for the first time girls have found a real rebel heroine to admire, who sings about their problems, temptation, lust, ambition, and pregnancy. A female performer who attracts men and inspires women, Madonna has recently signed the biggest record contract in the history of rock music.

anarchic form. Johnny Rotten of the Sex Pistols had this to say about punk style in 1977 . . . "Punk fashions are a load of bollocks (balls). Real punks nick (steal) all their gear from junk shops."

The reign of the first unprecedented punk style was relatively short-lived, as record companies strove to repackage punk music and style into more acceptable forms. The acts which emerged from the post-punk era were widely popular. Deborah Harry of Blondie, with her retro Marilyn Monroe look and blond locks, emerged as the queen of punk-chic, while Ian Dury and the Blockheads, the Boomtown Rats, Toyah, and the Pretenders developed sanitized versions of punk images. The New Romantics who followed hard on the heels of these bands, extravagantly costumed, included Adam Ant, Spandau Ballet, and Duran Duran, all of whom used their theatrical costume and images coupled with increasing use of promotional videos to encourage record sales.

The 1980s saw rock bands such as ZZ Top and Queen further develop their distinctive mass-appeal images, and many rose to new heights of self-parody through the decade, becom-

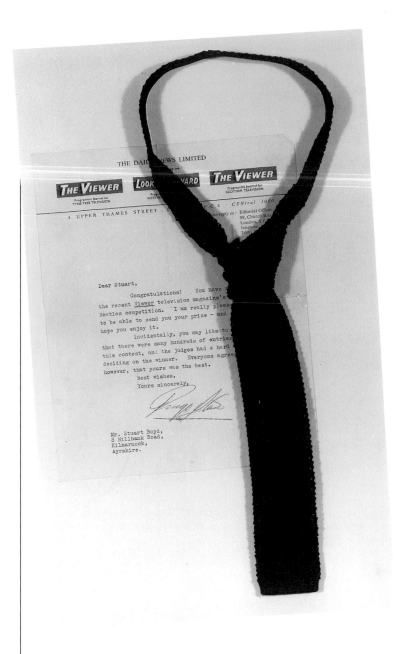

### Ringo's Tie

Ringo Starr's necktie made from silk and dating from 1964. The tie, together with the other three Beatles' neckwear, was one of four prizes in a competition in *The Viewer* magazine, a British journal for several television companies. The letter of authenticity is genuinely signed by Starr, not undertaken by a secretary which so often happened. This item was auctioned at the first rock & roll sale held in 1981 together with the Lennon prize which fetched a healthy premium over Starr's tie.

### John Lennon Jacket

This gray silk stage jacket dating from 1964 once belonged to John Lennon, and has a written "John Lennon" label confirming his ownership alongside the tailor's label. When it appeared in 1981 the estimated sale price was between £180 and £250, yet it actually fetched £850 – over $1200 and a high figure at the time.

### Classic Beatle Jacket

One of the collarless jackets that became a hallmark for the Beatles, this John Lennon stagewear from 1964 was auctioned in 1981 and described in the sale catalogue as being "edged with black velvet, with maroon lining and small pocket at one side holding a plastic plectrum."

### Lennon Stage Jacket

According to the tailor who made it, and authenticated it for the salesroom, this black gaberdine jacket, made for John Lennon in 1963, was based on jackets worn by the American vocal duo the Everly Brothers in one of their concert appearances.

### Lennon's Tinted Glasses

A pair of John Lennon glasses with smoky-gray plastic frames and mirrored, tinted lenses. Lennon began to wear his glasses in public to a greater extent in the latter days of the Beatles' history but initially, despite poor eyesight, he would never wear them on stage or in photographs. Later on he was able to afford contact lenses, but some of the early photos from the Cavern Club show him squinting quite noticeably.

### John Lennon Glasses, 1967

Lennon's fondness for the granny-style glasses extended to sunglasses. These glasses contained non-prescription lenses and were worn by Lennon during the summer of 1967. They were sold in 1991 with a letter from Julia Baird, Lennon's half sister, confirming this. This was an eventful summer for the group with the release of "Sgt. Pepper" and the death in August of Brian Epstein.

### Lennon Tie

Sold with a letter of authenticity signed by John Lennon himself, this 46 inch knitted silk tie had originally been donated by Lennon as the first prize in a contest held by *The Viewer* magazine in 1964.

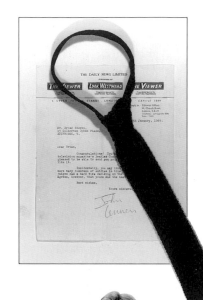

### Lennon's "Pocket" Coat

John Lennon had this special "pocket" coat made for him by designer Simone, part of the archetypal hippy team The Fool who went on to make the clothes for the Beatles' Apple boutique. The purple velvet jacket, dating from 1967, had three pockets on each side, two small round pockets under the lapels, and one small and large pocket on the inside. It was given to an employee by John Lennon during the spring of 1970.

### McCartney Beatle Suit

The epitome of the Beatles' "Beatlemania" image, this wool sharkskin suit with collarless jacket was made by West End tailor Dougie Millings (from a design by Pierre Cardin), whose name appears on the label alongside a property label inscribed "Beatles, Paul McCartney – Stage, 1963" that was sewn into the inside pocket.

### Lennon Movie Suit

This single-breasted suit, worn by John Lennon in the 1964 movie *A Hard Day's Night*, was made in black moygashel – a fabric of artificial fibers – by the Beatles' regular theatrical tailors D.A. Millings & Son, and was sold to a collector complete with a note from the tailor saying "John jammed the zip!"

### Debbie Harry's Nightdress

From the movie *Union City* released in 1979; the group Blondie were at the height of their success having had two U.K. number one singles and albums and their first U.S. chart success with the disco-influenced "Heart Of Glass." They would go on to score three further number one singles on both sides of the Atlantic. However, the same success did not transfer onto the big screen.

### Marc Bolan's Jacket

Marc Bolan's embroidered jacket dating from the early 1970s. Bolan is credited with being at the forefront of the glam-rock movement but his success was based on solid "rock meets pop" tunes. Time has treated the artist kindly, for while he was never as influential as David Bowie he has attained a status above other bands of the period.

### Bolan Waistcoat with Guitar

Marc Bolan's waistcoat and acoustic guitar. Made of imitation leather and tiger skin, the coat is embroidered with a letter "M" and was often worn by Bolan on stage. The guitar dates from 1965 and has a repaired neck. It has an interesting provenance, it was broken by Bolan in 1965 while at the Knightsbridge office of the producer Jim Economides. Bolan rejected suggestions that it could be repaired and left the guitar. It was rescued by a member of Those Fading Colours and was auctioned in 1990.

### Bowie Three-Piece Suit

From his "Glass Spider" European tour of 1987, David Bowie's three-piece tomato-red stage suit was signed "Bowie '87" inside the lapel. As with many such items, it appeared in auction with additional authentication in the form of a copy of the tour souvenir book showing Bowie wearing the suit.

### Boy George "Chameleon" Outfit

Boy George's costume as worn in the video for the number one single "Karma Chameleon". The outfit was donated by Boy George to raise money for The Arvon Foundation. George O'Dowd had been wearing such costumes for some years, his image merely being an extension of the reaction that was developing against the plain look of the Mod revival in London. While his look was an important feature of the media attention the group attained, the music was initially strong enough to justify the chart success.

### Karen Carpenter Gown

A beaded gown worn by Karen Carpenter. The item was sold by Sotheby's and "accompanied by a costume rental document." This illustrates that items which are not even owned by the artists in question, but merely worn, are of equal status to a collector. This particular dress is of the style generally associated with the artist especially in the way in which highlights her long thin frame.

### Bowie "Glass Spider" Suit

A suit worn by David Bowie on the "Glass Spider" tour of 1987. The jacket bears the label of Bergerie Di Cania, the pants a label of Nick Coleman. The jacket is inscribed inside in black felt pen "With many thanks for contributing to this auction, Bowie '89 (suit worn on '87 tour)" This refers to a Living Earth memorabilia auction in 1989 to which Bowie donated the suit.

### Ferry Debut Jacket

Bryan Ferry's tiger skin patterned lurex jacket as worn on the cover of the debut Roxy Music album in 1972. The LP was recorded at a cost of £5,000 in London and became a U.K. Top Ten hit. The image of the album with the foldout sleeve was an equally important feature. Ferry wished to portray "an image of ritzy nostalgic glamour" and he used a 50s style portrait for the cover together with similar images of the band within the cover.

### Dylan's "Rolling Thunder" Jacket

Bob Dylan's jacket by "Nudies of Hollywood" dating from 1976. The jacket was handmade by the late Mr. Nudie himself in size 40 regular. It was worn by the singer during his alliance to the "Born-Again Christian" movement and while on tour with the "Rolling Thunder Review." Dylan subsequently turned back to Judaism and handed the jacket down to Kinky Friedman, a member of the "Rolling Thunder" show.

### Fury Stage Suit

Billy Fury's stage suit from 1963. The suit, made by D.A. Millings & Son, is silver with a blue lining and has "Billy Fury 904" handwritten on the inside pocket. The outfit dates from Fury's most productive period, his popularity would wane slowly over the next two years as "beat" music dominated the charts.

### Billy Fury Bracelet

Billy Fury's gold and diamond identity bracelet, probably dating from the latter part of his career. Whilst Fury was very successful in the early 1960s, his weak heart prevented him from touring as much as he would have liked, and needed to, in order to sustain the hits. His 11 singles on Parlophone all failed to chart. The heart problem claimed him in 1983.

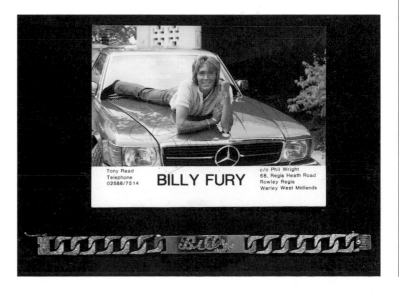

### Hadley's Ballet Suit

Spandau Ballet's Tony Hadley wore this silk suit in the video for the number two U.K. hit ''Gold.'' The suit was made by Chris Ruocco and was donated by the singer to be auctioned to raise money for The Arvon Foundation. The band started as a ''new romantic'' outfit and, with their first two albums achieved a significant following. Their third album pursued a more mainstream line and while this brought considerable success (for the first time in the U.S.) the band lost its direction, seemingly not quite knowing which audience to target.

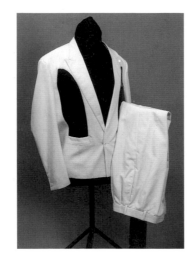

### Jimi Hendrix Hat

This hat could hardly have belonged to anyone but Jimi Hendrix. The size 7.5 hat is made of black felt with a red lining and labelled ''The Westerner''. The original black band is covered by a purple nylon scarf decorated with various gold-colored bucking broncos and jewelry. The image is pure Jimi Hendrix and this particular hat is the one worn on the cover of the Experience's U.K. number four album ''Smash Hits.''

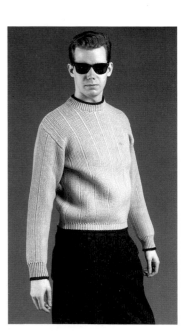

### Whitney Houston Two-Piece

A red two-piece outfit worn on stage by Whitney Houston. The cotton jacket and slacks, made by Fabrice, are also signed by the artist. Houston has an excellent pedigree for hit music: her cousin is Dionne Warwick, and her mother Cissy sang backing vocals for Presley among others. Before she was allowed to release a debut album, her mother and Clive Davies of Arista Records waited more than two years to collate a suitable collection of hit songs. Her first album yielded three U.S. number ones; her second had four.

### Holly Stage Jacket

A stage jacket and shirt from 1958 worn by Buddy Holly – and he is pictured wearing the jacket in the book *Remembering Buddy*. The three button design was popular with the Crickets who dressed in similar or identical stage outfits. Holly dropped the ''e'' from his surname but the nickname ''Buddy'' was used from his earliest childhood days at the suggestion of his mother who preferred it to Charles.

### Crickets' Crew-Neck

Buddy Holly fans will be familiar with the crew-neck sweater favored by the singer and his group the Crickets on many of their publicity shots. This one, *circa* 1958, belonged to Buddy and was light blue with a black trim around the collar and cuffs.

### Buddy Holly's Glasses

Synonymous with the name Buddy Holly are his glasses. "He made it O.K. to wear glasses," John Lennon once said, and he certainly paved the way for others – from the Shadows' Hank Marvin to Elvis Costello – to make dark-rimmed "specs" a part of their image. This pair dates from later in Holly's career, when he preferred a squarer frame than the earlier Rayban look.

### Buddy Holly Stage Suit

More than three decades after he wore it on his earliest tours, this charcoal-gray stage suit that once belonged to Buddy Holly appeared in a New York sale in 1990. The label in the collar informs us that it was designed by Irving's Design for Jeff's of Houston, Texas.

### Michael Jackson Stage Clothes

The stage outfit for Michael Jackson's "Bad" world tour. A highly sought after item made by the Western Costume Co., Hollywood, with individual labels bearing the artist's name. Jackson wore this outfit at various concerts throughout his year-long tour that started in Japan in September 1987, heavily sponsored by Pepsi. The tour became the biggest grossing ever, although some concerts were canceled due to lack of ticket sales.

### Jackson's World Tour Wardrobe

This collection of Michael Jackson stage wear dates from the 1987 "Bad" tour. The black fedora hat on the left is signed by the singer and will be familiar to Jackson video watchers. The black leather hat on the right is from the Australian leg of the tour and is by the makers of the famous original Aussie bushhat. However, it is the boots which are of the most interest. They are signed on the sole and while the other two items may be worth a substantial three-figure sum each, the boots would command well into four figures.

### Elton's "Yellow Brick Road" Suit

Made by Bill Whitten's Workroom 27 dating from 1973/4. The cream canvas jacket and slacks are painted and embroidered with the album cover artwork. Elton wore the suit with a yellow simulated silk shirt embroidered with the song titles. The double album, available as a limited edition on yellow vinyl, remains one of his most successful, peaking at number one on both sides of the Atlantic.

### Elton John's "Pinball Wizard" Boots

From the 1975 film *Tommy*. The Doc Martin-style boots are constructed from fiberglass with platform supports and metal callipers with leather straps for attaching to the legs. Elton played the role of the Pinball Wizard in the Ken Russell movie, based on the Pete Townshend rock opera concept album originally released in 1969. The soundtrack featured ''quintaphonic'' sound which was not only complicated to perfect but would also prove difficult to reproduce in movie theaters. It is said that Elton only agreed to play the role on condition he could keep the oversized boots. They were subsequently bought in the 1988 Elton John collection sale by the Managing Director of Doc Martins.

### Elton John's Pink Eiffel Tower Boater

The Herbert Johnson ''boater'' straw hat is pink with a scarlet hatband. The Tower is also pink and continued Elton's interest in illuminated accessories. Elton recently confessed that he was somewhat over-excessive with his costumes and accessories, but the more negative the reaction of his peers, the more tempting it became. Taupin never felt such histrionics were justified but ''at least he did it before anybody else.''

### "La Rocka" Elton John Jacket

A black leather jacket of a relatively calm design by Elton's standards. The printed Capitol records motif is of Gene Vincent's 1960 hit 'Wild Cat'. Elton's 1986 album was called "Leather Jackets" which may indicate a soft spot for this archetypal rock & roll gear.

### Elton John "Fluorescent Balls" Stage Suit

A jump suit by Bill Whitten's Workroom 27 dating from 1973/4. A completely outrageous outfit worn by Elton on his U.S. tour of 1974. The suit consisted of a wet-look lurex fabric applied overall with day-glow cork balls. The skull cap and removable collar had the balls supported on piano wire. While many of Elton's outfits have a discernable theme the idea behind this one escapes explanation.

### Elton John "General" Outfit

Made by Ret Turner and dating from 1983/4 together with an original sketch by the designer. Turner was responsible for many of John's outfits on the tour and it is particularly desirable for the collector to obtain both costume and sketch. After the split from lyricist Bernie Taupin in 1976, the 1983 "Too Low For Zero" heralded their reunion and a revival in Elton's chart fortunes particularly in the U.K. Although the two deny that the split lasted anything like this long (they did collaborate on several songs) it is clear in the quality of Elton's work since 1983 that he is at his best with Taupin. The outfit was worn on the tour to promote the new album.

### Elton John's Platform Shoes

These can be rather easily attributed to the early 70s. While platform shoes and high heels were all the rage, Elton managed to push the bounds of good taste to the very limits, if not beyond. Elton had no one designer for such items but examples came from Nunn Bush and Ferradini. The shoes were sold in "The Elton John Collection" in 1988, and one can safely assume that the purchaser will not be adding to their active life.

### Elton John Antique Brooch

Elton John's pearl and diamond brooch. The brooch itself dates back to 1900, although in Elton history it can be attributed it to his "Ice On Fire" period of 1985. Elton amassed a significant collection of jewelry: "I'm impulsive. If I see something I like,

I just buy it," he commented when his collection, not just the jewelry, were sold in 1988.

### Elton's Cartier Pendant

Elton John's onyx and diamond pendant by Cartier of Paris dating from 1920. This was probably bought by Elton in the early 1980s as he was photographed wearing it at the time of the "Too Low For Zero" album. In Phillip Norman's book on Elton, actress Nanette Newman recalls a trip to Cartier in 1972, "He went round the whole shop, picking things up and buying them. It was as if he was going round Safeways with a trolley."

### Elton John Brooch

Elton John's onyx and diamond pendant brooch by Cartier, his favorite jeweler. Elton wore this brooch on the cover of Sotheby's catalogue for the sale in which it was included. It dates, in Elton terms, to 1985. Elton followed a certain philosophy with the items: "It's a question of putting as much on as possible without looking like a Christmas tree."

### Annie Lennox's Boots

A pair of Annie Lennox's boots donated by the singer in aid of The Arvon Foundation and signed on both soles. She wore the boots throughout the "Revenge" tour and at the Nelson Mandela Concert in 1988. Lennox began working with Dave Stewart in 1977 firstly in the group the Tourists, and then together as the Eurythmics before splitting and embarking on solo careers. They successfully molded themselves into a significant album and live act while maintaining the ability to craft hit singles.

### Madonna's "Virgin" Shoes

A pair of Madonna's shoes which are signed and annotated "Express Yourself" on the sole of the left shoe. A size 38 they were used on "The Virgin Tour" in 1984, her first. Her self-titled debut album had been a moderate success on both sides of the Atlantic but the "Like A Virgin" follow-up was the turning point. It produced four hit singles plus an interest in her back catalogue numbers.

### "Blond Ambition" Madonna Stage Suit.

Madonna's gold stage suit worn on the "Blond Ambition" tour of 1990. The suit was sold with a magazine illustrating the singer wearing the suit on stage, together with a letter of authenticity. The tour proved highly successful, winning the Best Tour award in *Rolling Stone* magazine, and complemented a deliberately provocative period with singles such as 'Hanky Panky' and "Justify My Love," the video of which was banned. This was followed by the 1991 movie documentary detailing her life called *In Bed With Madonna*.

### Madonna Basque by Gaultier

A gold basque used by Madonna on her "Blond Ambition" tour of 1990. The costume was specially designed by Parisien couturier Jean Paul Gaultier and was offered as the first prize in a contest organized by MTV and Pioneer. The designer made many of the costumes used on the 54-date tour. The outfit was a development of the now famous "external bra" look which Madonna championed on her earlier tours.

### Sinead O'Connor/Mickey Rourke Jacket

A jacket donated by Sinead O'Connor to raise money for the Cancer Help Centre in Bristol, England. The garment was previously owned by Mickey Rourke and features a signed portrait of the actor. Although many stars donate items to be auctioned for charity, O'Connor is particularly vocal about the hypocrisy she sees within the industry, regularly boycotting many of the award ceremonies in protest at the manner in which "we are allowing ourselves to be portrayed as being in some way important . . ."

### Orbison "C&W" Suit

A western-style suit made for Roy Orbison by Mike McGregor. An interesting item as the singer was best remembered appearing in black, this being highlighted by the wearing of dark glasses. According to a popular story, the hallmark "Big O" dark glasses originated accidentally in 1963 after the singer left his standard prescription pair on a plane.

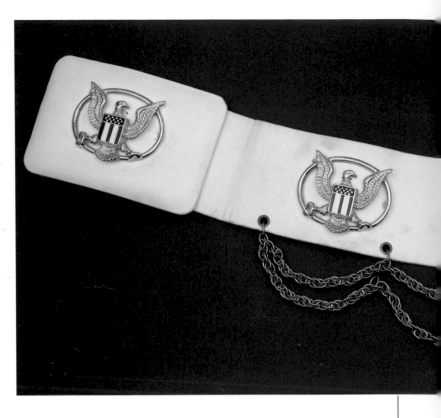

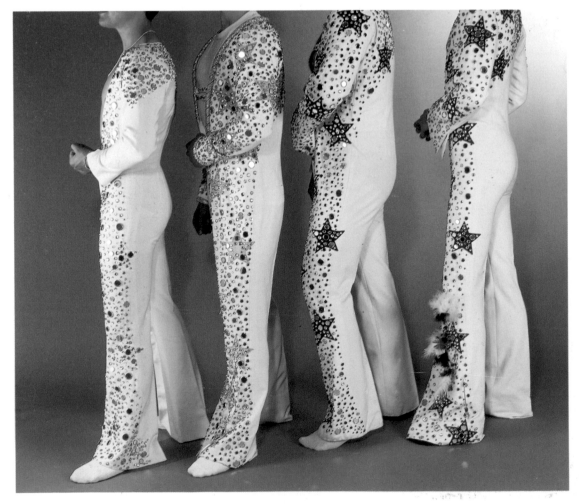

### Four Osmonds' Stage Suits

From their 1975 European tour, each suit is marked with a band member's name: Donny, Merrill, Alan and Jay. They were designed by Bill Belew and one can immediately see the similarity to some of the costumes he was designing for Presley at this time. Belew had made Presley's black leather outfit he wore on his 1968 TV comeback and continued to design most of Presley's more extrovert stage wear until the artist's death in 1977.

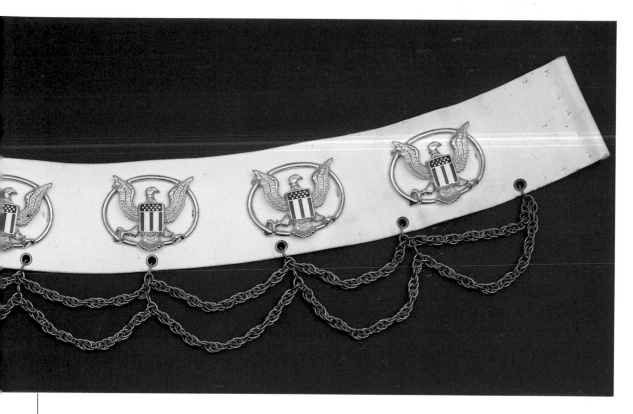

### Elvis Belt

A specially commissioned stage belt for Elvis Presley by Bill Belew. The belt is four inches wide and typifies the way that Elvis changed from rock & roller to Vegas performer. The reverse of the belt has the handwritten note "Elvis sample of belt Bill Belew" and is further initialled by Presley. The belt dates from the early 1970s and is believed to be a prototype for a series of belts for the singer.

### "Shooting Star" Outfit

An Elvis Presley stage suit designed by Bill Belew and often called the "Shooting Star" suit. A one-piece outfit with a matching cape with a gold lining, it was worn by the singer at his concert in Madison Square Garden in 1972. Elvis had made an encouraging return to recording and stage work in 1968 and was having his most productive chart success for many years. However, the rift with his wife in 1972 seems to have influenced a downturn in the quality of both his music and his life.

### Graceland Security Uniform

A security uniform from Elvis Presley's home, Graceland, which formerly belonged to Harold Lloyd, Elvis's first cousin. The jacket is waterproof with monogrammed "P" metal buttons and embroidered Elvis badges. The house is situated in 13 acres of land in the Memphis suburb of Whitehaven and is managed by the Presley Estate.

### Elvis "Concho" Jump Suit

Elvis Presley's silver "Concho" jump suit dating from his second season in Vegas in 1970. The suit appeared at auction in 1991 with this framed descriptive plaque showing the King performing. Later in 1970 Presley announced a small U.S. tour, his first since the heady days of the 1950s.

### Elvis Presley Jacket

A black suede jacket worn by Elvis Presley in concert in 1969. It was on 26 July of this year that the singer returned to stage work after an eight-year absence. His much-awaited debut was at the International Hotel in Las Vegas for a one-month stint, which was a great success. Presley gave the jacket to his hairdresser, Larry Geller, in 1972.

### Jacket Belonging to Elvis

You may think this is a collectible for Scott of the Antarctic fans but it is in fact a Coney jacket once belonging to Elvis Presley. The King gave it to a girlfriend, Tori Petty, in the spring of 1976, and it was sold in 1989 with documentation from George Klein, one of Elvis's closest friends, confirming this.

### Jump Suit Designed by Elvis

The white jump suit became the latter-day "Las Vegas" trademark of Elvis Presley, the epitome of 70s showbiz kitsch. This one, which the King wore on stage in 1973/4, was described as having "silk kickpleats, elaborate turquoise embroidery, jewel work, and zip front with custom plastic collar stay." It was designed, perhaps not surprisingly, by Elvis Presley himself.

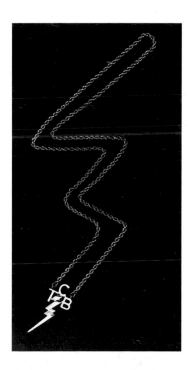

### Elvis Presley's "TCB" Medallion

Elvis Presley's "Taking Care of Business" 14 carat gold medallion from around the time of his death. The expression was originally used by Afro-Americans in the States especially in its "TCB" form, and that probably explains its appeal to Elvis.

### Elvis's Wristwatch

Elvis Presley's Patek Philippe gold wristwatch dating from the early 1970s. A standard watch but created by one of the best watch manufacturers. The watch is 14 carat as is the strap and was presented to the doctor who treated Presley for a dry sore throat, and it was sold in auction in 1986 accompanied by the two prescription slips for the singer.

### Engraved Elvis Wristwatch

An Elvis Presley wristwatch dating from 1970. The gold-plated, self-winding watch, made by Mathey Tissot, had block numerals enclosed by a ring with "Elvis Presley" written in raised letters. The watch was given away as appears to have happened frequently with Presley items, the recipient in this case being Presley's chauffeur.

### Prince' *Purple Rain* Costume

A cape with mask, gauntlets, and high-heel ankle boots worn by Prince in the 1984 film *Purple Rain*. This incredibly versatile performer had already produced five albums prior to the soundtrack for his movie debut. The 1980 "Dirty Mind" had stirred some interest in the U.S.A. but it was the 1982 album "1999" that began the gradual rise to stardom. The film *Purple Rain* was a typically cavalier move by Prince with the cast consisting predominantly of friends, not actors. While the quality of the music (two U.S. number ones) certainly attracted an audience for the film, its takings in excess of $60 million cannot be justified by that alone.

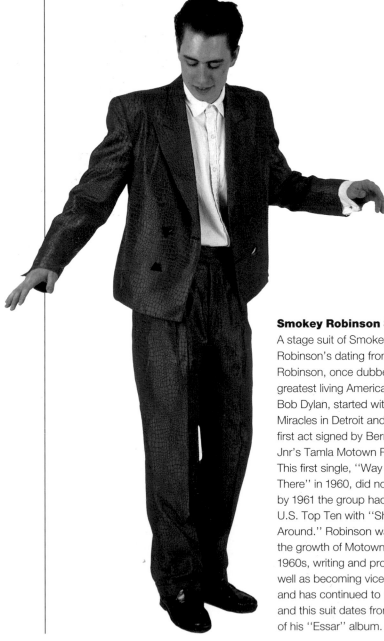

### Smokey Robinson Stage Suit

A stage suit of Smokey Robinson's dating from 1984. Robinson, once dubbed the greatest living American poet by Bob Dylan, started with the Miracles in Detroit and was the first act signed by Berry Gordy Jnr's Tamla Motown Records. This first single, "Way Over There" in 1960, did not chart but by 1961 the group had made the U.S. Top Ten with "Shop Around." Robinson was vital in the growth of Motown in the 1960s, writing and producing as well as becoming vice-president, and has continued to perform, and this suit dates from the time of his "Essar" album.

### Mick's Jacket and Vest

Mick Jagger's damask satin Kimono-style jacket and studded vest dating from 1977. This outfit was probably everyday clothing for Jagger and follows the loose baggy look that he still seems to favor today.

### Ron Wood Suit

The striped satin suit dating from 1967 was purchased from "Granny Takes A Trip" where Wood bought many of his clothes. This is the period before Wood joined the remnants of the Small Faces to form the Faces in 1969. After Mick Taylor quit the Stones in 1974, Wood joined the band initially for touring purposes only, claiming the Faces meant more to him. However, with Rod Stewart's solo successes the Faces were soon to disintegrate.

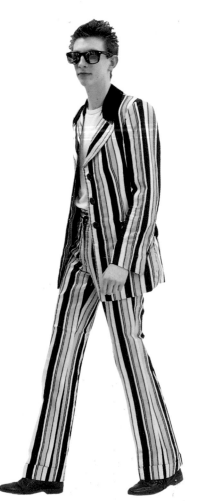

### Ron Wood Jacket

Dating from 1970, the printed satin jacket features Bonnie and Clyde-type figures and reflects how the Rolling Stones adapted their personal style to the psychedelic period.

### Jagger Jacket

A stage jacket worn by Mick Jagger in the late 1960s. The stylish Victorian coat is made of black cut velvet with red, brown and gold paisley designs. The Stones' stage outfits became significantly more adventurous with the advent of the "flower power" era and continued this way well into the 70s and 80s. With Jagger's exaggerated stage act they have made themselves the world's most sought after live performers.

### Sade Dress

A white lace dress worn by Sade on her 1988 world tour. The dress was auctioned to raise funds for The Arvon Foundation. After her stunning debut album "Diamond Life" (although Sade is a group name also) it proved difficult for the singer to break away from the "cocktail bar" sound and image. Predominantly an album artist, this dress was worn on the tour to promote her third album "Stronger Than Pride."

### Entwistle's "Who's Next" Suit

John Entwistle's suede suit worn on the cover of the 1971 album "Who's Next." This dates from the band's most productive period and proved to be their only U.K. number one album and was a relatively straightforward effort after the originality and controversy of "Tommy." "Quadrophenia," the band's next studio recording, was a return to the rock-opera style.

### Vicious Leather Jacket

Sid Vicious's first leather jacket which he bought at the age of 18. He wore it when he signed his A&M contract outside the gates of Buckingham Palace on March 10, 1977. The jacket originally belonged to a friend who shared a "squat" with Sid in Elgin Avenue, London. Having acquired the jacket Sid changed the decoration on it several times during his ownership.

**Keith Moon's Buffalo Coat**

U.K. groups who toured the U.S. in the second "British Invasion" of the early 70s had a predilection for going home dressed like extras from a Wild West movie, with buckskin jackets, stetson hats and leather cowboy boots. Not to be outdone, the Who's extrovert Keith Moon acquired this American Indian buffalo coat – a fur-lined garment heavily decorated on the suede outside with leather thongs, beadwork, buckles and geometric painted patterns.

**Who Football Helmet**

John Entwistle's MacGregor American football helmet as worn on the cover of 1974 album "Odds And Sods." Each member wore a helmet for the cover, with a letter at the front to spell "ROCK" and their first names signed at the side. Interestingly, Pete and Roger are wearing each other's helmets. The album was an Entwistle-inspired compilation of unreleased material and made the Top Ten in the U.K. and earned a gold disk in the U.S.

**Original Hendrix "Purple Haze" Lyrics**

Though remembered as an innovative guitarist rather than for his lyric writing, this earliest-known draft of Jimi Hendrix's "Purple Haze" – which appeared on his debut album "Are You Experienced" – generated a multi-thousand dollar price when it was auctioned in 1990. It includes alternative lyrics which were not to be found in the final version of the song, and a working title at the top of the page "Purple Haze – Jesus Saves."

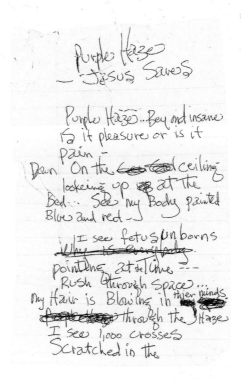

# Rock & Roll Art

Rock & roll art, within the context of this chapter, comprises album cover artwork and bass drum designs, works of art by the musicians themselves as well as accomplished professional artists. Also included in the chapter is manuscript material of original lyrics, which can provide intriguing insights into the lives and creative thoughts of the performers.

Early rock art, sampled from contemporary album covers, posters and programs, was conservatively styled and photographic rather than drawn. Exceptions were Elvis Presley's first British album (HMV CLP1093) released in March 1956 and Bill Haley's album, "Rock Around

▶

**Who Stained Glass**

In 1988 a group of memorabilia which belonged to John Entwistle was auctioned. This stained glass panel was one of several which Entwistle commissioned, each representing a different album cover of the group. Produced to the same size as the album covers, the 12 panels were designed to assemble into a stained glass window and included, as a centerpiece, a triple panel devoted to the "Tommy" cover.

The Clock" (Brunswick LAT8117) released in Britain in October that year. The album cover of "Elvis Presley" was decorated with a photographic portrait of Elvis, but what a portrait! Eyes shut, mouth wide open, a look of ecstasy on his face while he rocks his guitar, there was no doubt that the contents were going to prove uncontrolled. Bill Haley's album featured bright graphics on a scarlet background. If this cover itself didn't alert conservative record buyers to the musical style of the album, the sleeve notes left nothing to the imagination . . . "Let it rock – this is hard-driving stuff not for babies and grand-

### Banned "Butcher" Cover

The infamous "Butcher" cover for the U.S. issue album "Yesterday And Today." The photograph was also used in the U.K. to advertise the release of the single "Paperback Writer." Taken in a studio in Chelsea, London on March 25, 1966, the photograph consisted of baby dolls and animal meat. The cover was hastily withdrawn after an outcry and the cover – this one was still sealed with the record inside – is now a rare find. The band claimed the photograph was their "own idea of pop art satire" and was initiated due to the boredom of doing yet another photo session. The album still topped the U.S. charts on July 30, 1966. This was a particularly eventful time for the group in the U.S.A, for on July 31, Lennon's remarks about being "more popular than Jesus" were printed, which led to the odd Beatles record being used as a firelighter.

mothers, tough music for a tough generation." The more restrained performers of the time such as Buddy Holly and teen idol Ricky Nelson were portrayed in more conventional photographic poses.

As the marketing of groups became increasingly sophisticated, it was acknowledged that album covers were important to encourage sales. The covers had to be eye-catching and should portray the groups as vital and contemporary through the use of the latest trends in graphic design. The increasing complexity of album art during the 1960s can be highlighted just by looking at albums by the Beatles: their stark 1963 "Meet The Beatles," their Andy Warhol-influenced "A Hard Day's Night" soundtrack (1964), the mildly distorted "Rubber Soul" (1966) which pointed towards the use of hallucinogenic drugs and their revolutionary "Sgt. Pepper" retro cover designed by Peter Blake (1967). Album designs from other groups left their mark on the decade. Martin Sharp, an Australian artist who shared a flat with Eric Clapton in 1966 (and with whom Clapton wrote the track "Tales Of Brave Ulysses") created a swirling day-glo dream collage for Cream's "Disraeli Gears" (1967), while the Rolling Stones' album 'Their Satanic Majesties' with its applied three-dimensional photograph was said at the time of its release to be the most expensive album cover ever produced.

The circular "tobacco tin" design for the Small Faces'

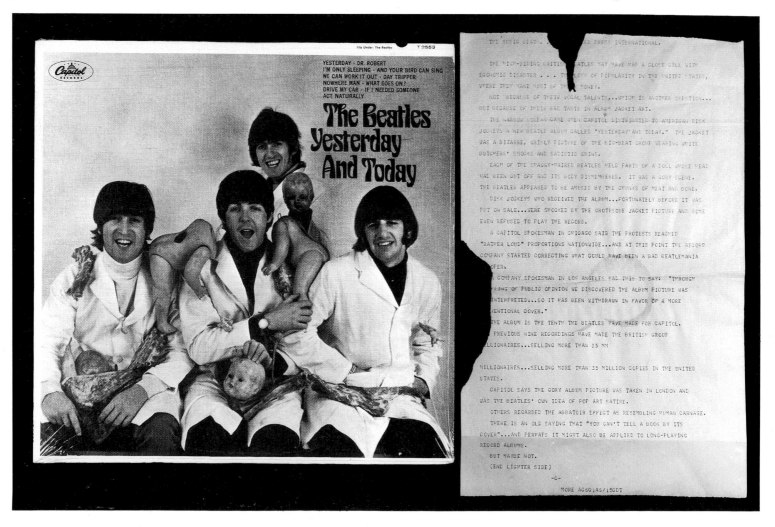

"Ogden's Nut Gone Flake" (1969) was revolutionary in a different way. Although the design won awards, its circular construction meant that the album cover had the disconcerting habit of rolling off shelves while its flimsy hinges ensured that the cover fell apart unless handled with great care.

Designs for album covers which were never used are interesting indications of contemporary codes of conduct at a time when most recording companies were owned by conservative pillars of society. The Beatles produced an album in America which was banned until repackaged in a more acceptable cover. Known in collectors' circles as the "Butcher's Sleeve," the original album cover to the American album "Yesterday And Today" was a gory color photograph of the four Beatles dressed in white coats, seated amongst hunks of raw meat and the dismembered bodies of dolls. Hastily withdrawn and reissued with an acceptable photograph of the band with a cabin trunk stuck over the offending cover, the original "Butcher's Sleeve" has become highly prized amongst collectors.

The original design for the Rolling Stones' album "Beggars Banquet" was the brainchild of Mick Jagger and Keith Richard who dreamt up a photograph of a lavatory wall with graffiti-

**Zeppelin Album Artwork**

After "Sgt. Pepper," album covers became more and more imaginative in their design, supergroups with supergroup budgets vying with each other for ever more original ways of packaging their 12-inch pieces of vinyl – sometimes to the point where there was more artistry in the sleeve than in the contents. The gimmick involved in "Led Zeppelin III" was the inner wheel which could be turned at the edge of the sleeve, changing the images that appeared in cut-out holes on various parts of the cover design. When the original artwork was sold, it was, therefore, more complex than most, comprising the five panels of the original mixed-media illustration, press proofs, a blank construction with the wheel, and two albums.

style handwritten song titles and credits. But the chairman of Decca, Sir Edward Lewis, banned the graphics and eventually the album was granted release provided the cover was changed (it finally went on sale with a plain buff cover bearing the letters "R S V P"). One album even had to be sold, like a dirty book, in a brown paper bag – this was the "Two Virgins" album (1968) which featured nude photographs of John Lennon and Yoko Ono on the front cover.

**Gentle Giant Drum Skin**

Bass drum skin logo handpainted with a design incorporating a variety of musical instruments. Made for the progressive British rock band of the 1970s, Gentle Giant, the drum appeared at auction with provenance stating that the instrument was used on all Gentle Giant recordings and live appearances between 1969 and 1971.

traits of band members at work. While some keep the bass drum logo tradition alive it can only realistically be for reasons of nostalgia rather than for the benefit of the first few rows of the vast audience.

The design of drum skin logos was certainly not covered by any art college syllabus in the 1960s, but it was from art college that many successful rock musicians moved into a career in music. In an interview in 1985 Bryan Ferry volunteered " . . . I suppose the network of the English art schools . . . were very important to the growth of the British music scene. So many future rockers attended them before and during my time – and many kids followed suit afterward because of us. The attraction

The Sex Pistols' desecration of an official Cecil Beaton portrait of HM The Queen – picturing her with a safety pin through her lips – in publicity material for their single "God Save The Queen," was part of an orchestrated graphic campaign to shock and outrage, and this particular image was banned by A&M records although the single was later released under Virgin with adjusted artwork. The artist Jamie Reid used ransom note-style lettering and day-glo colors to reach the group's target audience. This form culminated in the 1977 album, "Never Mind The Bollocks," the sight of which prompted a policewoman to file a report claiming that displaying the album with its obscene title contravened the 1889 Indecent Advertising Act (a claim which was subsequently overturned by a judge).

Many punk gigs were held in small clubs and municipal venues such as town halls. In the 1960s bands played live at small venues such as theaters, movie theaters and ballrooms with a line-up which may have included several performers and it was important that the band's name was prominently displayed. The bass drum skin provided a perfect site for arresting graphics and the name or logo of a particular band.

The Beatles used several different bass drum logos before settling on their best-known. John Lennon's original 1957 group, the Quarrymen, had their name displayed in upper case on their bass drum; 1962 saw the "B" of "The Beatles" waving insect-like antennae before the band decided on the two words in capital letters with the central "t" in "Beatles" enlarged.

Other bass drum logos represented here are those of Cream, AC/DC, the Who, Gentle Giant and Marmalade. Varying from carefully designed crisp, clean lines to less precise psychedelic multi-colored swirling clouds, these logos are very illustrative of the contemporary stylistic periods and may even have given a clue as to the manner of music likely to be played.

The heyday of bass drum art has passed. The band blueprint of a drummer and guitarists/vocalists/keyboard player which was *de rigeur* in the 1960s and 1970s has changed completely today. Solo artists have become increasingly influential in the music world, their style and personalities primarily visible through promotional videos. Contemporary bands are often formed without traditional drum kits, preferring electronic drum machines which produce relentless, complex rhythms at the touch of a button and without physical exhaustion. Performers today play vast arenas and are increasingly dependent on closed-circuit television which fills screens with close-up por-

**Jagger Portrait in Bronze**

Entitled "Jagger I" and numbered 21 from a limited edition of 50, this resin bronze portrait of Mick Jagger (15½ in. high) was executed by the British sculptor, John Somerville in about 1985. Showing Jagger in mid-performance, this work formed the basis of Somerville's later study in bronze entitled "Star Star."

### Lennon Drawing for *Daily Howl*

When John Lennon was still at school he whiled away his time when he should have been attending to more scholarly pursuits, producing a joke newspaper called the *Daily Howl*, in which he lampooned various members of the teaching staff. He left the bulk of these drawings, poems and short stories at his squalid student flat when he went off to play in Hamburg with the Silver Beatles, telling a flatmate he could keep them. Many later formed the basis of his first book *In His Own Write*, while others – like "This Is Not Robert Mitchum" – were to remain unseen until relatively recently.

was obvious when you consider that, in a society where a tradi-tional trade is customarily the thing, young people could leave a conventional school, get a government grant and go to an art college." John Lennon and Stuart Sutcliffe, the fifth member of the original Beatles line-up, attended Liverpool School of Art in the late 1950s. Keith Richard went to art college in Sidcup, Pete Townshend in London, Eric Clapton to Kingston College of Art, Godley and Creme were students at art school in Man-chester, while Bryan Ferry obtained a degree in Fine Arts at Newcastle University.

This chapter illustrates works of art by a number of rock musicians some of which have become well-known images. John Lennon's "Bag One" sequence of lithographs of himself and Yoko Ono (which included several intimate scenes) was seized by the police as "obscene publications" when first ex-hibited in London. Despite this notoriety, or perhaps because of it, this limited edition series became very popular with a wide variety of collectors, including Elton John who had a set of the

### Oxtoby Drawing of Elvis

"That's the way it was and is," this large pencil drawing of Elvis (25 by 28 in.) is by David Oxtoby and is dated 1975. The work portrays Presley as a youngster in the 1950s and seasoned performer of the mid 1970s with great sympathy and detail. Oxtoby became widely known during the 1970s for his visionary portraits of popular musicians, which were known collectively as "Oxtoby's Rockers."

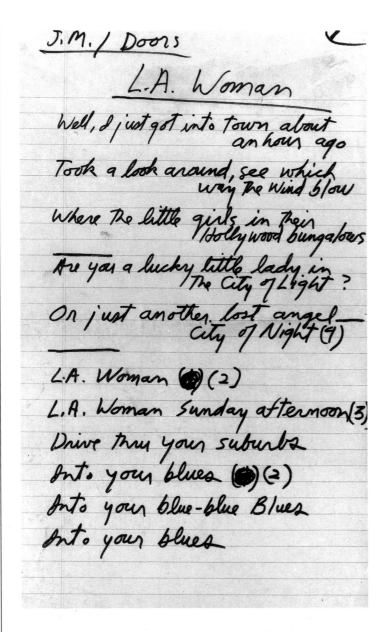

*J.M. / Doors*

## L.A. Woman

Well, I just got into town about
an hour ago
Took a look around, see which
way the wind blow
Where the little girls in their
Hollywood bungalows
Are you a lucky little lady in
The City of Light?
Or just another lost angel—
City of Night (4)

L.A. Woman (●) (2)
L.A. Woman Sunday afternoon (3)
Drive thru your suburbs
Into your blues (●) (2)
Into your blue-blue Blues
Into your blues

### Jim Morrison Lyrics
The Doors' final album, "L.A. Woman" was released early in 1971 just as Jim Morrison was leaving for Europe, to pursue poetry-writing – he was to die there, in Paris, later in the year. The lyrics, handwritten on three simple sheets of yellow legal paper, are initialled "J M /Doors" and were written in 1970, along with annotations regarding the vocal arrangements of the song, for the album's title track.

(photographer, designer and author), Barry Fantoni (painter and cartoonist), Bryan Organ (leading portraitist, subjects include the Prince and Princess of Wales), Andy Warhol (pop artist), Alan Aldridge and David Oxtoby. The latter two are particularly associated with portraits of rock & roll performers.

Aldridge is known for his illustrations inspired by Beatles songs, and for the cover of Elton John's hugely successful album "Captain Fantastic And The Brown Dirt Cowboy" (which held the number one slot in the U.S. album charts for seven weeks). Aldridge also created, among other rock based artworks, several amusing airbrush portraits of rock superstars including Bob Dylan and Elvis Presley.

David Oxtoby was responsible in the 1970s for an influential body of work entitled "Oxtoby's Rockers" which was, in the words of critic Graham Vickers, "an exuberant gallery of portraits dominated by early rock & rollers, often based on familiar received images but somehow brilliantly recharged with a life of their own. Even those to whom the music itself had meant little could now taste something of the unique excitement of rock & roll through Oxtoby's paintings."

While these masterly portraits attract an audience to whom the sitters may well be unfamiliar, manuscript material seduces the dedicated fan and rock historian. Important manuscript material seldom appears on the open market. Usually regarded as ephemeral, working drafts for lyrics were often thrown away as were playlists, old recording contracts and payment checks.

Undoubtedly Lennon and McCartney were the most successful singer/songwriter partnership in the history of rock music, but the tradition can be traced back to several 1950s performers including Chuck Berry, the Big Bopper, Eddie Cochran and Buddy Holly. Illustrated in this chapter are manuscript lyrics by Holly and the Big Bopper as well as more contemporary performers including Elton John, David Bowie, Bob Dylan, Jimi Hendrix and Jim Morrison, and both working and finished copy is represented. Working lyrics are perhaps of greatest interest to historians, showing the way in which ideas or emphasis may have developed during the composition process. Final versions of songs may be of more interest to fans, particularly if the lyric also bears an indication of chord sequences which indicates that the piece of paper was probably used during a recording or concert performance.

In all the various disciplines of rock & roll collectibles, rock art is the most perspicacious, illustrating so vividly contemporary life and style as well as illuminating performers' creative processes and innermost thoughts. Rock art and manuscript material are both extremely desirable and scarce, a combination which ensures that high prices are achieved when occasionally these rare collectibles appear on the open market.

Lennon lithographs in his private collection for many years.

A great deal of graphic talent has also been displayed over the years by musicians who received no art school training. John Entwistle, originally a French horn player with the Middlesex Youth Orchestra, displayed his aptitude for caricature drawing when his designs were used on the album cover of "The Who By Numbers," released in 1975. More recently, Ron Wood has held exhibitions of his work, largely lithographs and etchings representing fellow musicians, which are stylish, sensitive and capture the essence of the performer.

However fine the craftsmanship of the works of art produced by rock performers, it cannot be denied that most are sold to fans of their musical rather than artistic talents. It can always be speculated that their exploits would not have received the gallery exposure had the artist's name not been already well known in another profession.

This is not the case with other rock portraits – those undertaken by successful professional artists including Cecil Beaton

### John Lennon Cartoon

A typical piece of Lennon visual whimsy, this felt-tip drawing on yellow lined writing paper carries the title ''B'z in His Bonnet or Ants in His Pants'' and is signed ''John Lennon or else . . .'' Dating from the mid 1970s, it belongs to a Liverpool collector who purchased it at a memorabilia sale in 1982.

### AC/DC Drum Skin

Bass drum skins were a means by which bands, even in their earliest amateur days, were able to establish some kind of group logo. They constitute a unique record of a band at a particular stage in its career, and are therefore highly collectible. This skin for Australian heavy metal band AC/DC is handpainted (by whom is not evident), and is signed by the brothers Angus and Malcolm Young, who formed the nucleus of the group.

### Beach Boys Artwork

Original artwork for record sleeves are, by definition, extremely rare. These proofs for the front and back design of the Beach Boys' ''Smile'' were offered for sale in 1985 along with a xerox copy of a Capitol Records memo which discusses modifications in the design.

### Portrait of John Lennon

Apart from works by Stuart Sutcliffe, this is the only known portrait of John Lennon by a fellow student at Liverpool College of Art. It shows Lennon in typical pose leaning over the back of a chair in a college studio, wearing the glasses which were essential, given his chronic short sight. The artist, Anne Mason, was a classmate of John's and close friend of his wife-to-be, fellow student Cynthia Powell.

### Bronze of Paul McCartney

By David Wynne, it dates from the 60s and it is said that the sculptor did the sketches on which the bronzes are based at the Beatles' Paris concerts. McCartney is playing his ''violin'' bass guitar and this five-inch bronze is number four from a limited edition of 12. Wynne, a highly regarded contemporary sculptor, is perhaps most popularly known for his design of the commemorative British 50 pence piece with linked hands which celebrated the European Economic Community.

### "Sgt. Pepper" Blow-Ups

Various examples of Peter Blake's life-size blow-ups that he made for the ''Sgt. Pepper'' sleeve tableau have cropped up in memorabilia sales; among this selection, which appeared in 1987 – 20 years after the event – are Marilyn Monroe (top) and a bottom row consisting of psychoanalyst Carl Gustav Jung, pop singer Dion Di Mucci, film comedian Stan Laurel, and Hollywood child star Shirley Temple – plus a garden gnome signed by all four Beatles.

### Alternative "Sgt. Pepper" Drum Skin

When painter Peter Blake put together the tableau for the ''Sgt. Pepper'' cover, he engaged a real fairground artist called Joe Ephgrave to produce a drum skin in an appropriate style. Ephgrave actually produced two different versions; this is the little-seen ''alternative'' drum skin that belongs in a private collection. Should it ever go on the market, the collectors value would be immense.

### "Sgt. Pepper" Cut-Out Heads

The "Sgt. Pepper" montage consisted largely of cardboard cut-out heads mounted on poles of varying height, spaced in tiers two feet apart; a favorite pastime among fans was trying to identify as many of the faces as possible. Of the few cut-outs that have survived, these three appeared in the "Art of the Beatles" exhibition in Liverpool in 1984 – of New York painter Richard Lindner, movie comedian W.C. Fields, and an anonymous film starlet.

### Alternative Lennon Lyrics

This original manuscript of lyrics for John Lennon's "It's Only Love," in the singer's own hand, was particularly significant in that it included many alterations and differences to the final recorded version of the song and no less than nine extra lines of lyrics that never finally appeared in the published song.

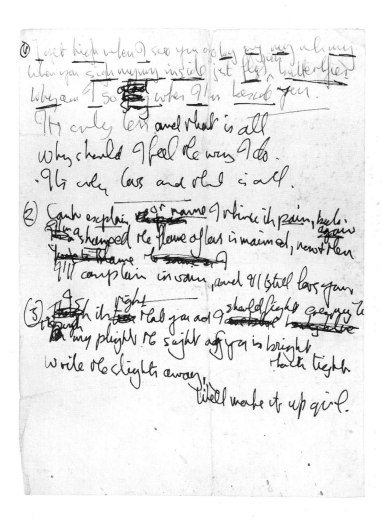

### Marlene Deitrich "Sgt. Pepper" Cut-Out

Immediately after the tableau for the "Sgt. Pepper" cover was photographed, most of the items disappeared as those present took away "souvenirs." Very little remains today – most of the three-dimensional montage was made up of cardboard cut-outs – but the life-size photographic enlargement of Marlene Dietrich did crop up in the first-ever rock memorabilia sale in 1981, signed by all four Beatles.

131

### Lennon "If I Fell" Lyrics

John Lennon's original manuscript lyrics for "If I Fell." The finished state of the piece indicates it was written for a rehearsal or for use in the recording studio. The lyrics are written on the inside of a folded Valentine card. The song was included on "A Hard Day's Night," the soundtrack from their first film which premiered on July 6, 1964. The film was nominated for two Academy Awards and was well received by viewers and critics alike.

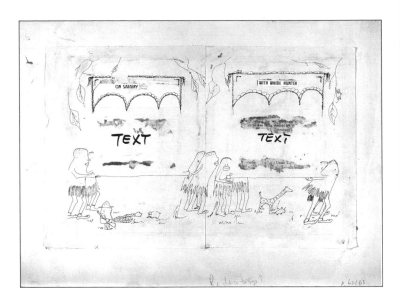

### Beatles *Melody Maker* Caricatures

James Hall Thomson, or Jimmy Thomson as he signed himself, was staff cartoonist at the *Melody Maker* weekly music paper in the U.K. through the late 60s and early 70s. His pen and ink caricatures captured the image of the four Beatles at various stages in the period of their transition from the world's biggest group to solo superstars. These four originals, mounted on card, appeared in a memorabilia sale in 1982.

### Lennon *In His Own Write* Drawings

John Lennon's first book of humorous writing and drawings, *In His Own Write*, saw him hailed as "the literary Beatle" when it first appeared in 1964. These preliminary drawings for the two-page spread "On Safari with the Whide Hunter" would undoubtedly command a higher price today than when they appeared on sale in 1984.

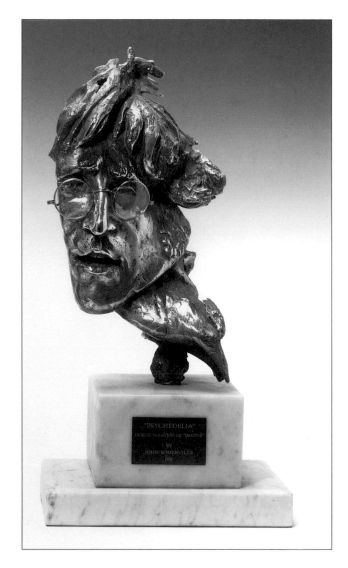

YOU CAN GO TO CHURCH AND SIGN A HYMN
JUDGE ME BY THE COLOUR OF MY SKIN
YOU CAN LIVE A LIE UNTIL YOU DIE
ONE THING YOU CAN'T HIDE
IS WHEN YOU'RE CRIPPLED INSIDE

### "Crippled Inside" Lennon Manuscript

This photocopy of John Lennon's original draft for "Crippled Inside" had the fourth verse of the song added in ink in Lennon's own handwriting; as with the works of literary names, these notations and scribblings are seized upon by collectors as unique samples of the artist's writing process in action.

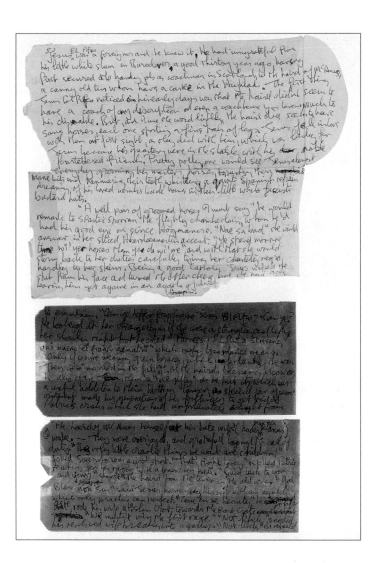

### Bust of John Lennon

Entitled "Psychedelia Unique Variation On 'Imagine'," this bust of John Lennon in polished bronze is by sculptor John Somerville. In order to achieve the desired effect, the mold for the bronze edition of nine was distorted at the wax stage of the process.

### Lennon's *Spaniard* Drafts

This original draft of what was to be the opening chapter of John Lennon's book *A Spaniard In The Works* belonged to Don Short, a reporter who traveled with the Beatles extensively during the 60s. He recalled in some detail how he acquired the document: "We checked into a country hotel somewhere between Birmingham and Leeds. After dinner John disappeared into the loo [bathroom] and emerged nearly an hour later clutching a torn white envelope and two brown disposal bags. He had scribbled notes all over them and at first I thought he intended showing me the lyrics of a new song he had written. Instead, he explained, it was the start of a "great new book." John thrust the pages into my hand – after copying the text into a clear exercise book – and said, "Here Don. They're yours. Flog 'em if you ever go broke . . .'"

133

### John Lennon Christmas Card

This Christmas card was hand drawn by John Lennon in wax crayon on a blank double album cover, bearing the legend "Apple Xmas '68 from John Lennon."

### Beatles Bronze

A reminder of one of several abortive attempts to have a permanent monument to the Beatles erected in Liverpool, this was one of two experimental 32 inch high bronzes produced by sculptor A. Curran and submitted to be considered for a full-scale public statue. Sufficient funds could not be raised and the 1978 project, intended for Mathew Street (the site of the Cavern Club) had to be abandoned.

### Lennon Collage

An unusual piece of artwork by John Lennon dating from 1966, this collage of news clippings, overwashed then framed and glazed, was given by the Beatle to a company called Curwen Prints Ltd. as payment for work carried out at their studio on his behalf, and were sold with two letters of authenticity in 1982.

### Yellow Submarine Cells
Animation "cells" from the Beatles' *Yellow Submarine* movie – the handpainted celluloids which, in their hundreds, go to make up moving sequences against a separately painted "still" background – have, not surprisingly, proliferated at sales in recent years. At 24 frames for every second of film, the 88-minute feature involved over 125,000 such cells in its production!

### Lennon "Bed-In" Drawing
On the now-celebrated occasion of John Lennon and Yoko Ono's "bed-in" at a Montreal hotel in 1969, Lennon drew this black felt-tip sketch. Many generally similar sketches appear on the market regularly.

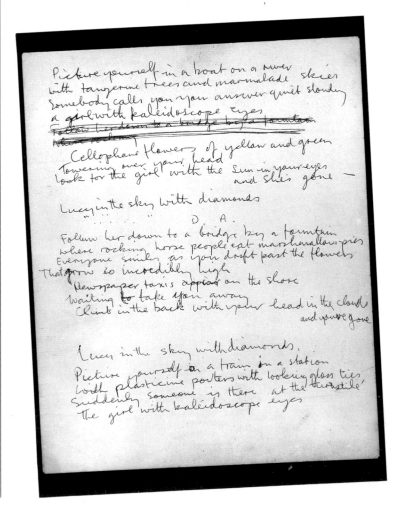

### Lennon's "Lucy In The Sky" Lyrics
Although John Lennon claimed at the time that the title "Lucy In The Sky With Diamonds" was originally uttered by his small son, Julian, and didn't refer to LSD, the lyrics are a knowing evocation of a hallucinogenic "trip," a shimmering surreal landscape full of gleaming images drawn from John's imagination and real life. "Looking glass ties," incidentally, quite possibly refers to a trendy 1960s Liverpool boutique called Looking Glass, (which sold pre-flower power, floral-print ties), rather than the Lewis Carroll *Alice* book.

135

### Handwritten "Help!" Lyrics

These lyrics for "Help!", handwritten by John Lennon, were sold with an autographed photograph from the same period (1965) and an explanatory plaque stating that the scrap of paper was "located" at the EMI Studios in Abbey Road.

## Lennon's Handwritten "Imagine"

These original lyrics of John Lennon's most famous post-Beatles song – "Imagine" – were written on board an aircraft following his and Yoko Ono's supposed "abduction" of Yoko's daughter Kyoko from a hotel in Palma, Majorca in April 1971. The lyrics, which include small differences to the final version, were scribbled on the back of a hotel bill; they would currently command a price of well into five figures in the salesroom.

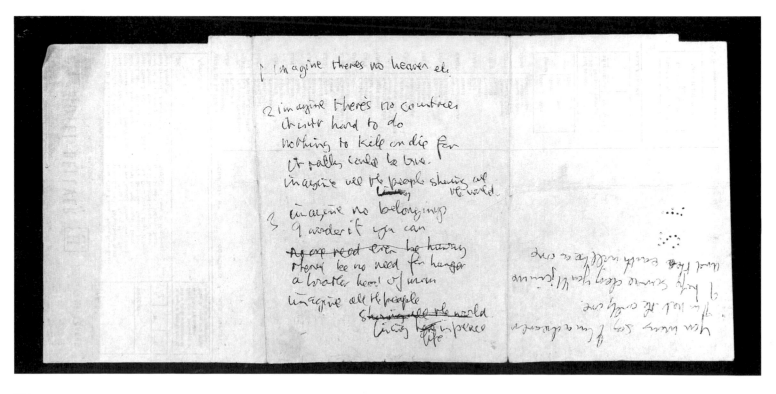

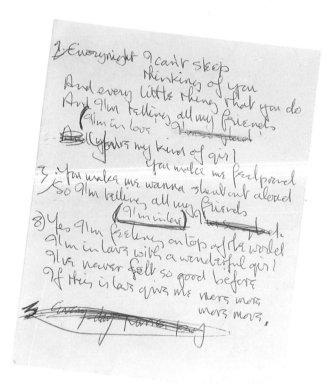

## Lennon Lyrics for the Fourmost

During the Merseybeat explosion of 1963, Lennon and McCartney gave a number of songs to other artists in the Brian Epstein ''stable,'' songs which the Beatles never actually used themselves, either on stage or on record. In Lennon's hand, these are the original lyrics for one such number, ''I'm In Love.'' It was utilized by the Fourmost, who had their first chart entry with another Lennon/McCartney composition, ''Hello Little Girl.''

## Lennon and McCartney Lyrics

Paul McCartney original manuscript for ''Little Child'' and a John Lennon set for ''Any Time At All.'' The Lennon lyrics, from 1964, are relatively complete suggesting that they were for use in the studio. ''Little Child'' dates from 1963 and was included on the ''With The Beatles'' album. In the U.S., it featured on ''Meet The Beatles.'' It was not until ''Sgt. Pepper'' that a U.S. album appeared with the same track listing as a U.K. release. Initially this was understandable as the US was over a year behind on Beatlemania, mainly because EMI's American subsidiary Capitol were slow to release their records. The British albums contained more tracks and so the spare tracks made more albums for the U.S. market. The biggest confidence trick was the soundtrack album ''A Hard Day's Night'' which had the five new tracks not featured in the film lifted altogether and replaced with instrumentals of old songs.

## ''Benny and the Jets'' by John Lennon

A rare example of a collage by John Lennon, this surrealistic juxtaposition of motorbikes, topless girls and Andy Warhol heads is dated October 1, 1974 and entitled ''Benny and the Jets.'' Size approximately 8 by 14 inches.

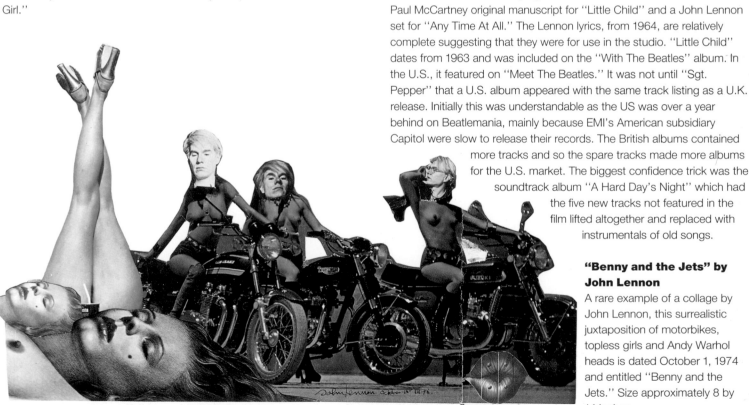

### Sutcliffe Self-Portrait

The Beatles' first bass player, Stuart Sutcliffe, was considered one of the most promising students at Liverpool College of Art, hence the dismay when he left college to play in Germany with the group. He very quickly developed – in Liverpool and then at the State Art School in Hamburg – a mature abstract style that belied his teenage years. This oil-on-canvas self-portrait is from an earlier period, 1958, when he was in his second year at Liverpool. (27 by 17.75 in).

### Artwork for John Lennon's Piano

This preliminary artwork in watercolor and marker pen was a design by Simon and Marijke – "The Fool" – for decorating John Lennon's upright piano, with a brightly colored landscape, typical of "psychedelic" illustration of the period. In shades of orange, yellow, green and blue it featured the then-fashionable ingredients of swirling fire patterns, winged goddesses and flying saucers.

### Lennon "Vicar" Drawing

A drawing by John Lennon, "The Vicar," which was described in a Sotheby's catalogue: "paper stained on the extremities, but the drawing undamaged." The 10 by 8 in. pen and ink drawing was mounted on card with an accompanying document of authenticity. It was, we are informed in the same catalogue entry, "presented to the vendor by the artist when he was working on the design of the two books by John Lennon, *In His Own Write* and *A Spaniard In The Works*."

### Stuart Sutcliffe Painting

An oil-on-board painting by Stuart Sutcliffe, entitled "Ye Cracke" (60 by 40 in). Sutcliffe attended Liverpool College of Art and became John Lennon's closest friend and a founder member of the original Beatles. Painted in 1959, the picture shows the interior of Ye Cracke, a pub in Rice Street, Liverpool, and a favorite haunt of students from the Liverpool College of Art. Sutcliffe and Lennon are the two central figures in the picture

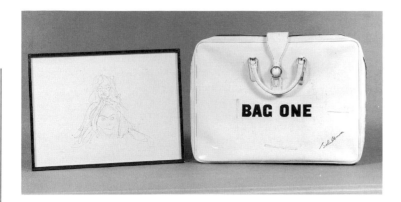

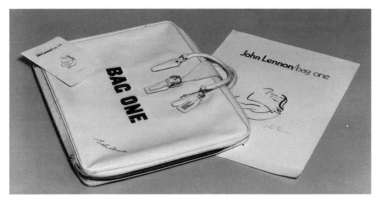

### John Lennon's "Bag One"

A limited edition collection of 20 lithographs that came in a presentation white PVC portfolio bag. This set – number 153 of an edition of 300 – belonged to Elton John; it came with a color photograph of Yoko Ono and Sean Ono-Lennon inscribed "To Elton/let's hope it's a good one!/ Love/Yoko & Sean," and was in Sotheby's sale entirely devoted to items from Elton John's personal collection of memorabilia.

### Beatles Drum Skin

The Ludwig Weather King bass drum skin that appeared in a London sale in 1984 carried the original handpainted Beatles logo that they used in their major touring days. It wasn't the group's first such logo – in their Cavern period their bass drum trademark featured two insect antennae growing out of the "B."

### Lennon Sculpture

A painted wooden cupboard, 79 by 114 cm (31 by 45 in), this sculpture by John Lennon was typical of the "minimalist" approach he shared with Yoko Ono, often presenting "found objects" as art. The title "Open & Shut" was presumably a pun (as in "open and shut case") as the work was originally donated by Lennon to an exhibition raising money for the defense in the *Oz* magazine obscenity trials in England in 1971.

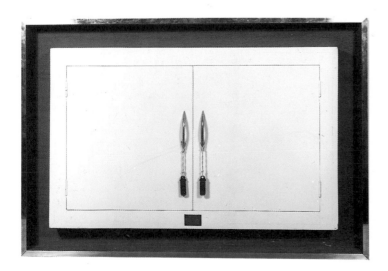

### *Yellow Submarine* Postcard

This postcard of the *Yellow Submarine*, marked "copyright King Features," was part of a collection of merchandise ephemera marketed in association with the animated film that included bulletin boards, stationery, and cut-out figures of the Beatles and the Yellow Submarine itself. The artwork, based on designs by Heinz Edelman, was executed by John Coates' TVC (TeleVision Cartoons), a London-based animation company.

## Big Bopper Lyrics

The Big Bopper, known as a Texas radio DJ under his real name of J.P. Richardson, had a huge hit on both sides of the Atlantic with "Chantilly Lace" in 1958, before perishing in a plane crash with Buddy Holly and Richie Valens, early in 1959. He wrote extensively – one posthumous success was "Running Bear" recorded by Johnny Preston – and these handwritten lyrics for the song "Walking Thru My Dreams" date from 1957.

## Bowie Screen Print

One of a set of five silkscreen prints by David Bowie entitled "Arcana Series" depicting tarot cards, this is the one representing "death" – the others being the moon, earth, a star and lovers. Number 17 of a limited edition of 50, the set appeared for sale in New York in 1985.

## Marc Bolan Lyrics

Marc Bolan's handwritten lyrics for his last number one "Metal Guru" in 1972. The song is about a car and continued Bolan's lyrical fascination for the subject although this was the most blatant praise of the can on wheels. Having had four consecutive number one singles of his official releases, T. Rex managed a further four Top Ten hits before falling slowly out of favor. However, unlike their namesake and many other bubble gum bands they were not extinct and Bolan was continuing to chart, if only in the lower regions, until his death.

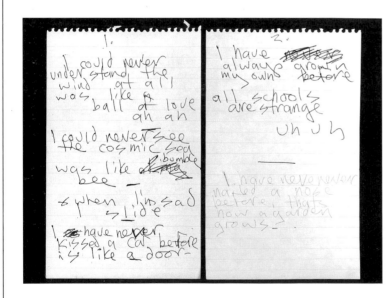

## Original Bolan Draft

From the album of the same name – which topped the British album charts in 1972 – these lyrics, handwritten in black and green ballpoint pen by Marc Bolan, are the original draft for the song "The Slider." Bolan has become widely collectible, and his prolific manuscript material often appears for sale.

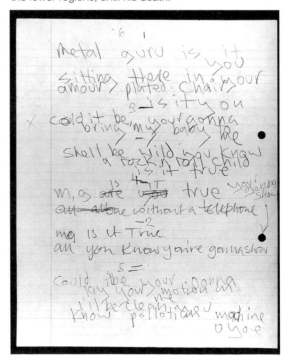

ROCK & ROLL ART

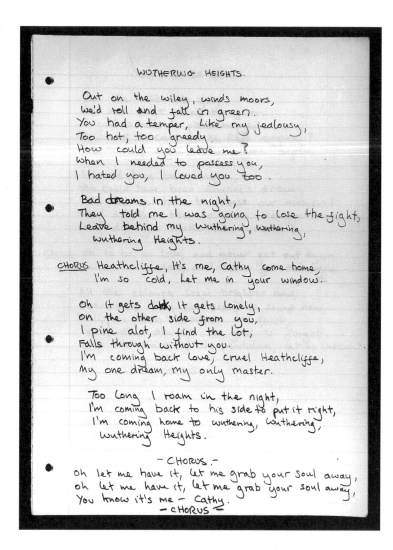

### Clapton by Ron Wood

"Eric Clapton II," a silkscreen print (23½ by 16½ in.) numbered five from a limited edition of 250. A sensitive portrait of the guitarist by a fellow musician, Ron Wood of the Rolling Stones, whose work has been exhibited to general acclaim in recent years. Signed both by the artist and the subject and dated 1988.

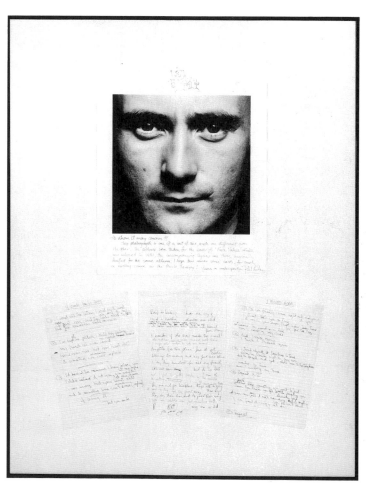

### Kate Bush Lyrics

The handwritten lyrics by Kate Bush for "Wuthering Heights," her first single which went to number one in the U.K. in 1978. It can clearly be seen that the song is inspired by the Emily Brontë novel. Bush signed to EMI in 1974 at the age of 16 but was nursed by the label to develop songs, dance and mime. Her first album "A Kick Inside" was the product of this and was skillfully produced by Andrew Powell and had a further input from Pink Floyd's Dave Gilmour who originally introduced the label to Bush. "Wuthering Heights" is an extraordinary song and it is surprising that "the suits" at EMI, having invested so much time in Bush, should have allowed her first release to be such an unusual and by no means certain hit. They of course claimed it to be perfect judgement.

### Phil Collins Lyrics

The lyrics for three of Phil Collins' songs from his "Face Value" album presented with a signed photograph. Collins donated this item to raise money for Music Therapy. The three songs are "If Leaving Me Is Easy," "I Missed Again" and "Roof Is Leaking," whose titles hint at the mood of Collins at the time. He claims the album was predominantly a product of his recent divorce and we can be grateful that his instinctive ear for a good tune prevented the release of an introspective and morose solo album.

141

### Eddie Cochran Portrait

Painted in oils, this artwork for a U.K. collection of reissues of Eddie Cochran tracks entitled "Portrait Of A Legend – Eddie Cochran," released on Rockstar Records, was by artist Bob Hunt. Cochran's legacy on disk has always seen more reissue activity in the U.K. than his native America; it was in Britain that his major following developed after his death in 1960.

### Cream Drum Skin

Bass drum skins during the 1960s were instantly recognizable logos for groups who performed live. This is the original handpainted bass drum skin used by Cream since about 1966 and was reputedly painted by Ginger Baker. The psychedelic writing and design on the Ludwig Weather Master (20 in. diameter) skin, overpainted the words "Ginger" and "Drum City" – reference to a well-known London drum store of the period. The skin was entered into a rock memorabilia auction by Cream's road manager who went on to work for John Mayall, Pink Floyd, and Ginger Baker's Airforce.

### Ray Cooper Portrait

By Bryan Organ, a 68 in. square painting in acrylic on canvas, this portrait of percussionist Ray Cooper – who, though from the world of classical music, through the late 1970s and early 1980s was best known for his work with Elton John – was part of the Elton John collection that featured in the special sale at Sotheby's in 1988.

### Deep Purple Candles

A group of five portrait wax candles (7.75 in. high) of Deep Purple, used in the design of the album cover "Burn" released in 1974. The photographer responsible for the album cover was Finn Costello, from whom the portrait candles were acquired prior to appearing in auction.

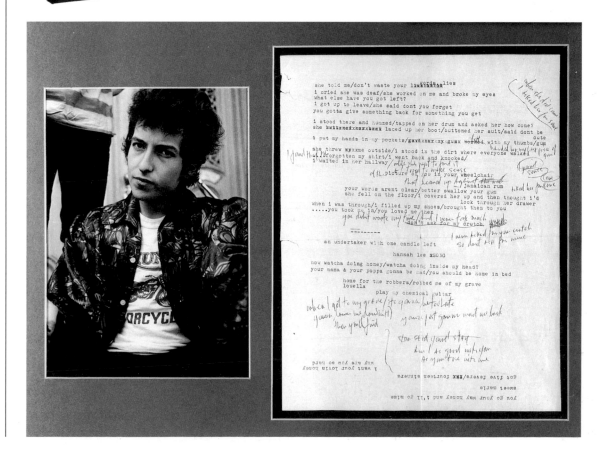

### Bob Dylan Lyrics

A combination of his own reclusiveness and the jackdaw-like activity of various fanatical devotees (the most famous of whom, A.J. Webberman, literally went through the garbage in the singer's trash can) has rendered Bob Dylan manuscript drafts far rarer than those relating to other artists, including the Beatles. All the more collectible, then, these handwritten lyrics for "Temporary Like Achilles," one of the songs on his mid 60s *tour de force* double album "Blonde On Blonde."

### Eagles Album Artwork

The original airbrushed artwork for the cover of the Eagles' 1976 album "Hotel California" (22 by 24 in.). The Eagles were one of America's most commercial and successful bands of the 1970s, following in the footsteps of the Byrds. At their peak the group had four chart-topping albums in the 1970s and sold over 40 million albums worldwide.

### Typewritten Dylan Lyrics

A page of lyrics by Bob Dylan from 1966. The typewritten lyrics are from "Fourth Time Around" but there are further fragments from other songs including "You Go Your Way & I'll Go Mine." During this year Dylan was hurt after an accident on his motorcycle and this led an absence from recording.

**ELO *Melody Maker* Artwork**

Original artwork being by definition unique, has an intrinsic collectors value, be it for an instantly recognizable album cover or immediately forgotten press advertisement. This artwork was for the latter, promoting the Electric Light Orchestra's "On The Third Day" album and tour, and appeared in the U.K. weekly magazine *Melody Maker* in 1973. (Courtesy of V&A Theatre Museum)

**Greg Lake's Artwork for ELP**

Two oils-on-canvas entitled "The Gnome" (30 by 20 in.) and "The Sage" (30 by 20 in.). Executed in muted shades by guitarist Greg Lake (originally the bassist/vocalist with King Crimson), the works were commissioned by Emerson, Lake and Palmer and designed for the cover of their 1971 live album "Pictures At An Exhibition." "The Sage" is somewhat reminiscent of the 1969 King Crimson album cover for "In The Court Of The Crimson King."

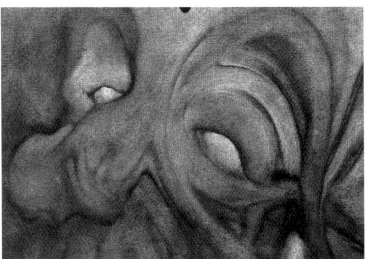

**Faces Magazine Artwork**

A mock-up of a tabloid newspaper page, this artwork for the Faces' single "You Can Make Me Dance Sing Or Anything" was for a December 1974 advertisement in the U.K. *Sounds* magazine. (Courtesy of V&A Theatre Museum)

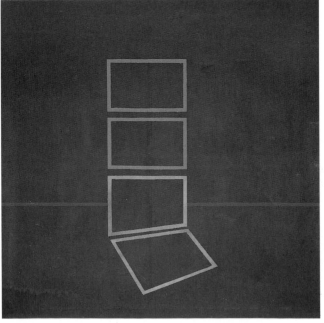

**Painting by Bryan Ferry**

Like so many other successful rock musicians, Bryan Ferry moved from art into the music industry. This acrylic-on-canvas of bright green squares against a pastel green background (30 in square) by Bryan Ferry is entitled "Zone." Executed in 1967, the picture was displayed at an exhibition in Newcastle in the late 1960s from where the original owner purchased it.

### Frankie's "Power" Sleeve Art

"The Power Of Love" was a UK Number One late in 1984 for Frankie Goes To Hollywood. This finely packaged single, (autographed by the group) was designed by Royston Edwards of the Accident (now Instinct) company, and reflects the post-modern "retro" style of the period in the renaissance iconography which is echoed in the centre-label crusader and outer-sleeve heart and crucifix motifs.

### Jimi Hendrix Portrait

Rock stars – since Peter Blake's early reference to Bo Diddley and Andy Warhol's Elvis images – have long been regular subject matter for painters. This 1973 oil-on-canvas portrait (12.25 by 12.25 in.) of Jimi Hendrix is by the noted British artist Patrick Proctor, and was part of the Elton John collection.

### Hendrix Artwork

Jimi Hendrix commissioned this painting, by Henri Matinez, in 1970, with the intention of using the picture as the cover for his next album. The album – the double record set tentatively titled "Cry Of Love" – was never to be, the work on it still unfinished at the time of the guitarist's death.

### Hendrix Drawings and Lyrics

This manuscript of lyrics with the caricatures on the reverse by Jimi Hendrix is an absolute gem. The cartoon is in the hand of Hendrix but also that of his girlfriend at the time, Cathy Etchingham. It is believed to date from November 1966, two months after Hendrix arrived in Britain. If this is accurate it is interesting that Hendrix depicts a riotous and often disapproving audience some time before he developed this image with the British press. Hendrix had played several gigs, by this time, in Paris and it was apparent, according to Mitch Mitchell, even on this short tour (supporting Johnny Halliday) that Hendrix, relatively shy off-stage, was a showman on it. The drawing is packed with wit, one of the best being the reference to ''Eric Clapton and the Sour Cream.''

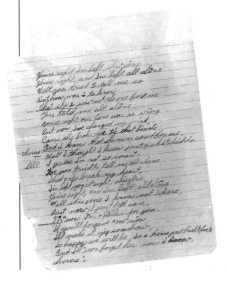

### Buddy Holly Handwritten Lyrics

These lyrics, handwritten by Buddy Holly, illustrate the largely shared repertoire of early rock & roll. ''You're Right, I'm Left, She's Gone'' was an early southern hit for Elvis Presley (though not written by him) while still on the Sun label, and it was during this period that Holly first met up with him. Significantly, Buddy Holly was soon to utilize mainly self-penned material for most of his hits.

### Portrait of Elton John

Elton John and Marilyn Monroe are linked inexorably through the song ''Candle In The Wind.'' The composition tried to see the world through Marilyn's eyes and, in this oil-on-canvas portrait of Elton John (60 by 60 in.) by Bryan Organ, the artist shows Elton wearing Marilyn's image over his heart.

### Elton "Wrap Her Up" Artwork

Artwork for singles sleeves crop up on a less regular basis than those for albums. This artwork for Elton John's 1985 Top 20 single "Wrap Her Up" was sold in a group along with similar items for his next single "Cry To Heaven" and the associated album "Ice On Fire."

### Elton by Oxtoby

Entitled "Bernie's Mate . . . Elton John," this arresting portrait of Elton John in action was executed in aqua-technique on canvas (60 by 60 in.) by David Oxtoby in 1977. Showing the performer wearing a pair of his outrageous trademark glasses of the period, this portrait was purchased by Elton John from the artist and remained in his private collection until sold through Sotheby's in 1988.

### Elton John Original Artwork

This 47 by 47.75 in. oil-on-canvas portrait of Elton John was the original artwork for the 1975 hit album "Rock Of The Westies," and was among the items in the singer's personal collection. The inscription on the back offers the only clue to its origin, "Record and Tape, Limited, Washington DC." It was signed by the painter, "Market," and titled after the album.

### Elton John Costume Designs

Two original design drawings for Elton John costumes. The Bob Mackie artwork dates from 1975, and the finished product was worn by Elton on the Cher *TV Special* of 1976. It was an elaborate outfit with yellow and orange overalls, together with a maribou feather trimmed cloak. The Ret Turner sketch is a "Matador" stage suit and dates from 1983/4 and includes fabric swatches for Elton's approval.

### Design for "Led Zeppelin IV"

Part of an original album sleeve design for "Led Zeppelin IV," this illustration in pencil and gold paint (38 by 23 in.) by Barrington Coleby was titled "View in Half or Varying Light," and appeared in the first sale of Rock'n'Roll and Advertising Art at London Sotheby's in 1981.

### Marmalade Drum Skin

Bass drum skin logo (21 in. diameter) for the British group, Marmalade, and used in their appearances on television programs including *Top Of The Pops*. The group started out as Dean Ford and the Gaylords, but changed their name to Marmalade in 1967 and adopted the "golly" figure which was used at that time by the jam and marmalade manufacturers, Robertson.

### Yoko Ono "Hammer" Piece

At the top of a ladder, this conceptual piece of participatory art invited the public to hammer a nail into the ceiling. It was at doing just this, during a 1966 exhibition of Yoko Ono's work at the Indica Gallery in London entitled "Unfinished Paintings and Objects Show," that John Lennon first met the Japanese artist, who was already well known on the *avant garde* art scene as a creator of such conceptual pieces and organizer of various "happenings" in New York, London and elsewhere. Despite its ephemeral nature, the minimalist "sculpture" does actually exist, as part of a private collection in Tokyo.

### Pink Floyd Manuscripts

Various manuscripts for Pink Floyd songs, mainly from the 1977 album ''Animals.'' Roger Waters was by now taking an increasingly senior role within the group, especially in the songwriting, and their final two albums before Waters left were predominantly his individual work.

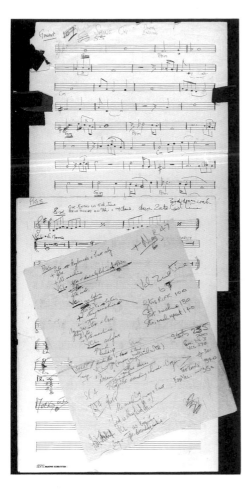

### Fiberglass Bust of Elvis

With no pretensions to being a work of art, this kitscher than kitsch fiberglass bust of Elvis incorporates aspects of his image – the late 1950s slicked-back hair with 1970s ''Las Vegas'' stage suit – transcending two decades, but still manages to look nothing like him. It was found by a collector as recently as 1991 in a grocers-cum-hardware store in Toronto, Canada!

### Bronze Bust of Elvis

This large bronze bust of Elvis Presley (17.5 in. high) appeared in the first ever rock & roll auction, held in December 1981. Sculpted by Debereux, it portrays a stylized image of the musician wearing a high-collared coat and dates from *circa* 1978. After his death in 1977, Presley artifacts were produced in great numbers to meet the demands of mourning followers.

### Ceramic Bust of Elvis

Even more so than John Lennon, since his death Elvis Presley has been commemorated three-dimensionally in literally hundreds of busts, statues and plaques which in most cases – as in this ceramic bust – served to perpetuate the bland 1970s ''Las Vegas'' image of the singer rather than that of the teenage firebrand who literally revolutionized music in the mid 1950s.

### Elvis Presley Bust

A bronzed bust of Elvis Presley (8.5 in high) by Jon Douglas in 1976. Sculpted before Presley's death in August 1977, styled naturalistically, the bust shows Elvis in the mid 1970s with fuller face and wearing one of his trademark high-collared jackets.

### Elvis Watercolor

"Archive Fan Mag 1 – Study of Elvis Presley," an Indian ink and watercolor portrait on brown paper (22 by 15 in.) by David Oxtoby, dated 1976. One of a series, this portrait was exhibited at the Redfern Gallery in 1977 with a group of other works by Oxtoby, based on rock musicians of the 1970s. The work was purchased and owned for many years by Elton John.

### Elvis by Aldridge

The British artist Alan Aldridge is particularly known for his illustrations inspired by Beatles songs and the artwork for the cover of Elton John's album "Captain Fantastic And The Brown Dirt Cowboy," but Aldridge portraits of other rock musicians are equally collectible. This airbrush-on-cartridge Aldridge portrait of Elvis Presley (24¾ by 18¾ in.) can be seen as a witty visual pun of the performer as a sex object. A contemporary described Elvis's stage performance in 1954 when "he started to move his hips real slow like he had a thing for his guitar." Alan Aldridge in this portrait has used his imagination to take things one step further . . .

**Ballpoint Portrait of Elvis**
A portrait of Elvis Presley (15 by 12 in.) executed in 1973 by the artist David Oxtoby, in an unusual medium – black ballpoint pen. This particular work admirably illustrates Oxtoby's skill as a draughtsman in the early 1970s using a difficult medium, and his ability to capture the mood and style of the performer.

**Oxtoby Elvis Lithograph**
Elvis Presley, rock & roll's original bad boy, is depicted in this lithograph in a pose similar to that of Marlon Brando in the film *The Wild One* (1953) in which Brando's character, a rebellious leather-jacketed biker, is asked what he's rebelling against – ''Whatta ya got?'' is Brando's reply. The artist of this lithograph, David Oxtoby, is perhaps best known for his portraits of rock & roll musicians and his work is sought by collectors both within and outside the rock industry.

### Jagger Sketch by Beaton

A real rarity, this pencil sketch of Mick Jagger that appeared at auction in 1989 was by society photographer Cecil Beaton, and carried a rubber stamp attesting to such, which read "Cecil Beaton From Miss E. Hose."

### Jagger Portrait

A far more sensitive portrait of Mick Jagger than afforded by most portraiture of the Rolling Stones singer, this crayon-on-linen weave by Oliver Messel, dating from 1974, was sold as part of the celebrated Elton John collection in 1988.

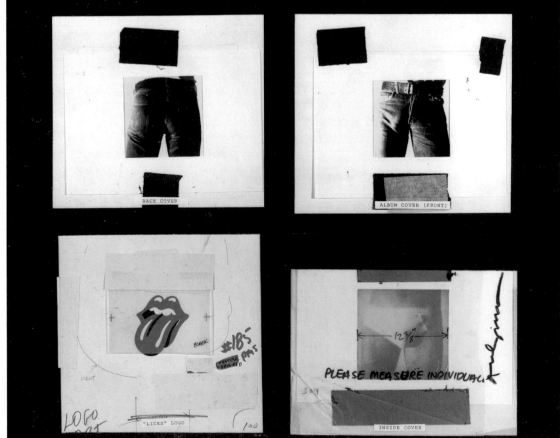

### Stones "Sticky Fingers" Artwork

The cover design, by Craig Braun, for the Rolling Stones' album "Sticky Fingers" was nominated for a Grammy award when it appeared in 1971. The original artwork, which sold for several thousand dollars, included as well as Braun's line drawings for the overall design, polaroid photographs of the Stones and the front and back "crotch" pictures, all by pop artist Andy Warhol.

### Bust of Mick Jagger

Like the similar bust he did of John Lennon, this 1980 study in bronze of Mick Jagger by sculptor John Somerville was created from a mold which had been cast after the original wax cast had been slightly altered – a method known as *cire-perdue* – to achieve the animated – and anguished – look that seems to be Somerville's stock in trade. It was entitled "Star Star Unique Variation on Mick Jagger No. 1."

### Pistols' "God Save The Queen" Artwork

The publicity campaign for the Sex Pistols' "God Save The Queen" was planned to coincide with the Queen's Jubilee celebrations in 1977. Jamie Reid worked on the image using an official Cecil Beaton portrait of the Queen which he obtained from the *Daily Express*. This is the artwork for the original cover, which was banned by the record company, A&M; the Sex Pistols then signed to Virgin Records and "God Save The Queen" was released two months later, at the end of May, with a different cover.

### Alternative Sex Pistols Artwork

"Anarchy In The U.K." was the Sex Pistols' first single, released in November 1976. Several ideas for the sleeve were tried out by designer Jamie Reid before settling for an image based around a torn Union Jack, a deliberate misuse of the British national flag. Among the artwork discarded in the process was this piece, now mounted and framed, with stapled lettering on a torn black paper background.

### Painting of the Rolling Stones

British pop painter Patrick Proctor exhibited widely in the 1960s and beyond, and this picture of the Rolling Stones titled "Ruby Tuesday" was first shown in a London gallery in 1967; the 39 by 29 in. oil-on-canvas was yet another item that found its way into the extensive collection of Elton John.

### Sex Pistols Album Proof

When the original lithographic proof for the Sex Pistols' "Never Mind The Bollocks, Here's The Sex Pistols" appeared in auction in 1988, it was accompanied by a proof, also by designer Jamie Reid, for one of several initial ideas for the album title that never materialized, "God Save The Sex Pistols" – following on from their hit of the same year (1977), "God Save The Queen."

### Springsteen "Backstreets" Lyrics

From his 1975 album "Born To Run," these handwritten lyrics for the song 'Backstreets' by Bruce Springsteen feature revisions in pencil and some alternative lyrics that never appeared in the final version of the number: "One soft infested summer me and Terry became friends tryin' in vain to breathe the fire we was born in." On two pages of white lined notepaper, they appeared in a memorabilia sale in New York in the summer of 1991.

### Oxtoby Portrait of Rod Stewart

This portrait of Rod Stewart in colored chalk (14 by 15 in.) by David Oxtoby is entitled "Royal Scot" and presents the spike-haired performer in a typical pose at the microphone. Exhibited at Alexander Postan Fine Art in 1974 this portrait was owned for many years by Elton John and displayed in his home until sold in 1988 in the series of sales known as "The Elton John Collection."

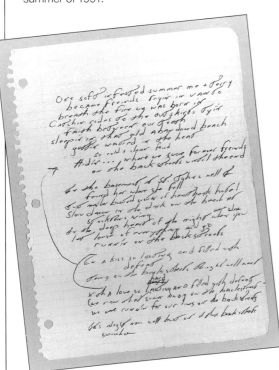

## Entwistle's Who Caricatures

John Entwistle, bass guitarist and founder member of the Who, was the first member of the group to release a solo album. In 1988 Entwistle sold a number of guitars and more personal memorabilia through Sotheby's including these two pencil sketches on lined writing paper of his fellow Who members, Roger Daltrey and Keith Moon. These were progressive designs by Entwistle for the final caricatures which were used for the cover of the 1976 album "The Who By Numbers."

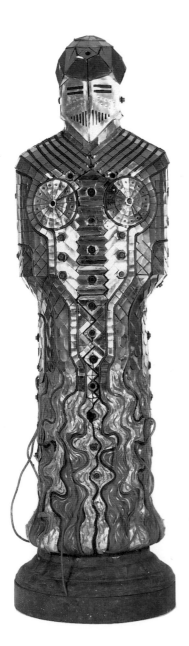

## John Entwistle Lyrics

John Entwistle's handwritten lyrics for "Dr. Jekyll And Mr. Hyde." The song was written about Keith Moon, and appeared as the B-side to the Who's 1968 single "Magic Bus." With Moon's character in mind, it takes little to assess the direction of the song, even without seeing these lyrics.

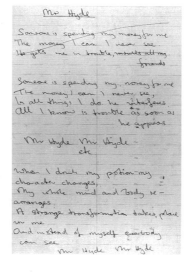

## Acid Queen Model From *Tommy*

The 1975 film *Tommy* was an important development in the history of the musical film, becoming an instant cult movie with lasting influence on a generation of moviegoers. This larger than life android female figure of the Acid Queen appeared in the film in several disturbing scenes and is made of papier-mâché, finished in silver with red plastic tubing.

## Frank Zappa Ad Artwork

Though it didn't chart at all in the U.K., and only made it to number twenty-three in the U.S. album list, this artwork for a *New Musical Express* advertisement for Frank Zappa's "Roxy And Elsewhere" in October 1974 has a collectible potential far outweighing the popularity of the album at the time. (Courtesy of V&A Theatre Museum)

# Rock Miscellany

Jukeboxes, unusual recordings, presentation awards and pop merchandise, all superficially disparate but linked inextricably to rock music and its performers. Covering a wide variety of objects from Beatles' stockings to signatures, and gum dispensers to gold disks, this chapter more than any other illustrates the diverse nature of rock & roll collectibles.

The jukebox is perhaps the most appropriate symbol of the rock & roll years and was undoubtedly responsible in part for the growth in the popularity of fringe music – from jazz and blues in the 1920s to Elvis in the 1950s.

▶

**The Wartime Wurlitzer**

An extravagance in illuminated plastic, the Wurlitzer 750 helped brighten wartime America (and elsewhere – thousands were exported) when it was introduced in 1941. Designed by Wurlitzer's Paul Fuller, over 18,000 units of the model were installed in locations through 1941. Fifty years later they command five-figure prices among collectors.

"Juke Joints" in the Deep South were unsophisticated structures, often little more than roadside shacks, where African-Americans would meet in the early years of this century to listen to each other play jazz and blues, drink moonshine and dance. In the 1920s, with the growing popularity of jazz music among the white population, suddenly recordings of "black" music by black performers were available. At the same time, electric phonographs with amplified sound were being produced and a new type of entertainment was born. Phonograph players with coin-operated mechanisms began to be installed in the juke joints. Popular from the start, these "Juke Boxes," as they soon became known, gave customers in small backwoods venues the opportunity to listen to the greatest exponents of jazz and blues for the price of a nickel.

The earliest jukeboxes were quite plain, solid-looking wooden cabinets, their restrained design based on phonograph chests which were so popular in the home – in a similar way, when radios became the most important centers of home entertainment and radio ownership became more widespread in the 1930s, jukebox design was heavily influenced by contemporary radio styling. The purpose of the jukebox was, of course, entertainment, and as the decade progressed, increasingly exotic veneers were used and the exterior designs became more attractive and glamorous in an effort to make the jukebox the focal point of any café, restaurant or club. One essential element of the design was the coin-slot mechanism and the important manufacturers, Wurlitzer, Rock-Ola, AMI, and Seeburg, made sure that the record selection and playing mechanisms were visible; they realized that customers would want to see something happening as soon as their coin was inserted, like any penny-in-the-slot amusement machine.

The repeal of prohibition on December 5, 1933 after 14 dry years rapidly expanded the market for jukeboxes; in 1933 it was recorded that 25,000 were installed but by 1937 the figure had risen to 225,000. Manufacturers realized that if people could once again linger over drinks in bars, there would be an increased need for instant, cheap musical entertainment, presented with a gloss of sophistication and glamour. In 1938, a style revolution took place in jukebox design when Seeburg developed the concept of the illuminated jukebox. A cabinet was produced with side panels of translucent plastic gently lit from behind by low-wattage bulbs; it was named the "Symphonola Classic" – a jukebox which glowed. This stylistic coup was an instant success and challenged the position of products from the other three manufacturers, prompting them to return to their own drawing boards to design illuminated machines.

The designer responsible for several of the most innovative jukeboxes of the era, which are today those most desired by collectors, was Paul Fuller. Born in Switzerland in 1899, Fuller at an early age was appointed head of the Interior Design department of Marshall Field, the elegant Chicago department store. In the mid 1930s he joined Wurlitzer and designed in rapid succession some of the most imaginative and desirable jukeboxes: the 700, 800, 750, 780, and the 850 which were manufactured between 1940 and 1941. Fuller specialized in combining sculptured plastics and decorative finishes with complex lighting patterns and

**The Seeburg Trashcan**
The first of a series of three models known as the Trashcan or the Barrel, the Seeburg S-146 Symphonia dated from 1946. It was distinguished by its contrasting features of a "traditional" simulated walnut body with illuminated red plastic columns, topped by a pink plastic dome lit from the inside by a revolving multi-colored reflector.

technical wizardry, to produce streams of dancing bubbles which enlivened the illuminated side panels.

Interrupted by the war, jukebox manufacturers were required to reduce their output by 75 percent and their factories were given over to the production of rifles, ammunition boxes and aircraft components. When peace came Wurlitzer continued manufacturing jukeboxes and Paul Fuller's retrospective 1015 was the first Wurlitzer to be produced after the war. But it was the 1100, Fuller's last jukebox design, which had the greatest influence of all the post-war machines. Bearing an uncanny resemblance to the upturned nose section of a B17F bomber (the "Flying Fortress"), the 1100 with its chrome and glitter heralded a new generation of jukebox design in the 1950s.

In the early 1950s with Rock-Ola retailing their machines with names such as "Rocket," "Comet" and "Fireball" and Chantal marketing their "Meteor" there was no doubt that jukeboxes wanted to be seen as an integral part of "space age" design. Another strong stylistic influence at the time was the automobile. The American industrial designer, Raymond Loewy, once quipped that a car was nothing but a "jukebox on wheels," and car imagery was widely used in jukebox styling, including chrome grills and fins, tail lights and curved glass panels mimicking the innovative wrap-around windshields. This generation of machine was shiny and brash, perhaps devised to attract people like the secretary in Detroit who admitted in 1952 that "Chrome is my favorite color."

In the 1950s, as had been the case in the juke joints of the 1920s, jukeboxes played music which was not aired on the radio and from the second half of the 1950s these machines were inseparable from the growth of rock & roll. Teenagers would get together in drug stores and diners to play the raw and raunchy R&B and rock & roll records which led in some towns to weekly lists being issued to jukebox operators by the local police departments informing them of record titles they were forbidden to play!

Jukebox production continued into the 1960s and early 1970s with some ingenious designs such as the Scopitone ST16, which projected 16 mm films of the recording artist performing the song title chosen. But with the growing demand for stereophonic sound (unsuited to jukeboxes), coupled with the reduction in the number of coffee bars and similar teenage haunts in favor of fast food venues and diskotheques, it was a matter of "when" rather than "if" jukeboxes would lose their popularity.

Their association with rock & roll culture have made classic jukeboxes from the 1940s and 1950s highly collectable today, with a number of outlets specializing in selling reconditioned machines. The most valuable are those which have been restored rather than reconstructed, since purists rate originality very highly. Small specialist manufacturers have also emerged, responsible for producing reproductions of some of the rarest and most desirable of Paul Fuller's designs, including the 1015; these machines provide a neat solution to accommodating the apparently incompatible bedfellows, modern technology and retrospective styling.

Over the last decade sales of 7-inch 45 rpm singles have declined, perhaps adding one more nail into the coffin of the jukebox, but the strong demand among collectors and enthusiasts for commercially produced records which are difficult to obtain through regular retail outlets has led in recent years to burgeoning record fairs now held regularly in many large cities.

Some early or very unusual recordings do occasionally appear in auctions of rock & roll collectibles including demo

### Ron Wood's Rock-Ola

Produced in 1973, the Rock-Ola 451 usually commands a modest price among collectors. Its dated design hasn't quite dated enough to evoke real nostalgia – it just looks a bit old-fashioned.

This particular model had the added premium of having belonged to Rolling Stone Ron Wood, and was offered for sale complete with his selection of 50 records (100 sides) that included the Faces and the Stones.

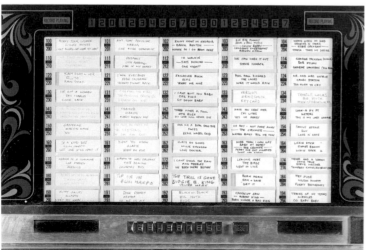

disks, acetates and reel-to-reel tapes which can prove extraordinarily valuable to historians. One example was a reel-to-reel tape of Jimi Hendrix in 1968 which came to light; with the labels written in Hendrix's hand, the series of tapes included such treasures as Hendrix playing an instrumental with Brian Jones. Studio reel-to-reel tapes were also uncovered which held perhaps the only surviving excerpts of "Lifehouse," a musical project conceived in 1971 by Pete Townshend as a follow-up to *Tommy* but later scrapped. Another diskovery was an acetate of the Beatles performing "Some Other Guy" recorded live at the Cavern Club in 1962 (a standard inclusion in many groups' repertoires at this time, the Beatles never professionally recorded or released the song).

Other recordings which fascinate enthusiasts are the personal record collections of well-known musicians which occasionally (usually posthumously) appear on the market. Such a tangible link to these performers, the collections clearly illustrate their musical influences and preferences, sometimes illuminating surprising anomalies. Jimi Hendrix's record collection, for example, included the predictable John Lee Hooker, Muddy Waters, Eddie Cochran, John Mayall's Bluesbreakers, and James Brown; but unlikely inclusions were Handel, Holst, and Nina Simone. Buddy Holly's collection of singles, which traveled with him and his Pilot Encore portable gramophone on tour, contained the Angelic Gospel Singers alongside the more obvious inclusions: Bo Diddley, Little Richard, Larry Williams, Ritchie Valens, Ray Charles, Bobby Vee, Peggy Lee, Doris Day and Jimmy Reed.

Buddy Holly was good about signing autograph books, in common with many performers – whether his contemporaries or present day stars. Judging by the number of these small volumes packed with signatures which appear on the market, it would appear that these little albums were as essential to a girl's purse as her lipstick and powder compact. Those who didn't have their autograph book with them when they spotted a star would use anything else that came to hand, such as a cigarette pack or paper money. The most valuable signatures, however, are those that appear on something directly linked to the reason for which the performer is famous, or relates to a particularly important event in the artist's history. These would include album covers, personal letters and concert playlists, tour brochures and programs, photographs, movie posters and song sheets. Significant value can be added to all these if they bear signatures: a printed cotton Beatles dress, for example, would realize about $200 in auction, but if it was the one which had been worn by an usherette at the charity premiere of the film *A Hard Day's Night* and had been personally signed by the Beatles, the value would rise to over $8,000.

Collectors should be aware, however, that many signatures acquired at the time were not written in the hand of the performer. While printed facsimiles are relatively easy for the amateur to spot, handwritten non-original signatures, known as "secretarial signatures," can be much more troublesome. Secretarial signatures of Elvis Presley and the Beatles are particularly common and at one stage about 70 percent of all Beatles signatures brought to Sotheby's for valuation proved to be secretarial

**Signed Presley Movie Poster**
Inscribed "To Hal, Best Wishes,
Elvis Presley," this poster for
Elvis's first movie *Love Me Tender*,
featured in a 1991 auction in New
York. The film, a western in which
he sang just a handful of songs,
gave Elvis a dramatic debut role
which had originally been
earmarked for James Dean.

or printed facsimiles. To add further confusion, band members
became adroit at signing for each other, as did their road
managers and assistants. A fan who may have queued at a stage
door, handed her program in for signature and received it back
again duly signed and annotated with her name, can be dis-
illusioned when told now that her program got no closer to her
idols than their road manager. The one crumb of comfort to the
disappointed fan is had performers personally signed all the
letters, photographs and autograph books that came their way,
they would certainly have had little time to write, perform or
record!

Most aspiring groups look forward to receiving their first
gold disk. The first glimpse of the presentation disk collection of
a successful artist can be awe-inspiring as one is confronted by a
wall or two completely covered with gold and platinum disks,
framed, brass-plaqued and glazed. The tradition of rewarding
excellent record sales with a "gold" award can be traced back to
1942 when Glenn Miller was presented with a gold record after
"Chattanooga Choo Choo" sold more than 1 million copies.

The Recording Industry Association of America (RIAA), a
trade association of America's foremost record companies, was
set up in 1952 and six years later, following the allocation of
numerous gold records on an *ad hoc* basis, the association introduced the gold record award accompanied by strict certification criteria. The formula which the RIAA devised covered both
albums and singles, requiring $1 million worth of album sales at
manufacturers' wholesale prices and 1 million copies sold for
singles.

The number of gold awards presented gradually increased
from 35 albums and singles in 1964 to 127 in 1974, and the following year the RIAA amended the standard for gold certification: 500,000 albums as well as $1 million in wholesale value.

The next development was the evolution of the platinum
sales award which was introduced officially in 1976 – authenticated album sales of 1 million copies and at least $2 million
wholesale value had to be achieved, or minimum single sales of 2
million copies. In February 1976 the first platinum album was
certified, the Eagles' compilation album, "Greatest Hits 1971-

1975." The first platinum single, in April 1976, was Johnnie
Taylor's "Disco Lady."

But the award certification system could be manipulated
since it was based on sales from record warehouses, turning a
blind eye to the generous sale-or-return policies between re-
tailers and record companies. In 1979 the RIAA closed the loop-
hole with a punitive 120-day delay between the first day the
record went on sale and the calculations for certification. This
measure seemed to work, and since 1980, certification has been
based on record sales 60 days after release date.

By the end of 1983 a total of 479 platinum certifications had
been granted and the most recent type of award, the multi-
platinum was officially launched the following year. Effectively, additional platinum awards are granted for every additional $2 million worth of sales together with sales of at least an
extra 1 million units; Michael Jackson's "Thriller" was one of the
first to achieve multi-platinum status with certified sales in excess of 20 million.

Sales of cassettes and CDs are, for RIAA certification purposes, included as album sales and naturally boost the figures
accordingly. The story with vinyl singles, whether 7 or 12 inch,
was a less happy one, with plummeting sales figures reflected by
a drop in gold single certification from 70 in 1983 to just three in

**Autographed Rolling Stones Album**
An original release copy of the debut album by the Rolling Stones,
autographed by the group on the back of the sleeve. The LP – entitled
simply "Rolling Stones" – entered the British charts in April 1964,
climbing to the number one position and staying in the chart for a whole
year. In the U.S. a slightly modified version was released later in the year
under the title "England's Newest Hit Makers/The Rolling Stones."

1987. To compensate for this, the RIAA radically adjusted their certification criteria and allowed vinyl EPs, cassette maxi-singles and 3-inch CD maxis to be counted as single sales; the decision proved highly successful with 125 singles achieving the revised level the following year. The yardstick for platinum singles, none of which were awarded in the years 1986 and 1987, was similarly altered with the new criterion being the sale of 1 million copies (including the "extras" specified with the new gold single formula); resulting in 30 certifications for platinum singles in 1989.

Surprisingly, perhaps, not every record which reaches the required number and value of sales to qualify for a gold or platinum award actually receives one. It is the performer's record company which selects those successful records it would like to be certified and applies to the RIAA for certification. Once certification is granted, the record company buys the official award plaques from a licensed plaque manufacturer through the RIAA.

Such personal and prestigious possessions appear on the open market surprisingly frequently. Perhaps donated to raise money for charity, given as mementoes to friends, lovers, or persistent fans, some presentation disks are the focus of fierce competitive bidding. The most sought after awards are naturally those presented to the recording artists by the record

### Wham! Presentation Set

An unusual presentation set to celebrate sales of the Wham! debut album "Fantastic" and three singles released from it. Very few could have recognized George Michael's talent by listening to the superficial and raw 1983 album (certainly Inner Vision records failed to appreciate the fact as they lost the group to Epic shortly after). A huge success in the U.K., "Fantastic" spent 116 weeks in the charts, peaking in the number one position.

### Stu Sutcliffe Draft Letter

A rough draft of an early attempt by the Beatles to get more work around Liverpool, in this letter from Stu Sutcliffe naming himself "manager." This was clearly before their first manager Allan Williams got involved with the group, and when for a short time they spelt their name "Beatals", so dates it from early 1960. Note the deletion of "Quar" (Sutclilffe was about to write their previous name Quarrymen)

company, but other disks are circulated which generally realize more affordable prices.

These include awards given to supporting musicians, members of the production team, particularly influential radio stations or DJs and, in one instance, from the recording artist to a soccer team! – this latter teeters on the borderline between presentation disk, merchandise and memorabilia.

Merchandise and memorabilia are some of the more lighthearted rock collectibles. The post-war baby boom had resulted in a large teenage population by 1960 and it was quickly realized that teenagers were an important new market, with money in their pockets but with interests and aspirations very different to those of their parents. The pop music industry was worth many illions of dollars a year, and in addition, a bewildering range of products were manufactured with a pop music theme designed to part teenagers from their money.

Today, merchandising concessions form an important part of any successful rock performer's income and they are carefully monitored. The story was very different with the Beatles who, in 1963, were the first group to find themselves the focus of concentrated attention from would-be merchandisers. Manufacturers were desperate to produce wallpaper, curtains, fabric, bedcovers, tableware, lamps, clothes, plastic guitars, lunch boxes, toys, jewelry and almost anything else which they believed would tempt a teenage buyer – with spare cash and with bedrooms to decorate, teenagers were certainly a ready market. The Beatles were the first group to set up a company to take over the assignment of merchandising rights. Known as Stramsact in Britain and Seltaeb (Beatles spelt backwards) in the U.S. the company certainly looked after the rights, but at a cost to the group of 90 percent of the profits!

The mass production of pop merchandise from the 1960s onwards benefits the enthusiast today who, with patience and perseverance, is still able to find unusual and interesting pieces to add to their collection at yard and tailgate sales, venues far removed both in price level and ambience from the plush interiors of international auctioneers!

### An American Classic

The most popular jukebox of its day, the Wurlitzer 1015 was the masterwork of designer Paul Fuller, ''the genius of the jukebox''; Wurlitzer distributed no less than 56,000 across the United States in 1946-47. It's hard to imagine now, but the name of the box used could determine the success or failure of a bar or restaurant, so the launch of the 1015 was accompanied by the biggest promotional campaign in jukebox history, involving napkins, swizzle sticks, tabletops, coasters, decals, billboards and national magazine advertising, all proclaiming ''Wurlitzer *is* Juke Box.''

A true collector's item with a current market price of anything up to $20,000.

### Rock-Ola Rocket

Ultra-modern in its time, this Rock-Ola Rocket 1434 featured a domed, clear plastic upper section which revealed the whole playing mechanism in action, and front side panels of ribbed plastic with chrome fittings.

From the very early 1950s, its appearance was pure science fiction compared to most other machines of the day. An ingenious mechanism involving two tone arms meant it could play the top or bottom side of any of the 25 records – most 78 rpm machines could only play the top side of a disk.

### "The Mother of Plastic"

Also known as ''The Mother of Plastic,'' the 1946 AMI Model A was revolutionary: it was the first jukebox to make extensive use of acrylic plastics, and the first to use colored fluorescent lights. Two revolving color cylinders, one on each side of the base of the box, were activated at the drop of the customer's coin, so the nickel in the ''nickelodeon'' bought sights to accompany the sounds.

### 1970s Stereo Rock-Ola

Along with 1950s American cars and pinball machines, jukeboxes have become status symbols for the home among affluent rock stars – this one came from the collection of Elton John.

Not a vintage model by any means, the Rock-Ola 464 from 1975, with its stereo speakers plainly visible at the front, shows that flamboyant design features could still be found on modern machines without trying to recreate the style of the 1950s.

### Musicmaker Panoramic

Jukebox design was considerably influenced by the participation element – the way in which customers had to make their record selection. Rather than simply pressing buttons in the conventional way, this magnificent Musicmaker Panoramic had a rotating index of the 200 selections operated by a clear plastic selector wheel located above the main speaker grill.

### Early "7-inch" Wurlitzer

One of the earliest Wurlitzers to play 45s – which dates it to 1957 at the earliest – the 1050 combined the new technology to stack and play 50 7-inch disks with the classic lines of its 78 rpm predecessors – bubble tubes, glowing lights and decorative molding.

### Late 1950s AMI Continental

The AMI Continental exudes a late 1950s contemporary cool with its "floating in air" curved title board, domed plastic cover and stylized eight-pointed star over the mesh speaker cover. A Continental in reasonably good condition can now command a sale price of well over $5,000.

### Animals' Gold Disk

A gold disk for "The House Of The Rising Sun" presented to Eric Burdon to commemorate the single reaching number one in both the U.K. and U.S. charts in 1964. An arrangement by Alan Price of a traditional blues song recorded by Josh White and Bob Dylan. Eric Burdon and the Animals went on to cut some raw and exemplary British R&B tracks in the 1960s. "House" was the first single not written by Lennon/McCartney to reach number one since the rise of Beatlemania.

### Bay City Rollers T-Shirt

Rollermania, like all cults and crazes, left behind its trail of throw-away ephemera; in fact the more disposable an item, like this cheaply printed T-shirt, the more collectable it is likely to become in the future. (Courtesy of V&A Theatre Museum)

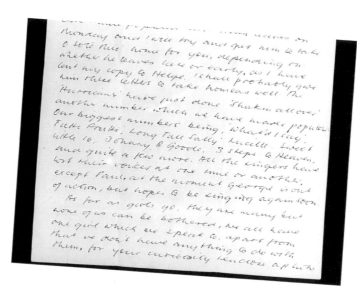

### Stuart Sutcliffe Letter

During their early 60s sojourns in Hamburg, bass player Stuart Sutcliffe was certainly the most prolific letter writer of the five Beatles, and his long accounts of their life there – particularly to his sister Pauline – now form a unique historical document of the group's embryo days. This one from 1960, put on sale in 1983, mentions one of their fellow Liverpudlian groups Rory Storm and the Hurricanes – ". . . I'm afraid he hasn't fooled anybody here and he must be very frustrated by the cheers which greet us at most of our numbers. We have improved a thousand-fold since our arrival."

### Sutcliffe Letter From Hamburg

Original Beatles bass player and painter, Stuart Sutcliffe and his Hamburg girlfriend Astrid Kirchherr, had a significant influence on the way the Beatles looked. This 1961 letter from Stuart to his sister Pauline, after he had left the group but was resident as an art student in Hamburg, describes with sketches a suit Astrid made for him, " . . . trousers without turn-ups . . . very tight hips and high like a Spanish bullfighter," which pre-empts the collarless look that the Beatles adopted just a couple of years later.

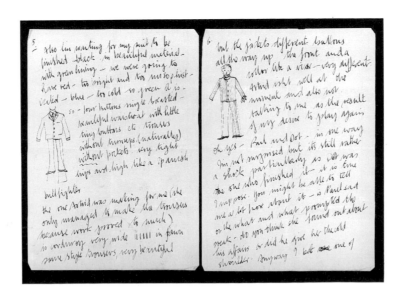

### John Lennon's Front Door

The epitome of British suburbia, this is the original front door – complete with decorative stained glass motif – from John Lennon's home "Mendips," just around the corner from his childhood haunts in and around Strawberry Fields. The present owners of the house at 251 Menlove Avenue, Liverpool, where John grew up with his Aunt Mimi and Uncle George, removed the original door and replaced it with a "modern" glass one when they moved there in the 1970s. The old door was relegated to the garage until it was acquired by a local collector in 1982. Subsequently the owners have had to change their front door yet again – to a solid hardwood type – due to the increasing number of visiting Beatles fans peering into the house!

## Lennon Work Permit

The most mundane bureaucratic documents are instantly collectable when they relate to a famous personality. These official papers concerning John Lennon's work permits in Hamburg in 1961 have changed hands for hundreds of pounds over recent years.

## Early Beatles Account Statement

This account statement from Brian Epstein's NEMS Enterprises dates from the period in Liverpool a few months before the Beatles had their first record release. Apart from the fact that roadie Neil Aspinall's weekly wage was £8, and the group's Cavern dates worth just £10 ($20), it also tells us that a week's gasoline criss-crossing Merseyside set them back £4.20. With the statement came an itinerary for the following week's gigs, complete with Epstein's personal instructions including "Give 'em a good night" and "I will expect a magnificent show." The back of the document, which appeared in the first rock & roll sale in 1981, lists numbers to be played on one of the dates. In Paul McCartney's handwriting; alongside a couple of originals – "Love Me Do" and "P.S. I Love You" – there are the American R&B covers like "Please Mr Postman," 'Some Other Guy' and "Mr. Moonlight," plus the group's then usual quota of old favorites including "Ain't She Sweet," "Darktown Strutters Ball" and the then current Frank Ifield hit "I Remember You."

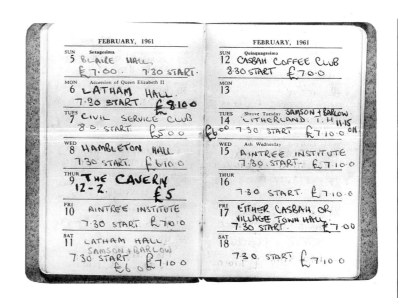

## Pete Best's Diary

The diary of Pete Best entitled "The Walton on the Hill Diary" with a light blue plastic cover which contains a record of the Beatles' bookings for the year 1961 with details of venues, starting times and fees. There are also several telephone numbers in the back including the Top Ten Club and the Cavern. The first mention of the Cavern is on February 9 for a fee of £5, but by July this fee had risen to £15, illustrating not only their popularity but how they changed the club from being predominantly jazz to "being beat."

## Beatle Fan Memorabilia, Liverpool 1962

In the days of their Liverpool popularity, before national success, the Beatles found time to answer their not inconsiderable amount of fan mail personally. This collection of memorabilia from those days – 1962 – included a letter from George Harrison (inexplicably dated 1966) and four signed photographs, attached to the back of two of which are plectrums (from George and John) and a cigarette butt (Paul), with a playlist scribbled on the back of a Cavern Club form.

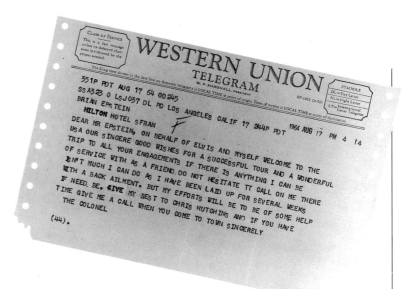

### Early Beatles Playlist

An early playlist by Paul McCartney for the Beatles dating from 1963 together with a page from an autograph book with the group's signatures. Despite the numerous autographs the band must have given over the years, a set can still command a considerable three-figure sum. Playlists are always of interest and these were often hurriedly written by each band member and then put on the concert floor for use during the performance, which could account for the damage to this one.

### Elvis Telegram to the Beatles

The first contact the Beatles ever had with their original rock & roll hero Elvis Presley was in this telegram to Brian Epstein from Elvis' manager "The Colonel" – Col. Tom Parker – offering a welcome from Elvis on the occasion of the group's first full U.S. tour in August 1964, and an invitation to help "if there is anything I can be of service with as a friend."

### "I Want To Hold Your Hand" Gold Disc

A presentation gold disk to commemorate more than 1 million American sales of the single "I Want To Hold Your Hand." Released in the U.S. in January 1964, the single entered the charts at number 45 but became the Beatles' first number one in the U.S. just two weeks later, qualifying for the prize as the fastest million-selling British disk in U.S. chart history.

### Beatles Hamburg Reissues

When the Beatles became really successful worldwide in 1964, the German-based Polydor label was quick to exploit the fact that the lads from Liverpool had made their first recordings for them. This was while they were working in Hamburg back in 1961 – partly as backing band for singer Tony Sheridan. Here are two rare examples of Polydor's bandwagoning, the Hamburg tracks repackaged as "Meet The Beat" (with an unknown band on the cover, in action at the Hamburg Star-Club), and a French release "Les Beatles" – both much sought-after by Beatles buffs and are regarded as rare records for collectors generally.

### Letter From George Harrison

Even after their initial taste of the big time, the Beatles still answered fan mail personally – for a while at least. This letter from George Harrison in the summer of 1963 urges a fan to buy their latest single "From Me To You" and "try to get it to number one." The letter was sold with other items belonging to the same Nottingham girl, including a postcard from George, a Parlophone publicity card signed by him, and a lock of hair!

### Beatles Flight Bag

A piece of merchandising obviously aimed at the jet set fan, very up market in the mid 60s. This "Air Flite" bag from 1964 was marked "NEMS Ent," and sold in 1987 with the accompanying leather belt.

### Beatles' Tour Itinerary

This itinerary for the Beatles' first full U.S. tour between August and September 1964 was prepared for George Harrison (and one assumes, the other Beatles) in a black notebook containing a letter from American Flyer's Airline, maps, flight itinerary with dates, flying times, distances covered, and aircraft seating plans. The number of venues visited in a short period rivals those of contemporary musicians on regular international tours.

### *Billboard* Award to Beatles

A "Special Achievement" presentation plaque awarded to the Beatles in March 1964 by the *Billboard* magazine for their unique top three positions in the U.S. "Hot 100" chart, when "I Want To Hold Your Hand," "She Loves You" and "Please Please Me" were placed one, two and three simultaneously.

### In-Shop Beatles Promotion Display

Even the promotion material for merchandise is collectable, like this cardboard stand-up display (U.K. 1964) which advertised both Beatles stockings – pictured in the "girls-magazine" style of 1960s illustration – and the current film release *A Hard Day's Night*.

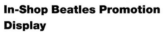

### Banknote Signed by the Beatles

"Just give me money . . ." Interesting to speculate whether this £1 note, signed by the Beatles "To Betty" and which appeared in auction in 1988, was originally the property of the autograph hunter or one of the Fab Four.

## Beatles Breakfast Service

The most-used image of the Beatles to appear on merchandise material was the Dezo Hoffmann portrait of the group in their gray collarless suits, usually modified in some way and more often than not without the photographer's permission. Typical of its use was on this breakfast service by Washington Pottery Ltd., which consisted of mugs, saucers, cereal bowls, plates, side plates and ashtrays.

## Nodding Beatles Car Mascots

A bizarre variation on the nodding dog, these Beatles "Bobb'n Head" dolls with spring-mounted, enlarged heads were manufactured by a U.S. company called Car Mascots Inc. and seemed to bear no similarity to any of the members of the group. But totally of their time and never to be repeated, thus highly collectable.

## Beatles Table Lamp

Apart from Mickey Mouse – and he had a 30-year head start – the Beatles probably appeared on more merchandise than anybody in history. These ephemesal treasures are now highly collectable of course; this lamp, which included all the trademarks of faces, signatures, musical notes and guitars, created considerable interest when sold in a London auction in 1990.

## Vintage Beatle Record Covers

Two Beatles record covers, both attracting a high premium at collectors fairs. The VJ release on the right was an early American album cashing in on their success in the singles charts, and included not only material from their debut U.K. album "Please Please Me," but "pictures and stories" covering such vital topics as their favorite foods, hobbies, color of hair and types of girls! This copy appeared in sale along with the notorious "Butcher" sleeve for the "Yesterday And Today" album.

### Beatles Bubble Gum Machine

What was basically an ordinary bubble gum dispensing machine suddenly became a Beatles Bubble Gum Machine by the insertion of a picture of the group inside the glass jar. Such was the pulling power of the Beatles' image in mid 1960s America, that this device was deemed sufficient to boost sales – which no doubt it did. The machine appeared in sale in 1984, where it was bought by a Liverpool collector on behalf of the local tourist board.

### Genuine Beatles Wig

Probably the most famous – or infamous – piece of merchandising that came to epitomize rampant Beatlemania was the Beatles wig. Outselling even the Davy Crockett hat of a decade earlier, this dubious headgear was worn by Americans "from nine to ninety!" and shows just how far product endorsement went in the Beatles' name. Sold in aid of the Samaritans charity along with this toupee was an unopened packet of micromesh Beatles nylon stockings.

### Beatlemania Ephemera

Another mixed bag of "mop top" merchandising, this collection sold in New York in 1985 included a Worcester Ware tray, an "official" ballpoint pen, playing cards, a lunch box copyrighted "NEMS 1965," a scrap book for all those news clippings, and the rage of 1964, the Beatles "Flip Your Wig" board game!

### "Mop Top" Beatles Dolls

The "mop top" aspect of their image was crucial in selling the Beatles to America on a mass scale, and items like these cheap "real hair" dolls perpetuated the caricature which the group themselves were already anxious to relegate to the past, a side of their career they were pleased to forget.

169

## Lennon Marriage Certificate

Described respectively as "Musician (Guitar)" and "Art Student (school)," John Winston Lennon and Cynthia Powell were married at Liverpool South Registry Office on August 23, 1962. Their wedding certificate appeared at the very first London sale of rock & roll memorabilia in December 1981.

## Acetate of "Yesterday"

A single-sided acetate of the McCartney song "Yesterday" from 1965. The acetate carries the label of the music publisher, Dick James, who managed the Beatles' own publishing company, Northern Songs, from 1963 until 1969, when he sold his share to ATV. The Northern Songs title was used as a joke against the famous Southern Songs publishers, but Lennon and McCartney diskovered later that they did not own their titles. McCartney tried to buy them subsequently but was beaten to it in 1985 by Michael Jackson who originally started buying songs on McCartney's advice. This acetate contains a version of the song that was rejected due to certain recording effects used on Paul's voice. It was George Martin's suggestion that they should use a string backing for the song although Paul initially hated the idea. However, once recorded, he loved it and the song became a U.S. number one in 1965 and a U.K. hit in 1976.

## Various Beatles Merchandise

Collections of Beatle's merchandise can give a normally grandiose salesroom the appearance of a toyshop. This colorful selection from a 1991 London auction included painting-by-numbers sets, a jigsaw puzzle, inflatable dolls, bubble gum cards, a bubble gum machine, brooches, a comb, four "Toby" jugs, and a set of egg cups!

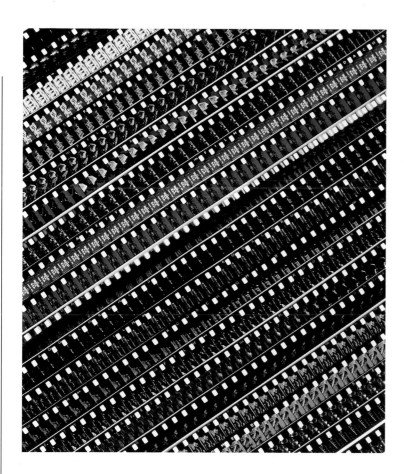

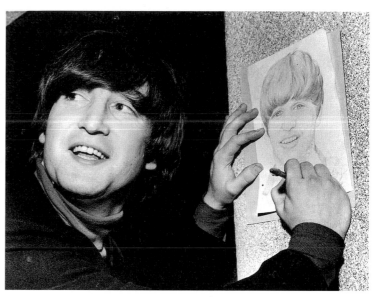

### Private On-Tour Film of the Beatles

A genuinely unique piece of memorabilia that sold for a five-figure price in 1986 was a private 8 mm silent color film taken of the Beatles on tour in 1965 and 1966 by their press agent, Tony Barrow. Of the three reels, two showed the group "behind the scenes" on their U.S. tour of 1965 – relaxing in their Hollywood hideaway in Benedict Canyon, surrounded by uniformed security guards while fans crowded on a ledge nearby overlooking the Canyon. Concert footage included a date in Atlanta in 1965 and the Tokyo Budokan Hall in 1966.

### John Signing Drawing Of Ringo

This photograph of John Lennon signing a fan's sketch of Ringo was sold in a London Auction along with the original sketch, signed by all four Beatles, plus a newspaper article and programme relating to the occasion, a concert at the Regal Theatre, Hull, in 1964.

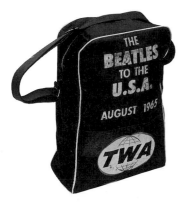

### Beatles U.S. Flightbags

These customized TWA bags were given only to the Beatles and their entourage for their third U.S. tour in August 1965. Today's travelers may consider such items rather strange but bags were a common airline feature until the price-cutting era of the late 1970s. This was the group's third U.S. outing and on this tour they met Presley. It is sad that two of the most influential talents of the rock era could not have performed publicly together.

### "Sgt. Pepper" Tracklist

Perhaps "rescued" from a late-night session at Abbey Road Studios, this handwritten track-listing by John Lennon for the "Sgt. Pepper" album was on the back of a brown envelope, but mounted under plastic with a reduced picture of the album cover realized over $2,000 in 1988.

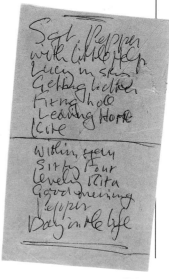

## Handwritten Arrangement for "Hey Jude"

The making of a hit. This playlist for "Hey Jude" shows how McCartney itemized the order for its constituent parts. The most common story behind the song is that it is about Julian Lennon and this is certainly McCartney's stated view. However, people still like to read more into it, and John Lennon was quoted as saying, as late as 1980, that he felt it was written for him. The song, which lasted for seven minutes and 11 seconds, is backed by a 40-piece orchestra and was recorded in late July of 1968.

## "Sgt. Pepper" Orchestration

The integrated use of orchestral session musicians reached new heights for a pop record on the Beatles' "Sgt. Pepper" album; all four members of the group signed this horn orchestration, presumably scored by George Martin, which relates to the central section of the title song.

## "Magical Mystery Tour" Gold Disc

Released as an album in the U.S. and a double EP in Britain, the music from the movie *Magical Mystery Tour* (a fusion of McCartney's catchy tunes and Lennon's desire to be different) was received much more favorably than the movie itself. After the death of Brian Epstein in August 1967, many felt that the made-for-television movie was the beginning of the Beatles' decline.

## "Hey Jude" Gold Disc

Presented to the Beatles for 1 million sales of "Hey Jude" in the U.S., this gold disk was given to the original auction vendor by George Harrison at Los Angeles Airport. The single was the Beatles' first release on their new Apple label and held the number one position in the American charts for nine weeks.

## Beatles Fan Club Records

A set of seven Beatles Fan Club Christmas records from 1963 onwards. The Beatles' output was generally high throughout their career, with singles being specially recorded and not just lifted album tracks which is normal practice today. Furthermore, they made a special record each year for their Fan Club members which were not for general release. The records were not finely constructed "pop" songs but informal jams in the studio with unscripted jokes and chat. The 1967 "Christmas Time Is Here Again" is as good as many a Christmas record that now makes number one (which perhaps is not saying much.)

### Apple Merchandise

The Beatles were the first group to be hounded by merchandisers seeking manufacturing concessions. They set up two companies to handle the assignment of their merchandising rights, and the teen market was flooded with all kinds of products aimed to attract the younger buyer. Most of these are British- or U.S.-made, such as the tiles by Proudholme Products of Brighton, and the Bobb'n-Head figures by Car Mascots, although the television is from Hong Kong. The Apple products are often the most collectible, as they were made for a shorter period and tended only to be available from the Baker Street Apple boutique. The Apple watch was designed by Richard Loftus, but the most bizarre item must surely be the teapot by Carlton Ware, for a truly appletizing cup!

### Apple Name Plate

This simple sign in brushed stainless steel with the word "Apple" inset in bright green, was from the entrance of the Beatles' famous office building (the roof of which was the venue for their "Get Back" performance in *Let It Be*) at 3 Savile Row, London.

### "Apple" Decorative Panel

When the Beatles' short-lived Apple boutique folded, they had the closing-down sale to end all closing-down sales. Designers "The Fool," who created most of the exotic clothing at Apple, also produced this brightly painted panel entitled "Apple" which was removed from the premises during the 1968 free-for-all.

### Apple Wristwatch

Old England had already brought out the "Flower Power" watch when the Beatles' Apple company commissioned an Apple watch simply bearing the apple logo as on the record label. With a simulated black suede strap, the watch — complete with suede carrying case — now appears at Beatles' conventions and auctions for around $1,000.

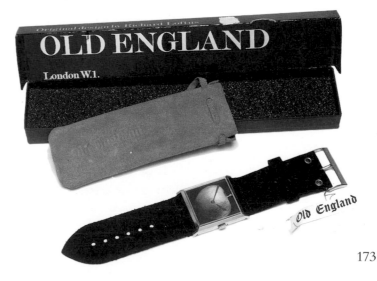

### Apple Singles Presentation Pack

"Our First Four," an Apple Records package of their first four single releases. The folder contains "Hey Jude," "Thingumybob" by Black Dyke Mills Band, "Those Were The Days" by Mary Hopkin and "Sour Milk Sea" by Jackie Lomax with an explanatory leaflet. It was an interesting start to the label's career with two number ones and two non-starters. The Hopkin single, a McCartney-produced traditional Russian folk song, knocked Apple 1 ("Hey Jude") off the U.K. top slot. This rare package rather summed up the future of the Apple label; unless a Beatle was involved somewhere in the recording, the record would not succeed.

### Glass Apple

This glass apple, made by Steuben Glassworks and signed by the manufacturer on the base, was presented by Paul McCartney to Alastair Taylor, office manager for the Beatles' Apple organization. When it appeared on sale in 1981 it was offered complete with the cardboard box that McCartney had wrapped it in – "dogs paw" sticky tape still intact – and the handwritten message "Paul's once now Alastair's."

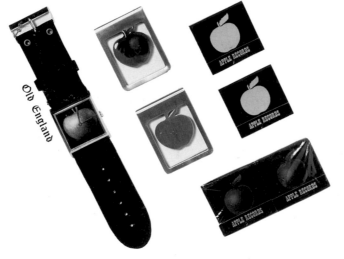

### Various Apple Objects

The Beatles' Apple logo, which was inspired by a painting by surrealist René Magritte owned by Paul McCartney, appeared on various types of merchandise including here the watch designed by Richard Loftus, money clips in stainless steel, and presentation packs of Apple Records matchbooks.

### Beatles GOSET Award

Among the plethora of awards showered on the Beatles during their career, some are remembered – like the annual *New Musical Express* readers' poll or the prestigious Ivor Novello Awards – while others have sunk into obscurity. This abstract figure in bronze, sold in 1981, falls into the latter category – it is the GOSET pop poll award for 1970 in which the Beatles won the International Section.

### Beatles Counter Display

Even something as transitory as a cardboard counter display, and slightly damaged at that, can have collector appeal. Printed in bright colors, this was a promotional item for the album "The Beatles Live At The Hollywood Bowl" released in 1977, and would achieve a figure in excess of $1,000.

### "Ballad Of John And Yoko" Award

Although only Lennon and McCartney performed on "The Ballad Of John And Yoko," it is still regarded as a Beatles single, and their last U.K. number one. The lyrics of the song upset many Americans – rekindling the Lennon and Christ controversy – and it only climbed to number eight in the U.S. This particular award was donated to a charity event on station WFIL, where Lennon sold it on air to raise money for Muscular Dystrophy.

### Apple T-Shirts

A collection of original promotional T-shirts for Apple and various individual Beatle projects. Despite the nature of the split all the former Beatles used the Apple label to issue their solo offerings, probably due to the nine-year contract the group had signed with EMI in 1967. These items dated from 1970 to 1974 and could fetch over $100 each today in unworn condition.

### McCartney *Melody Maker* Letter

The Beatles officially split on April 9, 1970 and this letter from McCartney to the U.K. music magazine *Melody Maker* dates from August of the same year. Although no longer together, the album and film *Let It Be* were released which kept the group in the public eye. The press blamed McCartney for the breakup and throughout the years rumors flowed that they would reunite. Some even suggested that a replacement would be found for Paul, who, by releasing his solo "McCartney" album almost alongside the Beatles' last effort, did little to extract himself from blame. It was not until McCartney was granted a "statement of motion" in January 1971 against the group (basically dissolving the partnership) that most people accepted it was finally over.

### Signed Big Brother Album

As autographed material became collectible, it would often arrive at sales elaborately mounted and framed, like this section of a Big Brother and the Holding Company album inscribed "To Stan, Love Janis Joplin XXXX" which came complete with a photograph of the singer and nameplate.

### Bee Gees Gold Disk

A presentation gold disk for the single "Night Fever" by the Bee Gees. Taken from the soundtrack of the hugely successful movie *Saturday Night Fever* (Paramount 1977) starring John Travolta, the album from the film is the biggest-selling soundtrack ever. the single "Night Fever" won awards for the "Most Performed Work" and "Best Selling A-Side" in 1978. With this single and four others, the Bee Gees became the first group in the 1970s to have five consecutive singles reach number one in the U.S. charts.

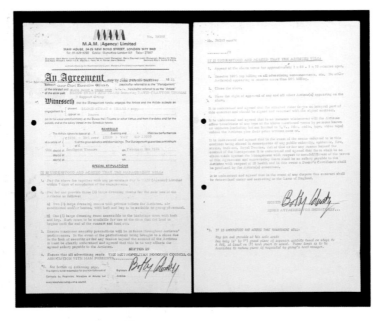

### Blood Sweat and Tears Contract and Letter

A contract for an engagement by the U.S. "jazz-rock" band Blood, Sweat and Tears in February 1976 as part of a U.K. tour that was subsequently canceled, sold together with the letter of cancellation. (From the Isaac Tigrett Collection)

## Booker T. & the MGs Award

This was a local music award given to Al Jackson, the original drummer with Booker T. & the MGs, in 1971 by the City of Memphis. As the house rhythm section at Stax Records, they were principal architects of the Memphis soul sound. In 1975 Jackson was shot and killed on a Memphis street. (From the Isaac Tigrett Collection)

## Boomtown Rats Silver Disk

A presentation silver disk for "I Don't Like Mondays" by the Boomtown Rats, presented to Johnny Fingers (the band's keyboard player). This single, voted the best single in 1979 at the British Rock and Pop Awards, was the Boomtown Rats' second British number one, in July 1979, where it stayed for four weeks. The lyrics were inspired by newspaper reports of a Californian schoolgirl who opened fire in her classroom and, when asked by police for an explanation, merely stated that she didn't like Mondays.

## Autographed Boy George Single

After the demise of his group Culture Club, Boy George had a U.K. number one with the first release under his own name, "Everything I Own," in 1987. The follow-up, "Keep Me In Mind," however, only just managed to scrape into the Top 30; this signed copy is inscribed: "to Emily, keep her in mind."

## Carpenters Contract and Letter

The 1975 appearance by the Carpenters at the Southport Theater, just north of Liverpool, England, was canceled due to Karen Carpenter's illness, the fact notified to the venue by the accompanying telegram. Both contract and telegram were subsequently sold in auction together. (From the Isaac Tigrett Collection)

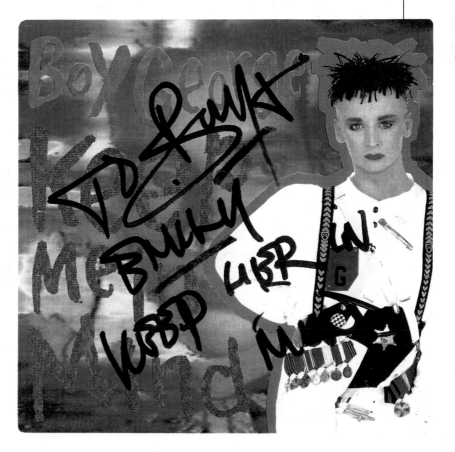

177

### Signed Chicago Album

Formed in the late 1960s, Chicago (initially called Chicago Transit Authority) used a large horn section to blend a rock approach into a jazz-style setting. Their first nine albums all made the U.S. Top Ten, with five number ones, and through the 80s they were still having occasional hits in the singles charts. (From the Isaac Tigrett Collection)

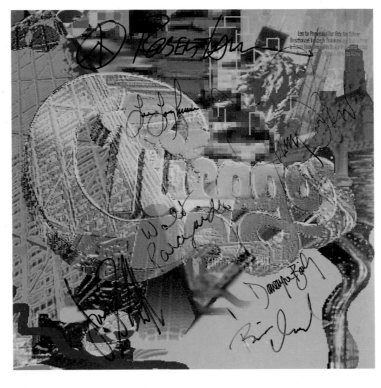

### Eric Clapton Gold Disk

An unusual presentation disk, not this time given to a recording artist for sales achievements, but presented by the recording artist to his favorite soccer team! The gold disk for the album "Slowhand" is mounted above a plaque detailing the occasion which Eric Clapton commemorated by presenting this award to West Bromwich Albion in 1978.

### Dave Clark Five Dolls

This hardly recognizable stand-up doll of Dave Clark, 5 in high, towers above the other members of his group, the Dave Clark Five, who only measure 3 in each. Made by the REMCO toy company in the United States, where Clark was always much bigger than on his home territory, they indicate the very young following that some of the British beat invasion groups attracted.

### Dave Clark Gold Disk

An unusual engraved gold disk presented to Lenny Davidson for the sale of 1 million copies of the single "Bit And Pieces." Entered into a rock memorabilia auction personally by Davidson, the lead guitarist with the Dave Clark Five, "Bits And Pieces" was released in 1964 and was their second chart success climbing to number two in the U.K. and number four in the U.S.

### Joe Cocker Gold Disk

A presentation gold disk for Joe Cocker's album "Mad Dogs And Englishmen" released in 1970. The album, of gold-colored metal, is mounted on ecru linen above a presentation plaque bearing the RIAA certified sales award logo. "Mad Dogs And Englishmen," the double album, commemorated an extraordinary tour of America in 1970 where Cocker was accompanied by an entourage of over 40 musicians (known collectively as Mad Dogs and Englishmen).

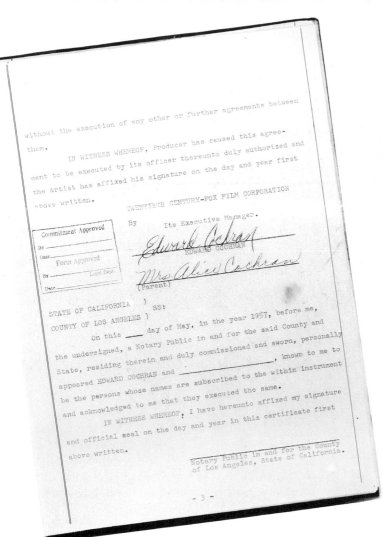

### Signed Eddie Cochran Programme

From the ill-fated British tour with Gene Vincent, this program must have been signed by Cochran literally days before his death on Easter Saturday, April 17, 1960. (From the Isaac Tigrett Collection)

### Eddie Cochran Film Contract

The original contract between Eddie Cochran and 20th Century Fox dated 1957. He is referred to as Edward in the contract which is signed by his mother, Alice, as Cochran was only 19 at the time. It consists of 49 pages, all initialed by Cochran, and is dated May 9, 1957. Cochran had already sung "Twenty Flight Rock" in *The Girl Can't Help It* and "You Ain't Gonna Make A Cotton Picker Out Of Me" in *Untamed Youth* during 1956 and clearly 20th Century-Fox were keen to add to the Presley-style bandwagon. It was not until 1959 that he performed in his next and final movie *Go, Johnny, Go!*

### Phil Collins Platinum Award

A rare triple platinum award presented to Phil Collins in recognition of sales of over 3 million copies of the Band Aid single "Do They Know It's Christmas?" The record which founded the charity, Band Aid, still holds the position as the best-selling single ever in the U.K.. "Do They Know" entered the charts at number one in 1984, re-entered in 1985 to peak at number three and was re-recorded in 1989 to climb to number one.

### Phil Collins' Signed Drum Skin

The skin is inscribed "Thanks for all your help. Luv Phil Collins" and bears an amusing cartoon self-portrait. While Collins may be a relatively new artist who does not perhaps fit into the traditional areas of rock & roll collecting, he is becoming more and more popular with collectors. His increased and continuing chart successes, which started when he joined Genesis in 1970 and took a surprising twist with the solo album "Face Value" in 1981, will reflect healthily on the market for his memorabilia.

### Cream Gold Disk

A gold disk for the Cream album "Disraeli Gears," their second album, released in 1967, following their 1966 "Fresh Cream" debut, and their first success in the U.S. where the album climbed to number four in the Top 40 album charts and remained in the chart for 50 weeks. Cream created the "fastest, loudest, most overpowering blues-based rock ever heard."

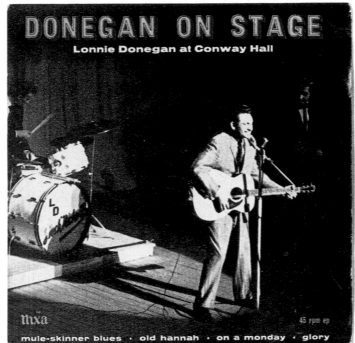

### Dire Straits Platinum Award

An extraordinary tenfold platinum award for "Brothers In Arms" by Dire Straits to commemorate sales of over 3 million. "Brothers In Arms" entered the U.K. album charts at number one and spent nine weeks in the number one position in the U.S.. To date, the album has spent nearly four years in the Top 75.

### Dr. Hook Gold Disk

A presentation gold disk for "Sometimes You Win" by Dr. Hook released in 1979. Formed in the late 1960s and originally called Dr. Hook and the Medicine Show, the band was led by the eyepatched Ray Sawyer, and they spent their formative years playing in small New Jersey venues. The band's first hit in the U.S. and Britain was "Sylvia's Mother" which came from their first album, "Dr. Hook" released in 1972.

### Rare Lonnie Donegan EP

The undisputed King of Skiffle, Lonnie Donegan's influence on British rock was incalculable as the prime inspiration for a generation of teenagers to take up the guitar. Originally planned as a live album, the four tracks on this now-rare EP (extended play) record from 1958 were all that could be released – the other songs, according to sleeve notes, were drowned by the ecstatic reaction of the audience!

### Signed Donovan Photograph

Donovan evolved from a denim-clad "British Dylan" to the epitome of the "peace and love" flower child, as instanced in this pastoral pose signed and dedicated "To the Museum of Rock Art – Donovan." (From the Isaac Tigrett Collection)

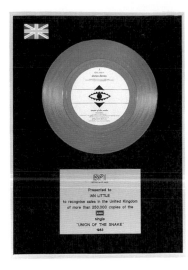

## Duran Duran Silver Disk

A silver disk to acknowledge sales of 250,000 for Duran Duran's "Union Of The Snake." With their roots in the New Romantic movement of the late 1970s and early 1980s, the group took their name from a character in the 1967 cult movie *Barbarella*. "Union" was the first single from their third album "Seven And The Ragged Tiger" and followed their first number one "Is There Something I Should Know" which had gone straight in the charts at number one.

## Signed Bob Dylan Novel

A copy of Bob Dylan's book *Tarantula* signed by the author and dedicated "to John and Yoko." This first edition was released in May 1971 and had been a long-anticipated debut novel having been written in 1966, although some feel the manuscript that was finally published dates from 1965. Dylan was desperate to write a novel but having finally done so he felt it did not merit publication ("It just wasn't a book, it was just a nuisance"). However, unofficial copies of the manuscript started to circulate and so it was decided to "let it roll." Not even Dylan's most ardent followers can muster up much enthusiasm for the work and his poems and prose are better represented in his songs and as footnotes on his albums.

## ELP Gold Disk

A presentation gold disk for "Welcome Back My Friends To The Show That Never Ends," a live album released in 1974 by Emerson, Lake and Palmer, presented to Greg Lake. The album spent five weeks in the U.K. Top 40 and 11 weeks in the U.S.A equivalent but climbed no higher than number four. The band split in 1979 and reformed again in 1987 but they have yet to equal the successes they achieved in the early 1970s.

## Fleetwood Mac Award

An unusual presentation set given to Stevie Nicks to commemorate 13 million sales of the Fleetwood Mac album "Rumours" which was the second album from the revised Fleetwood Mac line-up. First charting in 1977, "Rumours" won the Grammy award for the best album the same year. It spent 31 weeks at number one in the U.S. and over 440 weeks on the U.K. Top 75 (boosted by its availability on CD) and for once it is appropriate to describe a record as "a classic album."

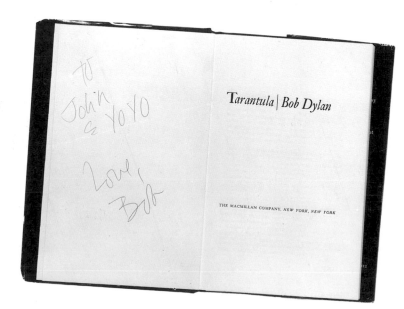

### Billy Fury Silver Disk

Presented to Billy Fury to commemorate sales in excess of 250,000 of ''Halfway To Paradise,'' a composition by Goffin and King. The single reached number three in 1961 and remained in the U.K. chart for 23 weeks. In common with many other recording stars of this period, the rise of the Beatles wrought a steady and significant decline in Fury's popularity and success.

### Signed Fleetwood Mac Notepaper

A signed sheet of Fleetwood Mac's Penguin notepaper to Elton John. Penguin Promotions organized the touring aspect of the band and was part of the self-management system, Seedy Management, that Mick Fleetwood and John McVie had established in 1974. It is unusual for a group to manage themselves, but Fleetwood Mac have a diverse and complicated history which saw them reject the conventional wisdom of ''the men in suits.'' In his recent autobiography, Fleetwood credits this self-determination as the reason why the band managed to stay together for so long. ''With the band running its own show, we couldn't take sides . . . and we were too smart to commit suicide.''

### Frankie Goes To Hollywood Gold Disk

A presentation gold disk for ''Relax'' by Frankie Goes To Hollywood. Released in November 1983 and banned by the BBC in January, ''Relax'' reached number one in the U.K. charts later that month. In total ''Relax'' spent 52 weeks in the singles charts; the single was featured in the 1984 movie *Police Academy* and reached number ten in the U.S. singles charts.

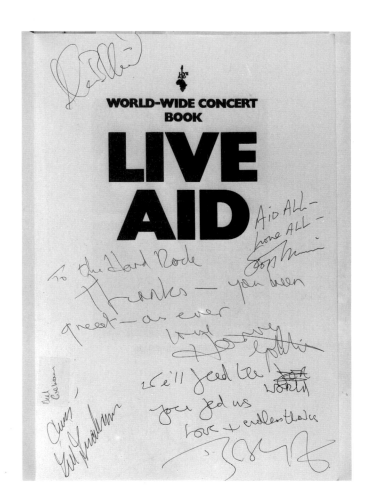

### Signed Live Aid Book

With a galaxy of stars' autographs throughout, this signed book of the Live Aid concerts also bore the messages ''We'll feed the world, you fed us, love and endless thanks Bob Geldof'' and ''To the Hard Rock, Thanks – you've been great – as ever, love Harvey Goldsmith'' to the Hard Rock Café chain who helped in the organization of the charity gig to end all charity gigs.

BILL HALEY And His COMETS
Decca Recording Artists

Personal Direction
Jas. H. Ferguson
801 Barclay Street
Chester, Pa. 2-3004

Exclusive Booking
JOLLY JOYCE
1619 Broadway, New York City
Room 716    PLaza 7-1786
Philadelphia: WAlnut 2-4677—2-3172

## Bill Haley Signed Photograph

A signed black-and-white publicity shot for Bill Haley and his Comets dating from 1955 with Haley's words "To Reg, keep swinging with the Comets, sincerely Bill Haley." The legend of rock & roll started here with the former country and western singer. His fifth single release, which started as the B-side to the flop "Thirteen Women," was "Rock Around The Clock," which spent eight weeks at number one in the U.S. and five weeks in the U.K. The song was featured in the movie *The Blackboard Jungle* which led to some unsightly scenes in movie houses up and down the country as the young audience tried to "boogie."

## Signed "Bangladesh" Album

"The Concert For Bangladesh" album signed by George Harrison, Ringo Starr, Bob Dylan, Eric Clapton and Billy Preston. You may think that Live Aid was the first, but you would be wrong. In 1971, prompted by an appeal from close friend Ravi Shankar, Harrison led two concerts at Madison Square Gardens to raise funds for the war-torn and starving Bangladeshi people. A host of rock performers also appeared and the subsequent triple album topped the U.K. chart. As a result of his efforts Harrison later received a "Child is Father to the Man" award from UNICEF.

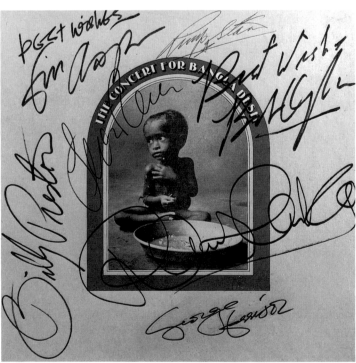

## Jimi Hendrix Gold Disk

A gold disk presented to the ex-studio session musician, Jimi Hendrix, for his debut album "Are You Experienced" released in 1967. "Are You Experienced" is an extraordinarily rich first album and one which many feel he never surpassed. The LP was certainly a market stall on which Hendrix displayed all his musical wares, showing supreme command of his instrument and the wah-wah pedal, original lyrics and controlled manipulation of feedback. With the album, Hendrix proved he was here to stay.

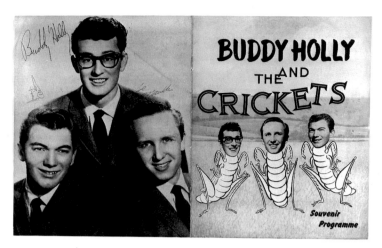

### Signed Buddy Holly Programme

A rare concert program for Buddy Holly and the Crickets dating from their English tour of 1958. A highly significant item as this was the only trip that the group made to the U.K. The tour was tremendously successful in promoting Holly and he continues to influence and inspire every new generation. For whatever reasons they are reissued, Holly's greatest hits compilations seem to be as regular as presidential elections, and they continue to make the U.K. Top Ten.

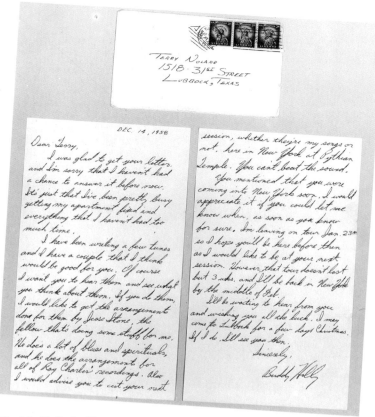

### Signed INXS Drum Skin

One of the most successful rock acts to come out of Australia, INXS really broke worldwide in the late 1980s with their Top Ten album "Kick" and the U.S. chart-topper "Need You Tonight" (a U.K. number two). The bass drum skin was donated by the band to a charity auction in Philadelphia. (From the Isaac Tigrett Collection)

### Buddy Holly Letter

Personal letters have always proved strong collectibles, partly because of the biographical insight they often provide into an artist's private life. This letter from Buddy Holly was written to singer Terry Noland, in Holly's home town of Lubbock, Texas, shortly after Buddy moved to New York, advising his friend about recording studios and offering him a song to record. Of interest to music fans is the mention of Jesse Stone as potential producer, whom Holly was using at the time and who, enthuses Holly, "does the arrangements for all Ray Charles' recordings . . ."

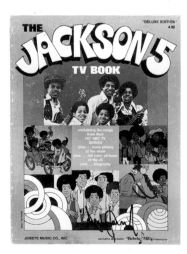

### Signed Jackson Five Book

It's over 20 years since the Jackson Five were big enough – like the Beatles before them – to have an animated TV series based on their characters. This book of the series contained music and lyrics of songs from the show, biographies and photographs of the real group, and was signed on the front by Michael Jackson, and inside by nine members of the Jackson family including parents Joe and Kathryn.

### Early Elton John Recording

An extremely rare copy of the 1969 album by the Bread and Beer Band. The main interest for the collector is the keyboard player listed as Reg Dwight. Elton John (or Reg Dwight as he was then known) was, at the time, working at D&M for Dick James as a songwriter with Bernie Taupin. They joined in November 1967 for $50 a week but found themselves pushed into writing commercial songs that neither of them liked. Elton would invariably take any opportunity to record and the Bread and Beer Band was a collection of D&M musicians. They recorded their first two tracks on December 2, 1968 at the Abbey Road studios. The result, ''The Devil's Gallop'' and the original ''Breakdown Blues'' was released as a single on Decca but met with little success. Undaunted, the group recorded ten further covers between March 19 and April 9, 1969 but the album was pulled after the test pressing stage. Elton had already released two singles under his adopted name and it is of interest that he continued to use Reg Dwight in 1969. He did not officially become Elton Hercules John until December 8, 1972 when he registered the change by deed poll.

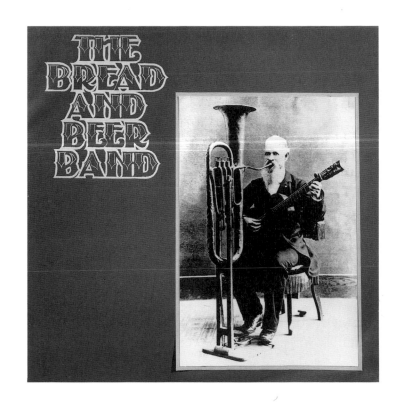

### Elton John Platinum Award

A platinum award for ''A Single Man'' by Elton John. Released in 1978 this was a doleful album and the first released after Elton had parted from his lyricist partner, Bernie Taupin with whom he had worked since 1967. After the split, Elton failed to have another Top Ten album success until the 1983 reunion with Taupin which led to the album ''Too Low For Zero.'' Presented personally to Elton John and in whose country home it hung until 1988.

### Elton John Cushion

Presumably manufactured as a promotional item, this blue denim cushion was embroidered with the cover design of the 1971 Elton John album ''Madman across the Water,'' while the reverse featured a list of the songs included on the record.

### Elton John Pinball Machine

Along with the Gottlieb company of Chicago, Bally are the world's best-known manufacturer of pinball machines. What greater honor, therefore, for self-confessed pinball freak Elton John than to have a machine designed around his own alter ego, Captain Fantastic. In fact two different ''Fantastic'' models were produced by Bally, both of which were part of the Elton John sale in 1988, this one also featuring Elton in his role as the Pinball Wizard in *Tommy*.

### Elton John Gold Disk

A gold disk for the double album ''Captain Fantastic And The Brown Dirt Cowboy.'' This award was presented to Elton John and was retained by him until entered into ''The Elton John Collection'' auction in 1988. Reaching number one in the U.S. album chart within a week of its release in 1975, ''Captain Fantastic'' charted Elton John's and Bernie Taupin's rise from obscurity. The track from the album ''Someone Saved My Life Tonight'' was released as a single and reached number four in the American singles chart in 1975.

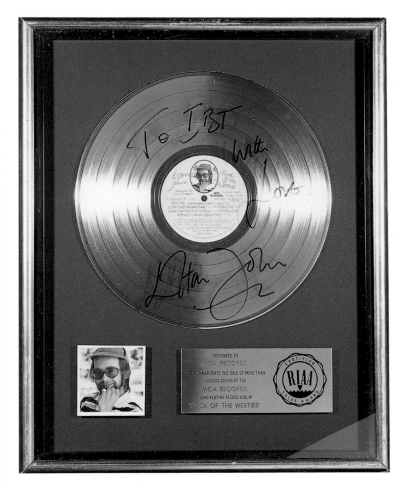

### "Rock Of The Westies" Gold Disk

A signed gold disk award for Elton John's follow-up album to "Captain Fantastic," "Rock Of The Westies." Despite only a lukewarm critical reception, the late 1975 release went on to top the U.S. chart and make the Top Five in the U.K. (From the Isaac Tigrett Collection)

### Signed Led Zeppelin Album

A signed copy of the third Led Zeppelin album which was released in October 1971 and reached number one on both sides of the Atlantic. This is the backrear of the cover; the front artwork features a revolving disk of images on a white background. The item features the signature of the late John Bonham — he died on September 25, 1980, and the band has not reformed since. The signature of a deceased artist does add to the desirability of an item.

### Kiss Trade Mark Registration

The 1970s band Kiss traded heavily on the fact that they were never seen in public without their extravagant make-up, so even their most dedicated fans didn't know what they really looked like. They became so obsessed with this – or at least with the publicity it garnered – that they actually had their individual make-up designs registered as trademarks! This plaque, sold in New York in 1989, featured four metal copies of the patent and trademark applications registration.

### John and Yoko's White Chess Set

Bought some years ago by a Japanese collector, the all-white carved ivory chess set was conceived by John Lennon and Yoko Ono, and is typical of the minimalist concepts in which the couple indulged through the early 1970s, heralded initially on the pop front by the Beatles' "white" album.

### Led Zeppelin Platinum Award

A platinum eight-track tape award for Led Zeppelin's fourth album. Known variously as "Led Zeppelin IV," "Zo-So," "Runes," "Four Symbols" or 'Untitled' (although the latter seems scarcely appropriate with so many alternative names in circulation), the album illustrates the broadening of the band with the addition of acoustic and folk-inspired material. The album spent two weeks at number one in the U.K. and remained in the Top 40 for 62 weeks. The epic track "Stairway To Heaven" included on this album is regarded by many as the band's finest and it became an anthem of the 1970s.

John Lennon — (Just Like) Starting Over

Produced by John Lennon, Yoko Ono and Jack Douglas

### Signed Lennon/Ono Single

A copy of the single "(Just Like) Starting Over" signed by John Lennon and Yoko Ono. The single, wryly titled after his five year lay-off, was released in the U.S. on October 24, 1980 only weeks before his death on December 8, making signed copies of some significance. The song was from the new album "Double Fantasy" which David Geffen had offered to release without hearing a track. This may not sound very brave considering Lennon's past chart successes, but it should be remembered that he was also responsible for some spectacular failures like "Two Virgins" released in 1968 and "The Wedding Album." Lennon fans will retort that these were not supposed to be commercial successes, but it illustrates the gamble that Geffen took.

### Lennon "Oz" Acetate

An acetate of John Lennon's unreleased song "God Save Oz" on the Apple label which misprints the title "Us." The song was recorded to help the editors of the magazine *Oz* which was on trial in the U.K. under various sections of the Obscene Publications Act for one particular issue. Lennon was keen to help all the "suppressed" at this time, giving money or moral support to various causes such as *Oz*. (In 1970 Lennon paid the fines, totalling £1,300, of protesters against a South African rugby game.) The song was never released and it was planned that someone else should record the vocals, although this appears not to have occurred.

### Lennon Gold Disk

A presentation gold disk for Lennon's "Mind Games" album which was released in 1973. After the uncommercial album 'Sometime In New York City' which was considered self-centerd and political, Lennon's "Mind Games" was a return to the style of his most successful solo album, "Imagine." Soon after the release of "Mind Games" Lennon and Ono separated and his moods and actions became increasingly volatile.

### Signed Madonna Albums and T-Shirt

Two Madonna albums and a T-shirt signed by the ambitious blonde although the "Who's That Girl" vinyl is a soundtrack to the movie of the same name. Madonna had the original film title, "Slammer," changed after she had written the song's lyrics. She contributed three more songs to the film in which she also starred but this did little to help it. The songs were successful and it remains much to her credit that the lady could continue to fail on celluloid while preserving her hold on the charts. The T-shirt is from Madonna's first U.K. tour which she bravely named after the movie. The "You Can Dance" album took its title from Madonna's spoken words on the intro to the U.K. number one "Into The Groove."

### Lennon/Ono Award

A *Disk and Music Echo* award to John and Yoko for U.K. sales of 250,000 of the single "Happy Xmas (War is Over)." Originally peaking at number seven in 1972, the single re-entered the charts in December 1980 after Lennon's assassination but was prevented from reaching number one by "(Just Like) Starting Over" which was released in November 1980 and held that position for five weeks.

### Lennon Lyrics for "Gimme Some Truth"

From his "Imagine" album, "Gimme Some Truth" was typical of the many tough-sounding songs that John Lennon was coming up with in the early 1970s. This piece of original manuscript was sold in a London auction – the last thing Lennon would have imagined at the time of writing it.

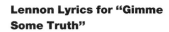

### "Flower Power" Wristwatch

With a bright pink leather strap and pink and gold face, this "Flower Power" wristwatch (*circa* 1968) designed by Richard Loftus, illustrates how even the most radical pop style is quickly absorbed into the cultural mainstream, thereby rendering it safe, respectable, and effectively dead. Nevertheless, as a period piece, the watch attracted three-figure interest when it went on sale in London in 1988.

### Mamas and Papas Dolls

Part of a series of Hasbro toys called Show Biz Babies, these 4 in. figures representing Michelle, John, Cass and Denny of the Mamas and Papas were packaged with an "autographed" photograph and "groovy" 7-inch flexi-disk "telling all" about each member of the group. Also in the same lot when they appeared at auction in 1991 were a set of Dave Clark Five dolls and a model of Peter Noone of Herman's Hermits.

### Bob Marley Platinum Award

A platinum award for the greatest hits album "Legend" by Bob Marley and the Wailers which was issued in 1984, three years after Bob Marley's death – the album received both gold and platinum certification in 1988. Probably the best known of the Jamaican reggae bands in the 1970s, Marley and his band produced rock-based reggae which made the Jamaicans sound as commercially successful abroad as it was popular at home.

### Bob Marley Badges

Bob Marley's espousal of Rastafarianism struck a note with many young people of West Indian origin in Britain. Even those who did not attempt to embrace the faith in all its ramifications, found a source of identity in the wearing of the red-gold-and-green, be it only in a piece of clothing or even a simple badge. Since Marley's death in 1981, anything directly associated with his brief years of real fame has become increasingly collectible over the years. (Courtesy of V&A Theatre Museum)

### Signed John Mellencamp Poster

Blues-influenced singer John Cougar Mellencamp has been highly regarded in his native U.S. since the early 1980s, though a lesser name in the U.K. and elsewhere; a situation somewhat remedied by the favorable critical reception accorded his 1987 album "Lonesome Jubilee," followed by this 1988 tour. (From the Isaac Tigrett Collection)

### George Michael Gold Disk

A gold disk to commemorate sales in Austria of 250,000 for the 1987 George Michael album "Faith," signed by Michael on the glass in magic marker. "Faith" went on to achieve sevenfold platinum status in America and was the album which proved George Michael was a genuine songwriting force, while illustrating his enthusiasm for producing "sculptured soul" and R&B based songs rather than classic pop.

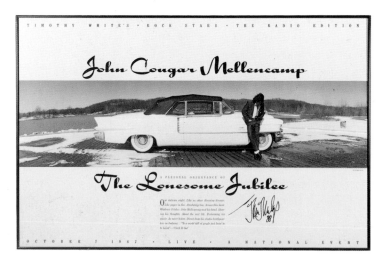

### Mindbenders Gold Disk

A presentation gold award for the single ''Groovy Kind Of Love'' by the Mindbenders which reached number two in both the U.S. and U.K. charts in 1966. It was presented to Eric Stewart, one of the founder members of the Mindbenders and entered into auction by him. Stewart later went on to form a band with Kevin Godley and Lol Creme which they christened 10cc (the name reputedly suggested by singer/producer Jonathan King).

### Signed Moody Blues Album

The Moody Blues formed in Birmingham, England, in 1964. Initially a typical British R&B group – their name came from a blues by Slim Harpo – they evolved into a ''progressive'' rock band in the 1970s. Their highly produced albums sold enormously worldwide, though this one – ''The Present'' from 1983 – was not one of the most memorable. (From the Isaac Tigrett Collection)

### Early Roy Orbison Record

Four years before he was catapulted into world stardom with ''Only The Lonely'' in 1960, Roy Orbison had a minor U.S. hit with ''Ooby Dooby'' as one of the Sun label's rockabilly roster. It was subsequently released in Britain on London Records, and featured on this much sought-after EP dating from 1958.

### Mott the Hoople Silver Disk

A silver disk award presented for U.K. sales of the single ''Roll Away The Stone'' by Mott the Hoople. Awarded to Morgan Fisher, the group's keyboard player and a vocalist, this particular award was unique in that Fisher signed the back of the mount in silver marker pen. A glitter rock band, the group fell under the protection and encouragement of David Bowie in 1972 who wrote and produced their first chart hit, ''All The Young Dudes.''

### Olivia Platinum Disk

A presentation platinum disk for the Newton-John album ''Olivia's Greatest Hits – Volume 2.'' Perhaps best known to a whole generation of teenage moviegoers for her role opposite John Travolta in the 1978 Paramount movie *Grease*, Olivia Newton-John's previous musical style had been based on country music, with hits including ''If Not For You,'' ''Banks Of The Ohio'' (both 1971) and 1973's ''Take Me Home Country Roads.''

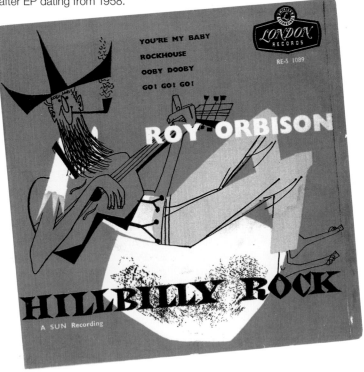

### Dolly Parton Badge

Never taking her image quite as seriously as the rest of the world, this badge of Dolly Parton-in-the-hay is an affectionate pastiche of the famous 1943 movie still of Jane Russell in *The Outlaw* – which caused a furore at the time, with her ample bosom supported by a specially built cantilevered bra, devised by aircraft designer/film producer Howard Hughes. (Courtesy of V&A Theatre Museum)

### Pink Floyd Gold Disk

A presentation gold disk for the double album "A Nice Pair" by Pink Floyd. The album is mounted above the presentation plaque engraved with Nick Mason as the recipient. "A Nice Pair" repackaged two earlier Pink Floyd albums, "The Piper At The Gates Of Dawn" (1967) and "A Saucerful Of Secrets" (1968) which were re-released in 1975 to continue the momentum caused by the enormous success of their 1973 album, "Dark Side Of The Moon." It spent 20 weeks in the U.K. album Top 40, and 36 in the U.S. equivalent.

### Pink Floyd "Animals" T-shirt

Like much good rock memorabilia, the promotional T-shirt was designed for the short rather than long-term and can now justifiably be viewed as a museum piece. The promotion campaign for the Pink Floyd 1977 Album "Animals" has become more a part of rock mythology than the album itself, after a 40-foot inflatable pig, similar to the one on the T-shirt, came loose from its moorings above London's Battersea Power Station while the band were shooting the album cover in December 1976. The Civil Aviation Authority issued a warning to all pilots in London airspace that a flying pig was on the loose. It was finally sighted at 18,000 feet over Chatham, Kent, then never seen again. (Courtesy of V&A Theatre Museum)

### Signed Freda Payne Photograph

When the hit songwriting team Holland-Dozier-Holland left Motown to form their own Invictus label, their first success was with Freda Payne's "Band Of Gold," a 1970 U.K. number one (number three in the U.S.). The signed picture was taken on one of her many visits to Britain in the early 70s. (From the Isaac Tigrett Collection)

### Pink Floyd Platinum Disk

A presentation platinum disk for Pink Floyd's "Dark Side Of The Moon" presented to Roger Waters and signed by him in black marker on the front glass. The album, which was released at an event held appropriately at London's Planetarium in 1973, was a staggering success. The sixth most successful album ever released in terms of weeks in the U.K. chart, "Dark Side Of The Moon" has spent 296 weeks there to date. climbing to number one in the U.S. album charts and spending 741 weeks in the album Top 200 to date.

### Pink Floyd Platinum Award

A custom-made platinum disk presented to Nicky [sic] Mason for the Pink Floyd album "Meddle" released in 1971. Despite the unusual style of the award, it was signed on the reverse by all four members of the group in black felt-tip pen and black and blue ballpoint. Pink Floyd were responsible in the late 1960s and early 1970s for some of the most fascinating "head music" produced. The album reached number three in the album charts and remained in the Top 40 for 82 weeks.

### Pink Floyd Autographs

Sets of autographs and photographs are often auctioned as one lot. This package consisted of three sets of Pink Floyd autographs consisting of four signatures on a promotional photograph, an autographed "Dark Side Of The Moon" album cover and a set of autographs from the earliest period of the band which included the legendary Syd Barrett.

### Police Platinum Disk

A presentation platinum disk for Police's album "Synchronicity" to commemorate sales of over 4 million copies. In 1982 a rock author was stimulated to write: "The Police are the rock band most likely to take over the world . . . they are the first band in years to have absolutely everything going for them." With their simple but instantly recognizable sound, the dramatic good looks of their lead singer (named Sting because of his trademark yellow and black striped sweaters) and their intelligent lyrics, the band attracted attention from the release of the "Roxanne" single in 1979 which reached number twelve in the U.K. charts.

### Elvis "Million Dollar" Bootleg

Truly legendary, the almost mythical tapes of the "Million Dollar Quartet" – an impromptu session at Sun Records in 1956 featuring Elvis Presley, Johnny Cash, Carl Perkins and Jerry Lee Lewis – finally appeared in the U.K. (in part at least) on this mid 70s bootleg pressing. Its appearance no doubt encouraged Charly Records, who had the U.K. rights to the Sun catalogue, to eventually release the whole session on CD, therefore rendering editions like this even more collectible.

"Authentic Studio Recordings, Memphis, Dec. 4, 1956"

### Elvis Presley Gold Disk

A gold disk to commemorate sales of over 1 million copies of the Elvis Presley single, "Burning Love." An old Dennis Linde song, "Burning Love" brought Presley back to the U.S. Top 10 in 1972 after an absence of two years. In Britain, however, he was enjoying his most successful period in almost a decade, with 13 Top Ten hits in just three years.

### Rare Presley South African Release

An extremely rare Elvis Presley album dated 1958 and on 10-inch format. The album is on the RCA Popular label with the catalogue number T31.077 and was pressed in South Africa by the Teal Record Co. The album, containing eight tracks, was never issued in the U.S. or U.K. and, as there is no record of Presley having sung with Janis, it was probably a marketing exercise to promote her material by coupling it with some Elvis tracks. As a result, the album is highly sought after by collectors.

### Signed Elvis G.I. Photograph

A signed photograph of Elvis Presley in the Army *circa* 1959. Elvis arrived in Bremerhaven, Germany on October 1, 1958 initially becoming a corporal and driving a jeep. It was during his service in Germany that Presley met Priscilla Beaulieu who was 14 at the time. Elvis left the army on the March 5, 1960 and immediately continued with his recording career. However, many feel that Presley's best recordings were behind him and, that with the exception of the Memphis sessions of 1969, it is generally agreed that he never came close to the inspiration of his pre-army recordings. There is a story that when Lennon heard of Elvis's death in 1977 he replied "Elvis died when he joined the army."

## Presley Sun Records / Early RCA Records

A rare complete set of Elvis Presley's Sun Records 78s and a later RCA Victor boxed set. Presley's career started in earnest when Sam Phillips, the owner of Sun Records, heard Elvis recording in his studio which he hired out to budding singers for $4. He teamed the singer with Scotty Moore and Bill Black and the result was "That's All Right" coupled with "Blue Moon Of Kentucky," released on July 19, 1954. It was after the local success of this that Presley signed with Sun Records and the follow-up, "Good Rockin' Tonight," was issued on September 9. The fourth Sun single, "Baby Let's Play House" and "I'm Left, You're Right, She's Gone" provided Elvis with his first national chart success by reaching number ten in the Country chart. In August 1955 Presley's final Sun release was issued, "Mystery Train" backed by "I Forget To Remember To Forget." By this stage it was clear that Sun could not offer the distribution or management skills that the artist warranted and so it became a contest for the major labels to bid for the Sun contract. RCA emerged the winner paying $35,000 on November 22, 1955, immediately reissuing all the Sun singles. The boxed sets shown here are British and are, by their very nature, a retrospective issue of Presley material. The "Mystery Train" song was issued in the U.K. in 1957 as the company tried to meet the demand for any Elvis material. Initially this material was distributed by EMI on its HMV label until July 1957 when RCA established its U.K. division.

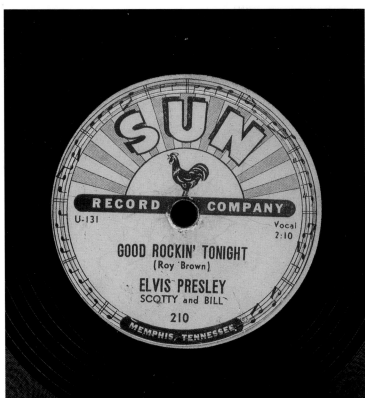

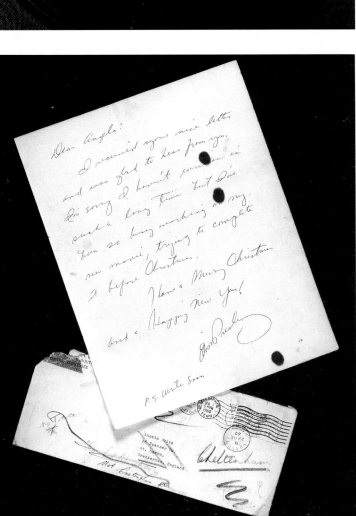

## Elvis Letter

A letter from Elvis Presley to an English fan, postmarked December 1, 1960. She was fortunate to receive it at all as it appears to have been incorrectly addressed but thankfully the British Post Office successfully re-directed it. It is amusing to note that Presley has added a "PS" asking the young fan to "Write soon." One would have thought that he would have had enough mail without encouraging it, but it is a revealing touch that highlights the real charm of the man. The movie referred to would probably have been *Flaming Star* which opened in the U.S. on December 20, 1960.

## Signed Elvis School Yearbook

A rare autographed Elvis Presley high school yearbook dating from 1953. The inscription reads "Best of luck to a very cute girl, remember me, Elvis." Elvis attended the Hume High School, Memphis, Tennessee until June 14, 1953, having achieved the academic heights of a diploma. He was initially very shy at school but toward the end he started to make more friends, dress well and by all accounts gave a bravo performance in the Christmas show of 1952.

Non-Com Officer in R. O. T. C., Vice-President Speech Club, Vice-President History Club.
**Awards:** Winner District Debate Tournament, Winner "I Speak For Democracy" Contest.

**ROBINSON, KATIE MAE**
**Major:** Commercial, Home Ec., English.
**Activities:** F. H. A., History Club, English Club, Vice-President History Club.

**RULEMAN, SHIRLEY**
**Major:** Home Ec., Commercial, English.
**Activities:** National Honor Society, F. H. A., Y-Teens, Latin Club, Jr. Cheerleader, Sabre Club, History Club, English Club, Honorary Captain in R. O. T. C., President Home Ec. Class.

**PRESLEY, ELVIS ARON**
**Major:** Shop, History, English.
**Activities:** R. O. T. C., Biology Club, English Club, History Club, Speech Club.

**PERRY, ROBERT EARL**
**Major:** History, Science, English.
**Activities:** Biology Club, T&I Club, Key Club, Baseball 4 years, Vice-President Key Club, Boys' Vice-President Senior Class, President T&I Club.
**Awards:** All-Star American Legion Baseball Team 1952, National Honor Society.

**SANDERS, MARY LOUISE**
**Major:** Commercial, Band, English.
**Activities:** Senior Band, Y-Teens, English Club, History Club, Historian of Band.

**SEALY, CAROLYN NAOMI**
**Major:** Commercial, Art, English.
**Activities:** Fifty Club, Y-Teens, Red Cross, Monitor, Sight-Saving Room.

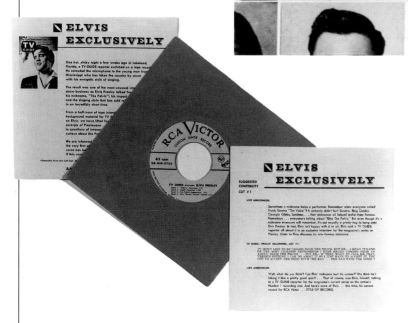

## Elvis Interview Disk

An interview with Elvis Presley entitled "Elvis Exclusively" on a 45 rpm disk issued by RCA Victor. The record was circulated by the American *TV Guide* magazine in 1956 and is shown here with the explanatory text and continuity sheet, making the item significantly more interesting to the collector. By 1956 Elvis was hotter than a Chevy manifold and was ideal material to promote magazines, shows and products. He was constantly appearing on TV specials such as *The Steve Allen Show* and *The Milton Berle Show* where his hip-swinging, pelvis-thrusting actions disgusted parents but energized the kids.

## Elvis's Driving License

Not in good condition, but valuable nevertheless, Elvis Presley's first driving license issued on March 24, 1952 for the State of Tennessee when he was still in high school. It is signed by Presley, though the signature is now well faded. Elvis drove trucks to provide extra money for the household, but progressed onto somewhat more luxurious means of transportation which can be glimpsed in the Cars Of The Stars.

### Pretenders Badge

Another early 1980s force to be reckoned with, who had more or less burned themselves out by the middle of the decade, the Pretenders – if only for their eponymous debut album – will be remembered with respect by all who scour the nostalgia marts for fragile relics of the seemingly indestructible. (Courtesy of V&A Theatre Museum)

### Pretenders Gold Disk

A presentation gold disk for the Pretenders'' album ''Learning To Crawl'' awarded to Chrissie Hynde, the vocalist and a guitarist with the group. The album, released in January 1984, climbed to number two in the U.K. album charts and spent 22 weeks in the U.S. album charts reaching number five (their greatest success in the U.S. to date), and went on to receive its platinum sales award.

### Signed "Prince's Trust" Program

An autographed souvenir program for the fourth ''Prince's Trust'' concert. The concert was held on June 20, 1986 at London's Wembley Arena and celebrated a decade of the charity, which was founded by H.R.H. Prince Charles in 1976. The program is signed by all those mentioned as well as others including Paul McCartney. The program was won in a competition on the BBC TV children's show *Saturday Superstore* in April 1987.

### Elvis *Tickle Me* Feathers

Elvis Presley's eighteenth film, the 1965 Allied Artists release *Tickle Me*, was typical of the depths of banality to which Elvis's moviemaking had sunk by this time. His $750,000 fee accounted for over half the budget, and in addition he was paid 50 percent of the profits; but starring Presley the film's success was guaranteed, helped along by publicity gimmicks like these ''Tickle Me'' feathers. (From the Isaac Tigrett Collection)

### Elvis Presley's Portable Telephone

Years before micro technology allowed portable telephones to become a part of everyday life, this rich man's toy was developed by the American Bell telephone company, involving a Vox transmitter and both push-button and dial facility to make calls. The one that appeared in auction in London in 1982 originally belonged to Elvis Presley – the initials ''EAP'' were still beneath the carrying handle – and was accompanied by a document of authenticity signed by Tom Parker, Elvis's manager, describing how Elvis gave the telephone as a gift to the vendor in 1971.

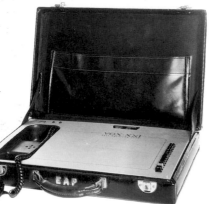

featuring

**BIG COUNTRY**
**SUZZANE VEGA**
**LEVEL 42**

**JOAN ARMATRADING**
**ERIC CLAPTON**
**PHIL COLLINS**
**RAY COOPER**
**JOHN ILLSLEY**
**ELTON JOHN**
**HOWARD JONES**
**MARK KNOPFLER**
**ROD STEWART**
**TINA TURNER**
**MIDGE URE**
**PAUL YOUNG**

### Signed Prince Single

A signed copy of the Prince 12-inch single "Mountains." This was the follow-up to one of Prince's best songs, "Kiss," taken from the semi-soundtrack "Parade." The album coincided with the release of the film *Under The Cherry Moon* and featured some of the songs from the film. This single is written by Lisa Coleman and Wendy Melvoin of the Revolution, Prince's backing group which was disbanded at the end of 1986. Few can deny the genius of this artist, and while he may infuriate his fans and record company executives alike with his occasional failures and misjudgments, his very adventurous style gives him a cult following in collecting circles.

### Prince Badges

Despite a risqué image and even more outrageous lyrics, Prince has managed to bridge the gap between the outer limits of what is permissable in rock content and presentation, and mainstream acceptability. The crossover into major-league status came with his 1984 album and movie *Purple Rain*, and with it all the promotional paraphernalia of stickers, T-shirts, posters and, of course, button badges. (Courtesy of V&A Theatre Museum)

### Prince Playlist

Even the most recent of memorabilia can command a price if the artist associated with it is deemed important enough. Prince ranks as a superstar, so the handwritten playlist from his Wembley concert of July 25, 1988, along with a signed album and ticket and program from the concert, appeared in a London salesroom less than a year later.

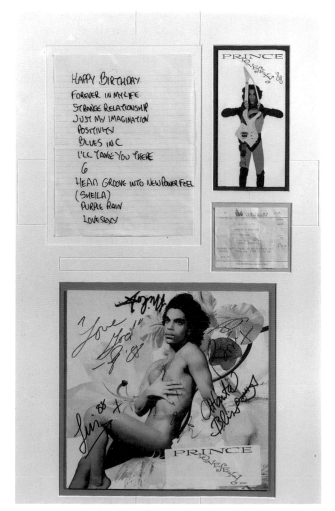

### Prince Bootleg

Banned because of its sexually explicit lyrics – first in the U.S., then in Britain and other territories – the "Black Album" by Prince has gained true notoriety, hence the thousand-dollar price tag attached to the few copies of the bootleg around, which itself was only pressed in a limited edition of 2,000.

### Procol Harum Award

An Ivor Novello award given to Procol Harum in 1967/8 for "A Whiter Shade Of Pale." Procol Harum was formed around pianist Gary Brooker who wrote the song with lyricist Keith Reid. Brooker used various combinations of musicians in the band over the years and for a time the line-up was almost the same as his previous band, the Paramounts. Harum never surpassed the success of this U.K. number one and split up in 1977 (but have reformed recently). In that year the song won, together with Queen's "Bo Rap," the Best British Pop Single 1952-77 at the British Record Industries awards.

### Cliff Richard Acetate

Cliff Richard's first acetate recording dating from 1958. This HMV 10-inch disk features a white "Special Recording" label listing the songs in blue ballpoint pen. Side One is described as "Cliff Richard and the Drifters, Breathless" and Side Two, "Lawdy Miss Clawdy" with the same credit. The song was recorded at the HMV record store in London's Oxford Street for £10, just after Richard had changed his name from Harry Webb. At this stage Hank Marvin and Bruce Welch were not part of the band which would later become the Shadows – changing the name so not to clash with the U.S. Drifters.

### Early Cliff Richard Contracts

These three contracts from the early days of Cliff Richard's career represent a slice of British pop history, and if they had been relating to vintage Beatles engagements would have attracted perhaps five times the modest £400 estimate suggested in a London sale in 1987 – such is the nature of the market. They all cover engagements by Cliff in late 1958 with his group the Drifters – who were soon to change their name to the Shadows when they diskovered there was already a Drifters in the U.S. – arranged by promoter Arthur Howes, who gave the rock & roller his first professional job in September, on tour with the chart-topping Kalin Twins.

### Rolling Stones Pay Check and Accounts

The Rolling Stones" first pay check dated September 4, 1963 together with a sheet of accounts listing the payment, and a page from *Melody Maker* listing the acts appearing at the "3rd National Jazz Festival" on August 11. The check is made payable to "Eric Easton" who signed up as the band's manager for three years, having seen them perform at the Crawdaddy Club on April 28, 1963. The Festival performance was only weeks before their first TV performance and hit single "Come On." Before long, £30 would not secure one Rolling Stone let alone five.

### Reading Festival Badge

Badges commemorating specific events such as rock festivals are sought after by collectors. The National Jazz and Blues Festival, which evolved into the Reading Rock Festival, started in 1959 and continues today. This badge from Reading 1976, although it was presenting strictly rock by this time, still carries the trumpet-on-chair logo of the old National Jazz Federation who founded what has now become an annual institution in Britain. (Courtesy of V&A Theatre Museum)

### Rolling Stones Acetate

An extremely rare acetate of the Rolling Stones *circa* 1963, recorded at the independent IBC Studios in London, with a version of Bo Diddley's "Road Runner." The acetate was sold in auction in a Decca singles cover, which suggests it was during their audition or early contracted period with the label. (From the Isaac Tigrett Collection)

### Rolling Stones Gold Disk

A presentation gold disk for "(I Can't Get No) Satisfaction" by the Rolling Stones. Released in July 1965, the Richards/Jagger composition with its distinctive riff, distorted sound and questionable lyrics became the sound of that summer. The single was the Stones" first U.S. number one; it remained there for four weeks and gave Richards and Jagger the confidence they needed for their compositions. It held the number one position in the U.K. charts for two weeks in September. With five cover versions released of this song, only "White Christmas" has charted more times in so many different years.

### Signed Stones Tour Programme

A brochure from the Rolling Stones" first U.S. Tour in June 1964 which is signed by each member of the group. Above it is a ticket from a concert in October 1964. The Stones arrived in the U.S. on the first of that month having already had three hit singles in the U.K.. At this stage, the Jagger/Richards songwriting partnership still lacked a certain confidence and all the hits had been covers. They had not yet had a hit in the U.S., but within a year they would have topped the charts twice, very much to their Satisfaction.

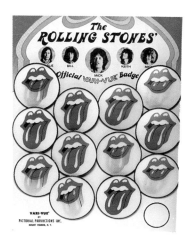

### Rolling Stones Badge Display Card

The Rolling Stones" "licks" logo was adopted in 1971 as their record label design and has been used by the band in various ways ever since. This store display holds 12 "Vari-Vue" buttons and dates from the early 1970s.

### 'Stones Gold Album

A presentation gold disk to Charles Watts for the Rolling Stones" 1968 album "Beggars Banquet." This album was released a year after the half-hearted success of "Their Satanic Majesties Request" and was the last to be recorded before the death of Brian Jones. "Beggars Banquet" restored the group's rock & roll band credentials with the definitive Stones' tracks "Street Fighting Man" and "Sympathy For The Devil." The album reached number three in the U.K. and number five in the U.S.

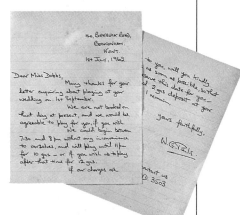

### Bill Wyman Letter

A letter from W.G. Perks (aka Bill Wyman) offering the services of the group at a wedding on September 1, 1962. Wyman changed his name on January 10, 1963 when he was introduced at their first Marquee Club concert as Lee Wyman. "Lee Wyman" was the name of a colleague of Bill's in the RAF and he had always thought it was much sexier than "Bill Perks" (no argument there). At this stage guitar player Brian Jones was known as "Elmo Lewis" so the young(ish) bassist saw no reason why he should not change as well. In June 1964 he therefore changed his name by deed poll but decided against losing the "Bill."

### Dave Lee Roth Signed Album

Lead singer with the internationally successful Van Halen, Dave Lee Roth went solo in 1984, producing a string of hits under his own name – including this 1986 U.S. Top Ten) entry, "Skyscraper." (From the Isaac Tigrett Collection)

### Signed Paul Simon Programme

The "Graceland" album and tour – from which this is an autographed program – was a milestone in popularizing "world" music, with Simon's use of musicians from South Africa, despite considerable controversy. (From the Isaac Tigrett Collection)

### Sonny and Cher Dolls

Jumping on the Barbie bandwagon, these 12-inch lookalike dolls of husband-and-wife hitmakers Sonny & Cher were marketed along with a "designer's collection" of separate outfits to clothe the dolls. Fifteen Cher outfits (designed by Bob Mackie), and eight for Sonny, were offered with the dolls at a London auction in 1990 estimated at $600–$1,000.

### Roxy Music Gold and Silver Disks

A double presentation award for the album "Avalon" by Roxy Music (1982). The last album which they made under this name, it spent 57 weeks in the U.K. Top 40 and climbed to number one. Unusually, the award comprises two disks, one of gold-colored metal the other of silver-colored metal; both presented to Bryan Ferry. This award was made even more desirable to collectors by having Bryan Ferry's signature in black felt-tip pen on the reverse.

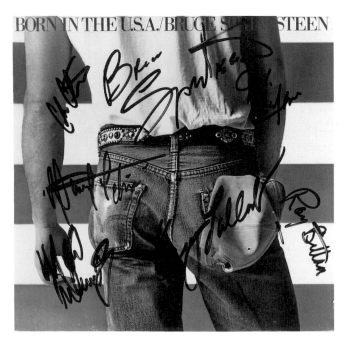

### Signed Springsteen Album

Bruce Springsteen's "Born In The U.S.A." album, signed by the Boss and members of the E. Street Band. Springsteen is one of America's most important rock artists, having achieved almost cult status since his 1975 "Born To Run" album. The "Born In The U.S.A." album of 1984 is his most successful to date, and elevated him to international star status. After its release in the U.K. his six previous albums all entered the charts and he achieved his first Top 10 single hit.

### Early Bruce Springsteen Memorabilia

Between 1969 and 1971, Bruce Springsteen led the band Steel Mill in his native New Jersey, his first real stepping stone to ultimate acclaim with the E. Street Band. This collection of memorabilia sold in New York relates to that period, and included concert tickets, free passes, local posters and flyers, a business card from his first band the Castiles, a Castiles fan club card and a rare Asbury Park Bruce Springsteen puzzle game where you are invited to find the titles of Springsteen's songs. Asbury Park was the district of New Jersey where Springsteen grew up, and "Greetings From Asbury Park N.J." the title of his debut album in 1973.

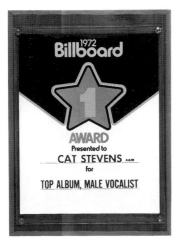

### Cat Stevens Award

An unusual "*Billboard* No 1 Award," awarded to Cat Stevens in 1972, the year that saw the release of his album "Catch Bull At Four" which spent three weeks at number one in the U.S. album charts and a further 23 weeks in the album Top 40. Stevens had success with three successive albums, "Teaser And The Firecat" which reached number two in the U.S. album charts and stayed in the Top 40 for 37 weeks, and "Tea For The Tillerman" reaching number eight and staying in the Top 40 for 44 weeks.

### Cat Stevens Australian Award

A special award to Cat Stevens for achieving the equivalent of 23 Australian gold records for his three albums, "Mona Bone Jakon" (1970), "Tea For The Tillerman" (1970) and "Teaser And The Firecat" (1971). This unusual Australia-shaped award was entered into a rock memorabilia auction by Cat Stevens" road manager (between 1975 and 1982).

### Rod Stewart Silver Disk

A silver disk for £150,000 worth of sales of the Rod Stewart album "Blondes Have More Fun," which made the number three spot in the British album charts in 1978, presented by the organizing body of the U.K. record business, the BPI – British Phonograph Industry.

### Sting Platinum Disk

Formed in 1952, the Record Industry Association of America is the trade association of U.S. record companies, and introduced gold records to mark million-selling disks in 1958. Times have changed, as have record sales, and now the million target is commemorated by a platinum award, like this one awarded to Sting in 1987 for album and cassette sales of "Nothing Like The Sun."

### Stiff Records Badge

Badges, especially those linked to a particular record release or tour, have an essential collectability, though often at the modest level of the junk shop, bric-a-brac stall or fan convention. Stiff Records – pioneers of the U.K. New Wave in the late 1970s – celebrated their "Be Stiff" package tour of 1978 with a number of badges, including the "U.S. road sign" logo that was the trademark of the trek. (Courtesy of V&A Theatre Museum)

### Supremes Signed Photograph

The Supremes – Florence Ballard, Diana Ross and Mary Wilson – signed this picture in their mid 1960s heyday, before the departure of Ms. Ross to superstar status. The photograph was part of a miscellaneous collection of autographs of Motown artists that included an early signed color portrait of Michael Jackson.

### 10cc Silver Disk

A presentation silver disk for the hugely successful single "I''m Not In Love" by 10cc. Released in 1975, "I''m Not In Love" topped the British charts in June and reached number two in the U.S. the following month. The second single to be released from the album "Original Soundtrack," it was considered an unusual choice for a single release at the time. This single, however, is repeatedly voted the best pop record of all time.

### Thin Lizzy Gold Disk

Donated to a rock memorabilia auction by Thin Lizzy to raise money for an appeal for a cancer research charity, this gold award was presented to the band itself for their double album "Live And Dangerous" released in 1978 – by far their most successful album which spent 62 weeks on the U.K. Top 40.

### 10cc Awards

Two Ivor Novello awards for the 10cc hits "Rubber Bullets" and "I'm Not In Love." The Manchester group had their first single success in 1972 with "Donna" (a fine imitation of the American sound of the late 1950s) which reached number two in the U.K. charts. It was "Rubber Bullets" which gave 10cc their first number one hit the following year, while "I'm Not In Love," released in June 1975, reached number one in the U.K. and number two in the U.S.

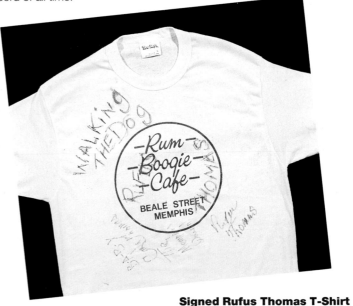

### Signed Rufus Thomas T-Shirt

An early star on the Memphis music scene, and the celebrated Stax label in particular, Rufus Thomas initially recorded for Sam Phillips on Sun. Born in 1917, on leaving high school he traveled the South with the Rabbit Foot Minstrels as a comedian and song-and-dance man. He hit the big time with "Walking The Dog" in 1963, but has remained loyal to the local soul scene for most of his career. The T-shirt promotes the Rum Boogie Café, a popular blues bar on Memphis'' fabled Beale Street. (From the Isaac Tigrett Collection)

### Three Degrees Contract

A standard Variety Artists Federation contract used extensively on the British club, ballroom and theater circuit, for a Three Degrees concert in 1974. They were bigger in the U.K. than their native U.S. at the time, helped no doubt by the fact that H.R.H. Prince Charles named them as his favorite performers! (From the Isaac Tigrett Collection)

### T. Rex Award

A *Disk and Music Echo* award to T. Rex for 250,000 British sales of the single ''Ride A White Swan.'' The first chart success in the U.K. for the group who had recently shortened their name to T. Rex, ''Ride A White Swan'' reached number two in 1970. Micky Finn had replaced Steve Peregrine-Took in the group and this single showed a marked change from the group's earlier, primarily acoustic, compositions to a much more commercial sound.

### T. Rex "Hot Love" Award

A special award presented by *Disk and Music Echo* to T. Rex for 250,000 British sales of the single ''Hot Love.'' The first British number one for Marc Bolan and T. Rex in 1971 where it remained for six weeks, ''Hot Love'' attracted a wide following from younger audiences. Known as teenyboppers this new generation of fans became increasingly hysterical in their adulation.

### T. Rex "Get It On" Award

Presented to T. Rex for British sales of 250,000 of the hit single ''Get It On'' by *Disk and Music Echo*. A Marc Bolan composition released in the U.K. in 1971, the single reached number one in Britain and, under the title ''Bang A Gong,'' was the only single success for the band in the U.S.

### Signed Tina Turner Album

The Tina Turner album ''Foreign Affair'' signed and dedicated ''To the Barrow Family.'' This is the inside cover of the foldout sleeve and shows Tina in typical performing pose. This was her third album since starting to record for Capitol Records. Having already completed a world tour for the ''Break Every Rule'' album in 1987/8, she performed a further 121 dates in 1990. Through these efforts she has become one of the most popular live female acts in the world, playing to a record 180,000 fans at one concert.

### Twist Instruction Book

Instigated by R&B singer Hank Ballard and popularized by Chubby Checker over 30 years ago, the Twist was the last great worldwide dance craze that virtually everybody could do – hence its popularity. This coffee-stained book (Espresso of course!) exploiting the craze would now fetch several dollars at collectors fairs.

### 2-Tone Records Badges

Prominent at the time with their black-and-white chequered logo, the Coventry-based British firm 2-Tone Records specialized in a racially integrated version of West Indian ska as post-punk dance music. Bands on the influential independent label included the Specials (who founded the label), Madness, the Beat and the Selector, and as a force for social as much as musical change during the late 1970s, its place in youth culture history is assured. (Courtesy of V&A Theatre Museum)

### Signed "U.S.A for Africa" Poster

Forty of these posters were signed by the various artists involved in the recording of the Michael Jackson/Lionel Ritchie composition "We Are The World." The total concept of "U.S.A for Africa," which included most of the usual marketing accessories like T-shirts and videos, raised over $44 million for famine relief. The single sold 7.4 million copies and the album 4.4 million. The single featured 44 artists in total and was recorded on January 28, at the A&M Studios in Los Angeles. This particular poster with 22 signatures was auctioned on station KLO to raise funds for the Red Cross.

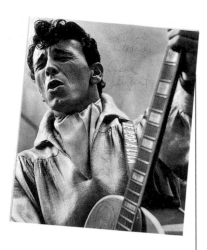

### Signed Gene Vincent Photograph

A signed photograph of Gene Vincent dating from 1956 with the inscription "To Toni, Regards Gene Vincent." The photograph is from the most important and exciting period in Vincent's life. He was married to 15-year-old Ruth Ann Hand in February and was signed to Capitol Records on the strength of winning their "Elvis Soundalike Sweepstake" in April. His only U.S. Top 10 hit was "Be-Bop-A-Lula" in July, despite it starting out as the B-side. Vincent is a more significant influence than his chart statistics indicate and, along with Elvis, was one of the first young white rock & rollers.

### U2 Platinum Disk

A platinum disk presented to Bono to commemorate the success of U2's "Rattle & Hum" album which was released in 1988. The band's first U.K. number one single, "Desire," came from this album. The release of "Rattle & Hum," a combination of live and studio recordings, was followed by a feature film of the same name which detailed U2's "Joshua Tree" tour. This particular presentation disk was donated by Bono to raise money for the charity, The Arvon Foundation.

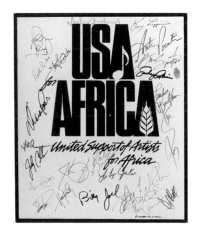

### Wham! Fan Club Badge

Wham!, the U.K. vocal duo of George Michael and Andrew Ridgley, were enormously successful through the first half of the 1980s with a string of Top 10 hits that included four British number ones and two U.S. chart toppers. Now all that remains, with George Michael a solo star in his own right, is the inevitable ephemera. (Courtesy of V&A Theatre Museum)

## Who "Tommy" Gold Disk

A presentation gold disk for "Tommy." The album is the soundtrack of the movie released in 1975 and spent nine weeks in the U.K. album chart climbing to number two, and 47 weeks in the U.S. album chart. *Tommy*, the highly successful and influential 90-minute rock opera was Townshend's concept and it is particularly noteworthy that this disk was presented to Townshend himself.

## Who Tour Ephemera

Obviously one of the road crew, the name Dick Parry features on many of this Who tour material which included itineraries between 1979 and 1982, backstage passes, travel and hotel details and a number of guest passes. Tours covered included the "Quadrophenia" and "It's Hard" treks, and the whole package appeared in a London salesroom in 1988.

## "Who Are You" Gold Disk

A presentation gold disk for "Who Are You" by the Who. Released in August 1978, the album spent nine weeks in the U.K. album Top 40 but only reached number six, while climbing to number two in the U.S. where it spent 13 weeks on the charts. It was the last album to be recorded by the original group of Daltrey, Entwistle, Moon and Townshend. Only a month after the record's release, Keith Moon, the band's wild and charismatic drummer, was found dead in his apartment from an overdose and was replaced by the former Small Faces drummer, Kenny Jones.

## Who "Quadrophenia" Gold Disk

A gold presentation disk for over $1 million worth of sales of the album "Quadrophenia" originally released in 1973 by the Who. A heavily orchestrated musical epic, "Quadrophenia" (a story of double schizophrenia) was an ambitious project which only received acclaim when linked with the successful 1979 film of the same name after which a re-mixed movie soundtrack was released.

## Who Platinum Disk

A presentation platinum disk presented to Peter Townshend for the album "The Story Of The Who" released in 1976. After the release of their well-received album "The Who By Numbers" in 1975, the band had a quiet year in 1976 apart from double billing with the Grateful Dead in concert in California. The inactivity of the year is reflected by the release in the U.K. of this compilation album, "The Story Of The Who" which was never a U.S. issue.

## Signed Press Photo of Early Who

A group changing its name early in its career makes anything bearing the original name even more collectible — such as this color picture signed by the future members of the Who when they were still called the High Numbers, cut from the pages of the 60s U.K. fan magazine *Fab*.

# INDEX

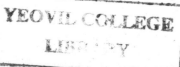